ADVANCED MOULDMAKING AND CASTING

Nick Brooks

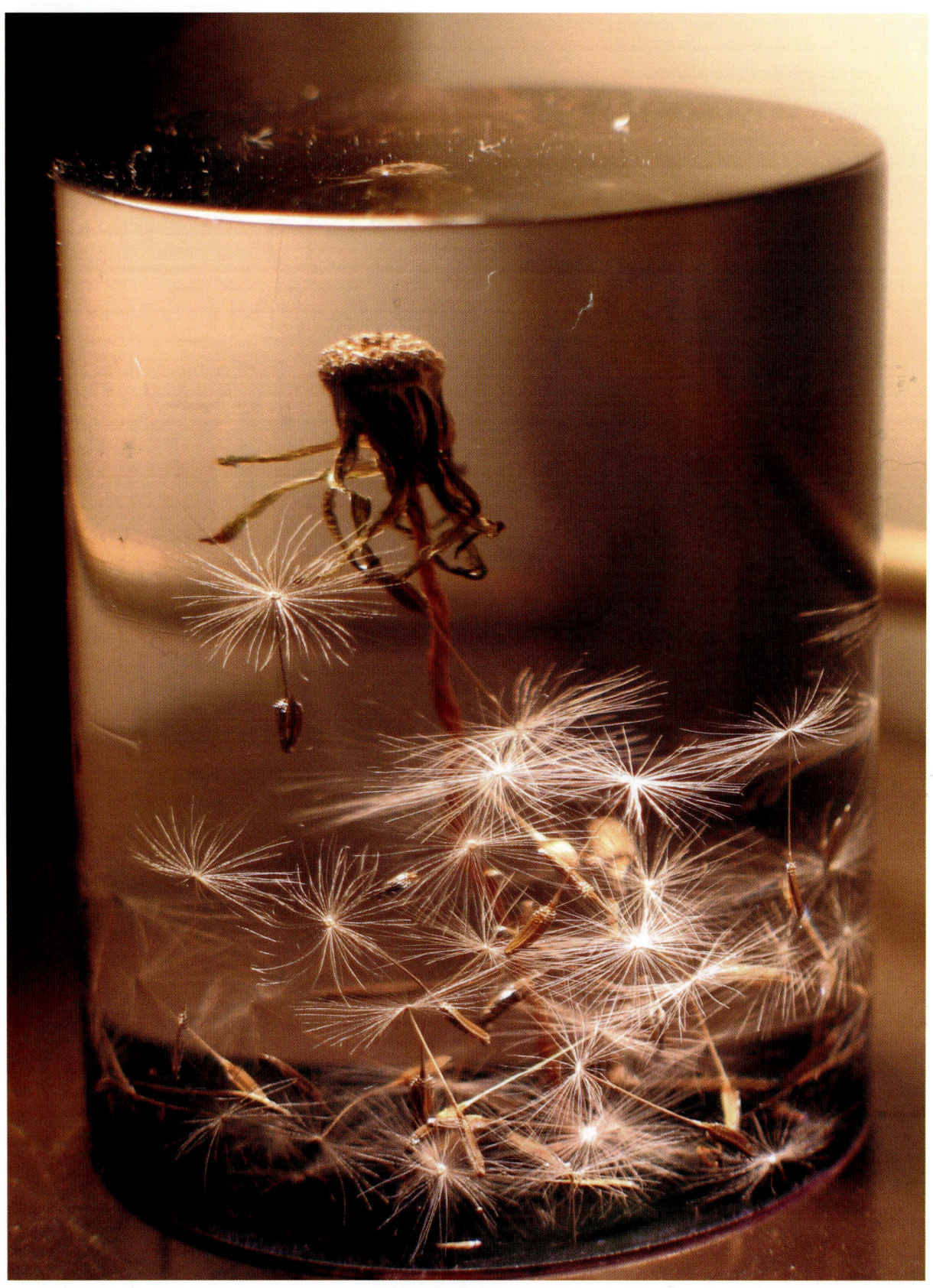

Embedded polyester resin.

ADVANCED MOULDMAKING AND CASTING

Nick Brooks

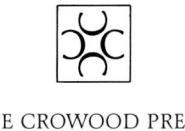

THE CROWOOD PRESS

First published in 2011 by
The Crowood Press Ltd
Ramsbury, Marlborough
Wiltshire SN8 2HR

www.crowood.com

British Library Cataloguing-in-Publication Data
A catalogue record for this book is available from the British
Library.

ISBN 978 1 84797 310 8

Disclaimer
The author and publisher do not accept any responsibility in
any manner whatsoever for any error or omission, or any loss,
damage, injury, adverse outcome, or liability of any kind
incurred as a result of the use of any of the information
contained in this book, or reliance upon it

DEDICATION
To Linki and Jake

Typeset by Servis Filmsetting Ltd, Stockport, Cheshire
Printed and bound in Malaysia by Times Offset (M) Sdn Bhd

CONTENTS

FOREWORD

What is the purpose of moulds and casts? And why does the Royal Academy of Arts mount an exhibition of Modern British Sculpture using in its poster a detail of an exact replica over 2 metres square of part of Olaf Street in London, made by the Boyle Family in 1966?

By making moulds and casting from them a unique and new form can be transformed in its material. A more durable or more beautiful or more expressively appropriate material is substituted for the original material, which was in its time appropriate for the discovery of the form. This is the use of making moulds and casting in the origination of an individual work of art.

Alternatively, a form recognized as valuable can be produced en masse, as a multiple, as we call works of art that no longer rely on their uniqueness to gain prestige. The same process is used in industries that make useful objects, indistinguishable from each other. The 100,000,000 sunflower seeds in the installation *Sunflower Seeds* by Ai Weiwei at Tate Modern in 2010 must set a record for quantity cast. It also set a record for the individuation of multiples. Each cast was finished and coloured by hand, and it may be said that no two are identical. The unique also remains important in utilitarian productions, as millions of 'crowned' teeth in the mouths of old people can testify.

The reproduction of objects mirrors biological reproduction itself. Humanity, instinct with a sense of its own value, has the urge to reproduce sexually. The same urge goes back billions of years to the earliest form of life. From its beginning, society created what we now call works of art, as religious objects for use in ritual. An artist was required to conform to a traditional mode of representation, and religion might even require details to be incorporated that could not be seen by the worshipper. In medieval Japan statues of the Buddha were cast in lacquer. These figures sometimes hid carefully cast feet within shoes that have only been broken open by accident more recently. The combination of a liquid that sets with fibrous reinforcement was the basis of Japanese casting technique. The liquid was drawn from the lacquer tree, the fibre was hemp or cotton. The expansion of Buddhist monasticism was such that in 700CE the Emperor ordered every household to plant lacquer trees. A connection between then and now can be seen in the use of contemporary resins with glass fibre reinforcement.

Putting metal aside, with its dependence on high temperatures, clay, plaster and wax form a triumvirate of traditional materials, whose strengths and weaknesses complement each other. Things made in any of them can resist entropy. The first sculpture that Degas exhibited failed to gain critical approval. Thereafter he left in wax many wonderful works, suitable for casting in bronze. They have survived, with some disputed distortions, the best to be finally cast in a more durable material. Posthumous fame has conferred similar resurrections on many pieces of sculpture by twentieth-century artists for whom recognition came late.

Around 1900CE an awareness of the interplay between positive and negative versions of the same surface developed, perhaps because of the ubiquity of moulds and casting. Abstract sculptors such as Gabo came to work with thin sheet surfaces having visual access to both sides. The language of Cubism invited sculptors such as Zadkine to integrate both within a single figure. The exchange of negative and positive was demonstrated on a grand scale by Rachel Whiteread's *House* which stood at 193 Grove Road in London from 1993 to 1994. There, the mass of a wall was converted into a narrow space, and the volume of a room was converted into a solid block.

In his influential essay 'The Work of Art in the Age of Mechanical Reproduction' (1936), Walter Benjamin wrote:

'from a photographic negative one can make any number of prints; to ask for the 'authentic' print makes no sense.' He deplored the exaggerated value placed on the uniqueness of art objects, and the mystical aura with which they were endowed. He thought that from 1900 onwards the technical means existed to free art from its roots in religious practice, free it, he hoped, to engage with the practice of politics.

In the post-modern situation a variety of aesthetic convictions exist alongside the political. Consider Brian Haw's protest against the UK government's policies in Iraq. From 2001 till 2006 he camped in Parliament Square. He assembled some 600 banners and other items of protest. Everything in that assemblage was reproduced by the artist Mark Wallinger, in an installation *State Britain* at the Duveen Galleries, Tate Britain, in 2009. In such projects as this, the skills of mould-making and casting can play a crucial role. After their Olaf Street Study in 1966, the Boyle Family went on to replicate 100 randomly chosen sites in London. From that they proceeded to a global selection of samples to represent the earth. Whatever the motives and aesthetic convictions of a sculptor, the methods of making moulds and casting from them, which are taught by Nick Brooks, and which he has described with such clarity in this book, will prove of immense value.

Ken Adams
Former Senior Lecturer at St Martins College
of Art and Design

INTRODUCTION

In producing *Advanced Mouldmaking and Casting* my aims are to provide a book that can be used both to advance levels of pre-existing skills and to introduce new techniques and materials that may not have been used previously by the reader. The content builds upon and goes beyond the fundamental techniques and principles described in the precursor to this book, *Mouldmaking and Casting* (The Crowood Press, 2005).

Some of the processes and materials covered are 'traditional', and the reader may have had some experience of them before. Hopefully this book will address any problems encountered with these. Other processes and materials in the book are relatively new to the subject, being in use in industry but only recently available on the smaller-scale domestic market. It is hoped this book will encourage further levels of exploration and experience of the subject.

Mouldmaking and casting is, of course, not a finite process and the reader may choose to reinterpret certain processes. The options for a particular project are often multiple and varied depending on the requirements of the maker. The aesthetic, economic and timetabled requirements of the particular project in hand will all inform those options in a multitude of different ways. Having the specifications and technical practices for the processes and materials is only the foundations for a project; what the maker does with that information is what ultimately informs and inspires the work. It is hoped that this book can be a part of that process.

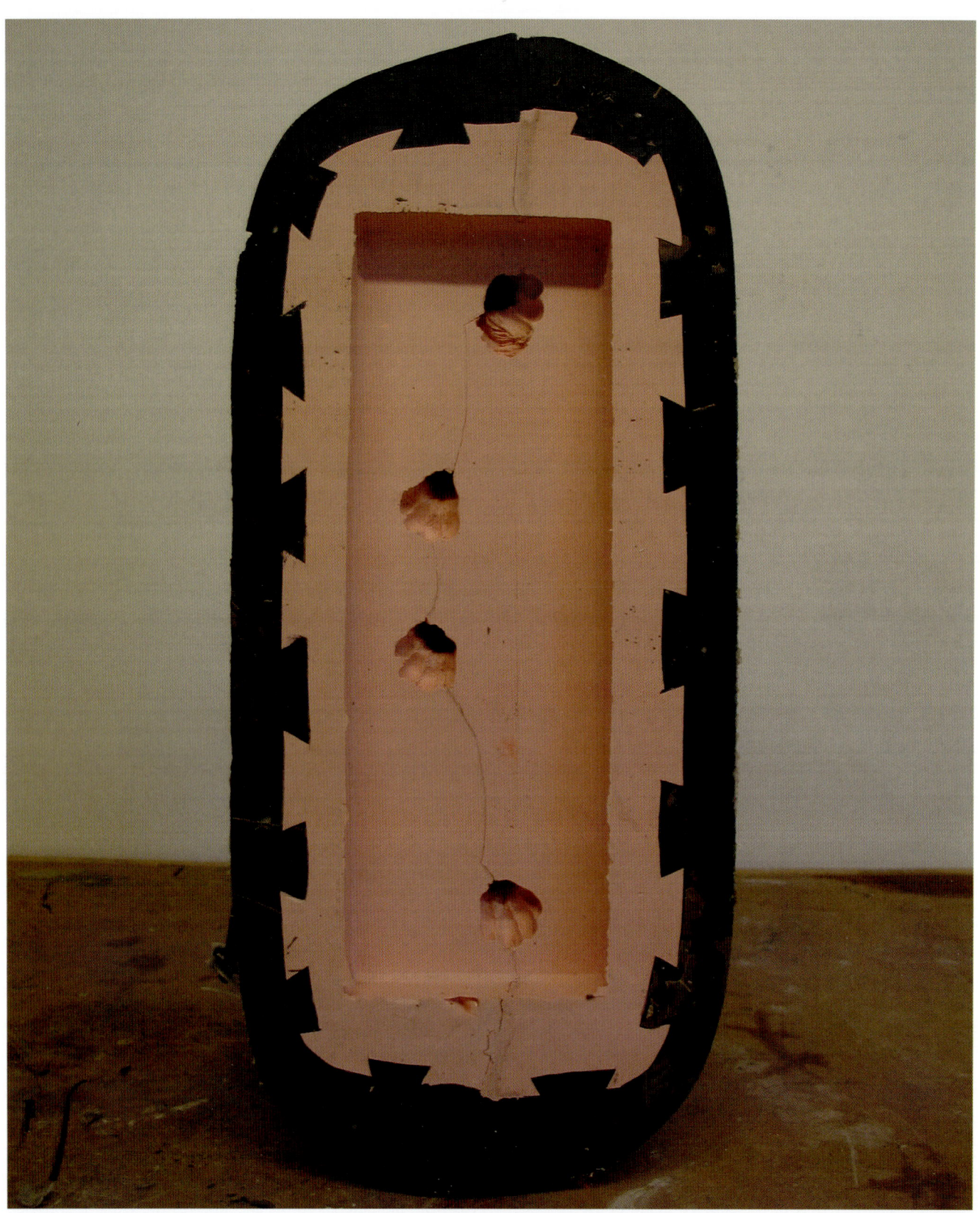

Multiple piece 'cored' silicone rubber mould.

CHAPTER ONE

MULTIPLE-PIECE 'CORED' SILICONE RUBBER

Creating multiple-piece 'cored' moulds can be quite complex to execute so the aim of this book is to cover the process in detail. Silicone rubber as a versatile and accurate mouldmaking material has been around on the domestic market for a long time and has been a key part of the generic mouldmaking process in the commercial trade for years.

From very simple blocks to highly complex multiple-piece moulds, silicone rubbers can cover almost every mouldmaking eventuality. The 'cored' mould allows the mouldmaker to aspire to ever more complicated mouldmaking challenges.

The Core

The 'core' refers to a separate internal mould piece that cannot be reached from outside the original form being moulded. The core is supported by external mould pieces that hold it in place within the mould. To understand this fully and to proceed at this level of mouldmaking it is important to have at least an academic understanding, or preferably practical experience, of the principles of mouldmaking and casting and multiple-piece mouldmaking that are explained in the precursor to this book, *Mouldmaking and Casting*.

A mould core allows the mouldmaker to capture an area of difficult-to-access detail on an original that cannot be captured with other pieces. Access to this sort of area may be difficult because of undercutting into it that would not allow removal of the mould pieces, or demoulding of castings from the mould. A core may not always be strictly necessary but it can sometimes help greatly in the production of a mould and subsequent casting from it.

The necessity or usefulness of a core is best illustrated with a practical example: in this case, creating a mould from a model of a four-legged animal. If a mould were to be taken in two pieces on either side of the animal, as may seem logical, each mould piece would have the negative space of two whole legs of the animal within in them. This would work as a mould in principle, but it would make removal of the mould from the original difficult and the demoulding of a cast, in a less durable material, even more so. With the legs of an animal being much thinner than the body the mould pieces would have to be pulled down each leg and removed like a sock. On a large scale this may be practical, but on a smaller scale the removal of the mould in this way, particularly if the casting material is not very durable, may be problematic if not impossible. The answer is to create a seam down either side of each leg using one core mould piece that creates the inside leg seam of all four legs.

The core piece is created first, as one whole piece. The outside two pieces are then created over this to make the outside seam lines of the legs and the rest of the body.

This will allow the mould to be separated from either side of each leg and the core piece to be pulled away from between them. Demoulding in this way will create minimal stress on the relatively delicate leg sections of the casting.

Understanding the principles of this example will hopefully help in making decisions on the potential advantages of creating cored moulds in other mouldmaking situations. See Chapter 8 for an illustrated example of casting in this mould.

PROJECT

Specification

A three-piece silicone rubber and two-piece fibreglass case mould. From Polyurethane resin model figure of a lion on a base. Size: 320mm (L), 110mm (W) and 200mm (H).

Time Required

Approximately 7–8 hours of working time.

Materials

- Silicone rubber (Siliastic 3495, supplied by Notcutt Ltd);
- gel coat polyester resin (all polyester resin products supplied by Alec Tiranti Ltd);
- general-purpose polyester resin;
- polyester resin pigment;
- polyester resin catalyst;
- a heavy fibreglass mat;
- acetone;
- vegetable oil;
- spray wax release agent;
- grey clay; and
- roofing bolts and wing nuts.

Tools

- A modelling board;
- dispensing and mixing containers;
- wooden spatulas;
- brushes (1in and ½in);
- scissors;
- a palette knife;
- a craft knife;
- wooden clay tools;
- a rubber kidney clay tool;
- a looped wire clay tool;
- a clay harp;
- disposable rubber gloves;
- a spirit level;
- an electric jigsaw or hacksaw blade in a holder; and
- an electric drill.

Method

SET-UP AND PREPARATION

As with any project, careful preparation before the start of the job is crucial. Knowing the material quantities and tools needed, undertaking repairs to the original and setting-up the working area will all help to complete the job accurately and efficiently. (Tip: make sure you have enough materials to complete the job before you start. Running out of material halfway through the job is at least a waste of time and, at worst, a loss of previously executed work.)

THE MOULD CORE

The first piece of the mould to be created is the core piece, around which the other two mould pieces will be made. This is created in the space in between all four of the animal's legs.

1. Apply a clay wall onto one side of the animal to block off the outside area of the legs on that side. Make sure the clay wall only covers the outside half of the two legs. Seal the clay wall from the outside by pinching it to the surface of the original model.
2. Ensure that the area of contact on the inside of the clay wall and the original is at right angles using a clay tool.
3. Create registration indents on the inside surface of the clay wall. This will provide 'nipple and cup' registration between the mould core and the outside mould piece.
4. Set the original on its side, clay wall down, on a modelling board. With a spirit level ensure that it is level between the two lowest points of the legs. (Silicone rubber will be poured into the void between the legs of the animal so it will need to rise to a 'level' within.)
5. Spray wax release agent within the core space.
6. Mix a batch of silicone and pour it into the core space to a midway line on the outside of the top two legs.
7. Allow to set fully.
8. With a small mix of silicone, stick pre-set and cut registration blocks on the top surface of the core. This will provide registration of the core into the other outside mould piece.

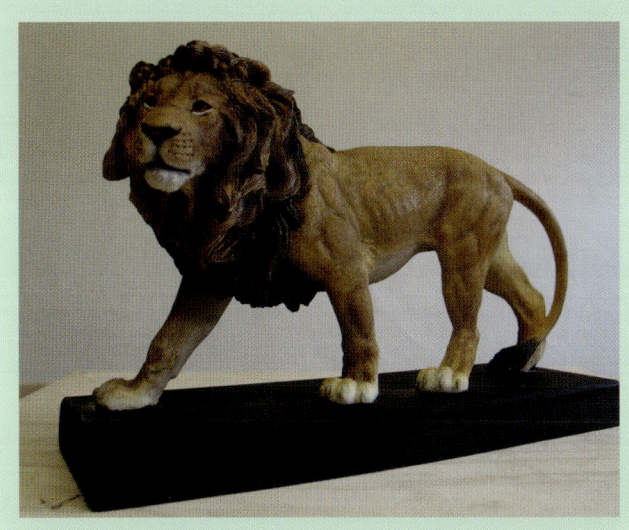

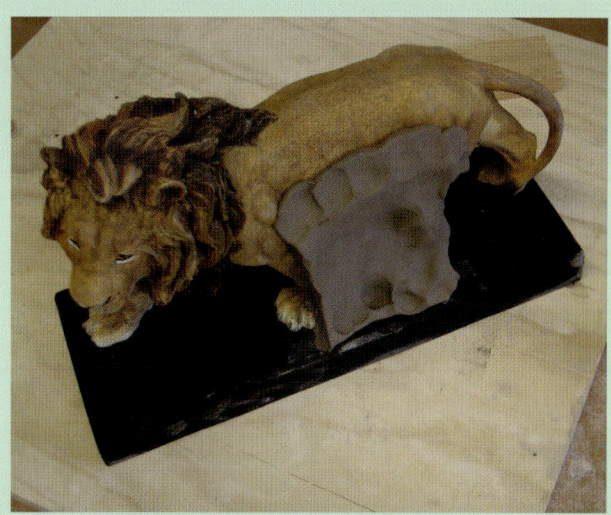

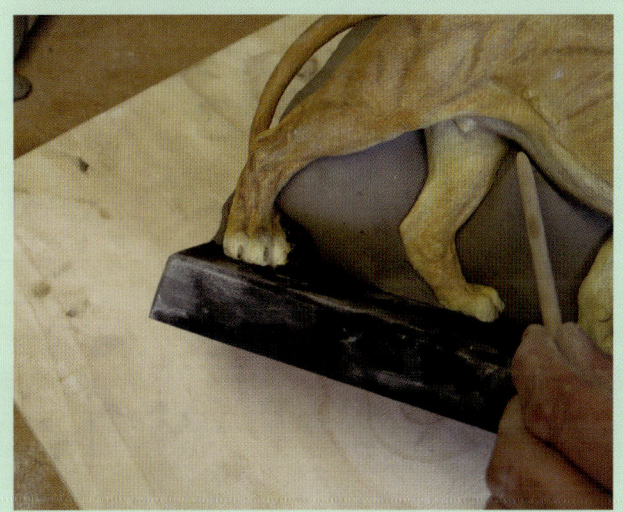

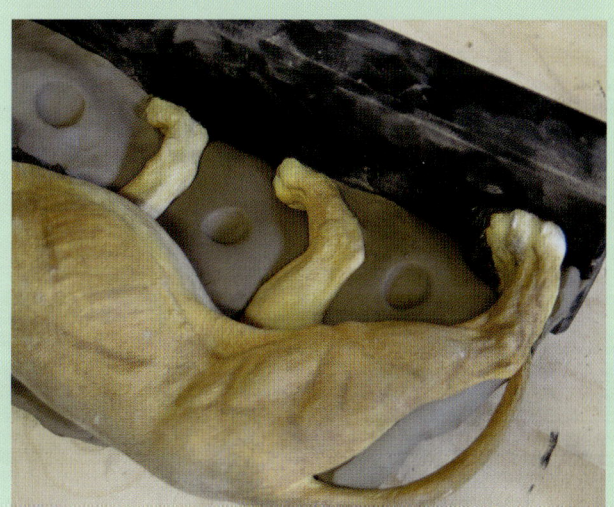

TOP LEFT: **Original model.**

TOP RIGHT: **The first wall is placed to define the 'core'.**

MIDDLE LEFT: **A clean perpendicular join is created on the inside of the wall.**

MIDDLE RIGHT: **Registration indents are applied.**

RIGHT: **A level is set across the legs.**

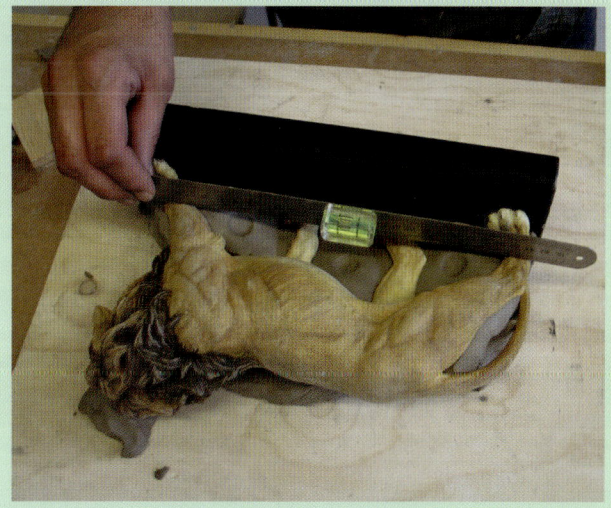

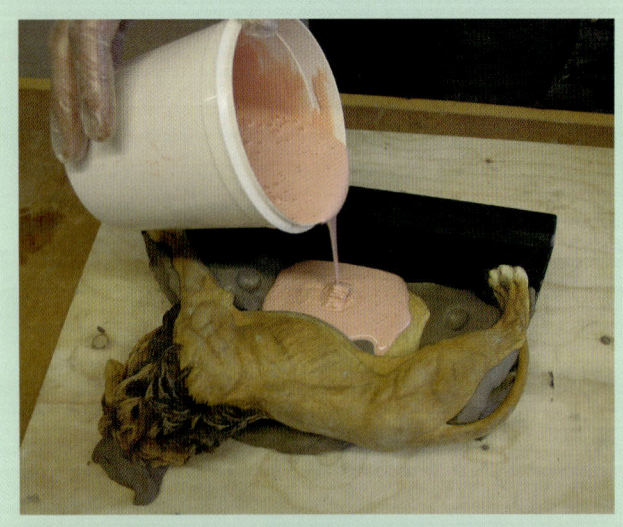

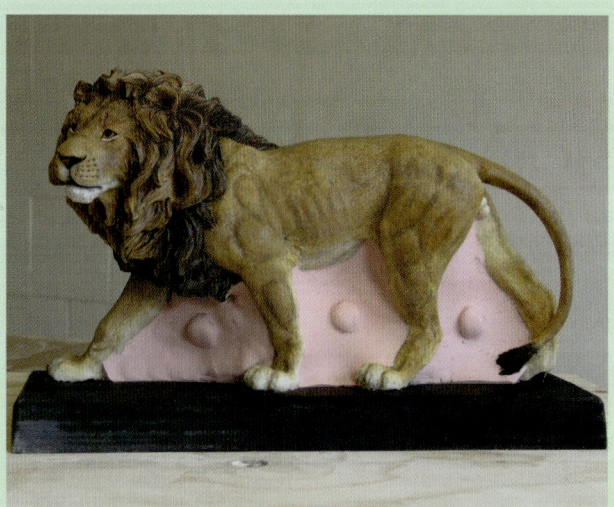

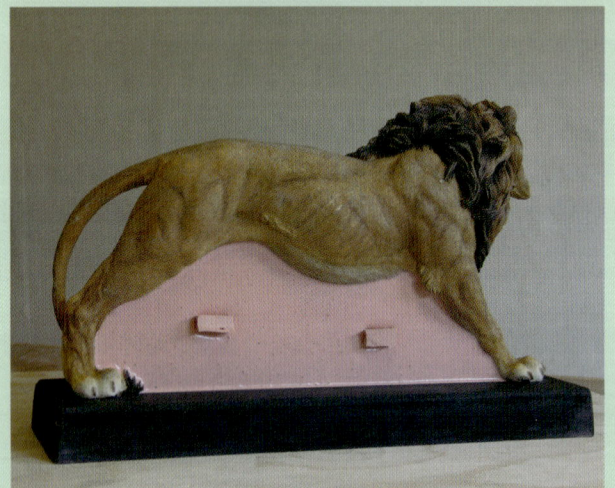

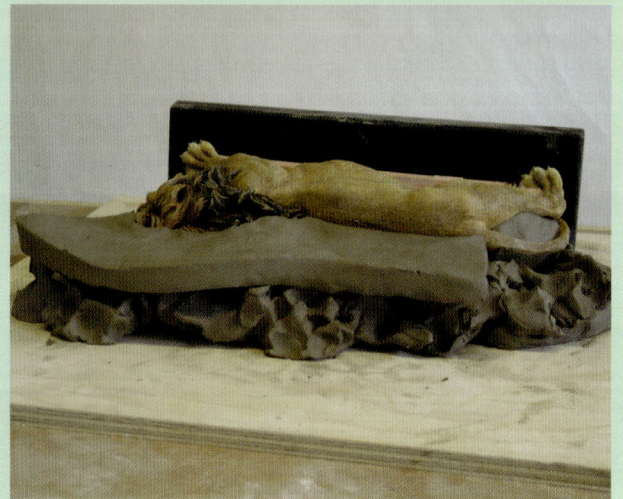

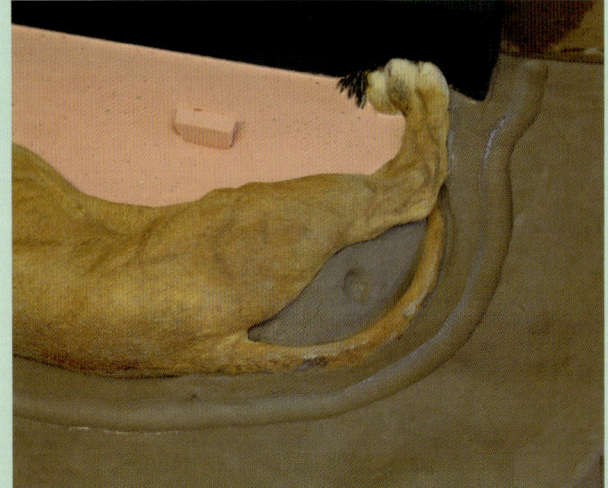

TOP LEFT: **The liquid silicone core is poured.**

TOP RIGHT: **The set core, showing registration indents.**

MIDDLE LEFT: **The set core, showing registration blocks.**

MIDDLE RIGHT: **A clay bed and top slap are created.**

LEFT: **A registration 'pinch line' is cut.**

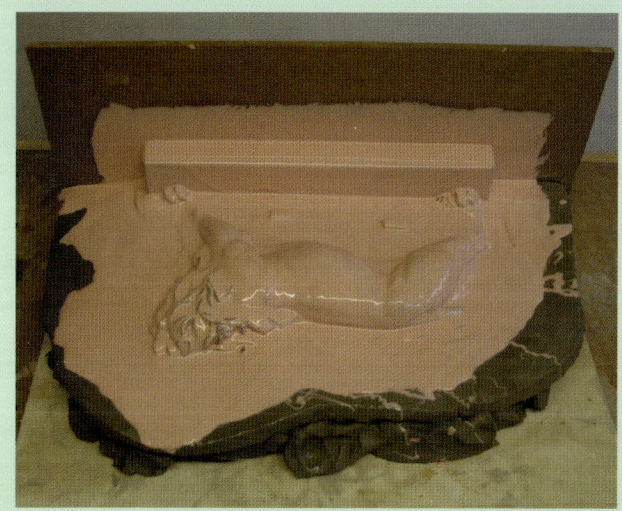

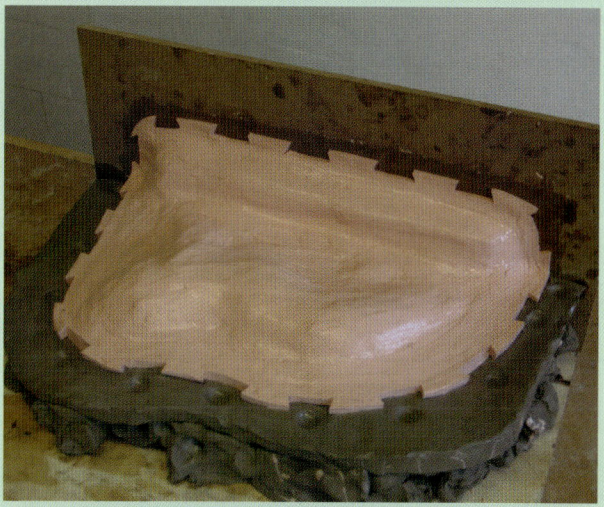

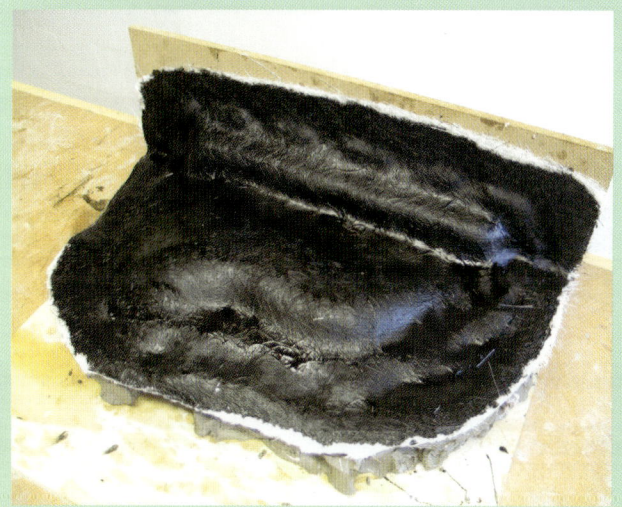

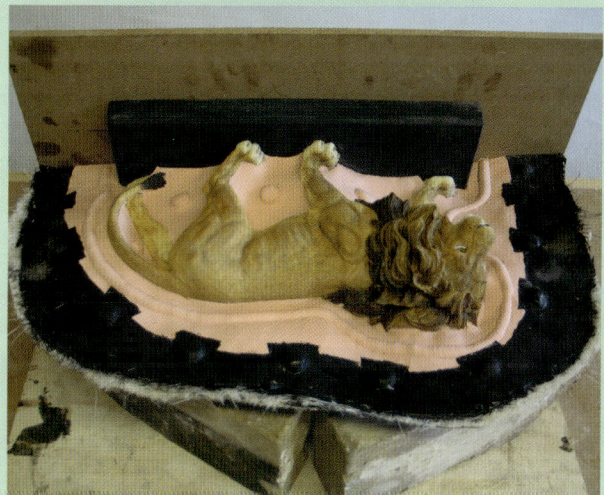

TOP LEFT: The first silicone coat is applied and allowed to set.

TOP RIGHT: A thixotropic coat is applied, allowed to set and registration dovetails are cut.

MIDDLE LEFT: A polyester resin and fibreglass case is created.

MIDDLE RIGHT: The mould is flipped ready for the second half of the mould to be made.

RIGHT: The second silicone half is created.

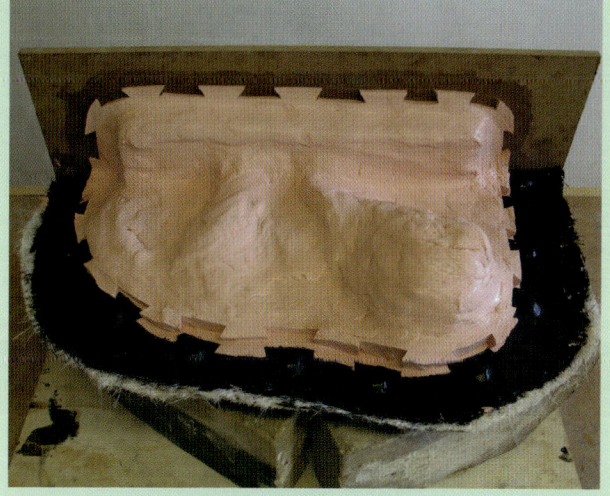

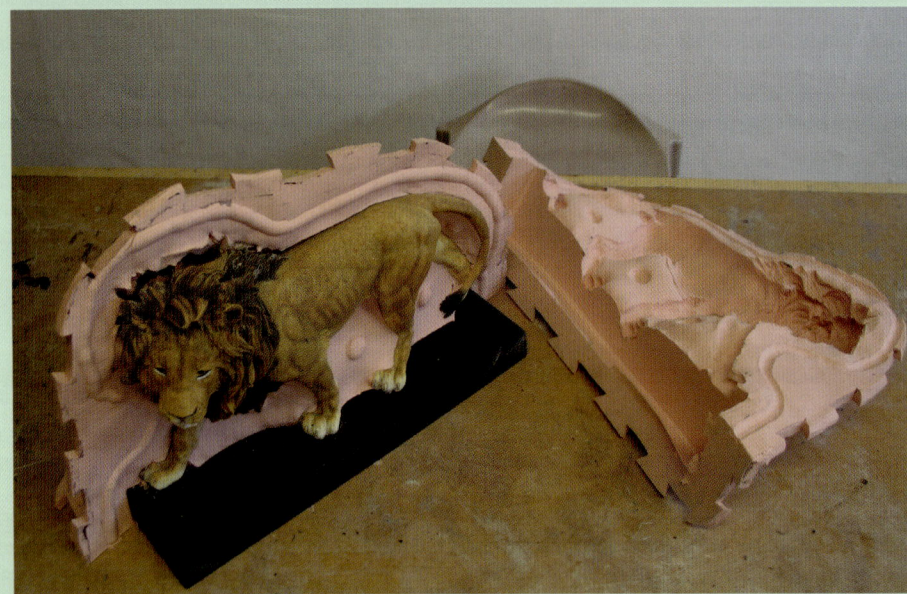

The two outside mould pieces are removed to reveal the core inside.

THE CLAY BED

With the mould core created, the first side mould piece enclosing it can be made. A clay bed needs to be created to build to a midway point around the original.

1. Define where the midway point surrounding the original is and mark it or commit it to memory.
2. With small pieces of clay build up a rough clay bed to within 10mm of the division line.
3. Smooth the top surface.
4. Using a clay harp set at 10mm, cut a slab of clay.
5. Roughly cut to shape and place it on top of the rough clay bed.
6. With a clay tool make the connection of the clay bed and the division line around the original. Ensure that the point of connection between clay bed and the original is at a right angle.
7. Smooth the surface of the clay bed with a rubber kidney clay tool. Use vegetable oil to allow the kidney to smooth the surface without dragging.
8. Using a looped wire clay tool, create a pinch line in the clay bed around the original 10–15mm out from the point of connection with the clay bed.
9. Because the model has a base the mould will need to encompass this. Secure a board against the underside of the base so the mould can be created around it.
10. Apply spray release agent to exposed surfaces of the core, original and board against the base.

THE FIRST SIDE MOULD PIECE AND CASE

The next task is to create the first side mould piece against the exposed area of the mould core and exposed half of the original using the brushable thixotropic silicone paste method and fibreglass case methods (see *Mouldmaking and Casting* for details).

1. Apply wax spray release agent to the exposed clay bed.
2. Paint on silicone detail coat and allow it to set fully.
3. Lay up the thixotropic coat to mould thickness and allow it to set fully.
4. Cut registration 'dovetails' around the silicone extending on to the clay bed. This will register the silicone into the fibreglass case.
5. Create the fibreglass case to support the silicone. Allow it to set fully.

THE SECOND SIDE MOULD PIECE AND CASE

1. Remove the board against the base of the original.
2. Keeping the previously created core, mould piece and case and the original together, carefully flip the whole mould over to reveal the second side of the original.
3. The second side of the original and mould core can now be seen sitting within the first side mould piece and case.
4. Remove the clay bed and mould core clay wall.

5. Carefully clean any clay debris off the exposed original, mould core and exposed flange of the first side mould piece with a sponge. Ensure all surfaces are dry.

6. Reset the board against base of the original.

7. Apply spray wax release agent to all surfaces.

8. Create the second side silicone piece and supporting fibreglass case as above.

TRIMMING, DRILLING AND OPENING THE MOULD

Now the mould is complete it can be trimmed, drilled and opened.

1. Remove the board against the base of the original.

2. With an electric jigsaw or hacksaw blade in a holder trim approximately 10mm off the outside edge of the fibreglass case flange. This is to remove the rough edge of the case flanges to a good edge and expose the seam line between the pieces of the case.

3. Trim the case flange around the opening of the mould in the same way.

4. Sand the surface of the fibreglass case for safe handling.

5. Drill 6.5mm holes at 40–50mm intervals, approximately 20mm out from the original around the case flange. These will accommodate M6 nuts and bolts to secure the mould pieces together.

6. Introduce a thin blade knife between the two case pieces and separate them.

7. Remove the case pieces from the silicone and peel away the two outside silicone mould pieces from the original. Sometimes the case including the silicone will come away in one operation.

8. Carefully remove the mould core from the original. There will be an 'easy' direction to pull the mould core away from the original, depending upon the position of the legs.

9. With the mould removed, all pieces can be washed, dried and reassembled with the nuts and bolts ready for use.

10. When reassembling first secure both side pieces of silicone into their supporting cases. Next secure the mould core into one of the side pieces. Lastly secure the second side piece.

11. When tightening nuts and bolts secure them in opposite pairs in sequence a little at a time until firm. This will ensure the seam line of the mould is secured evenly all round and not squeezed tighter at one point.

12. Do not over-tighten the nuts and bolts as it may distort the core inside and compromise the seam lines.

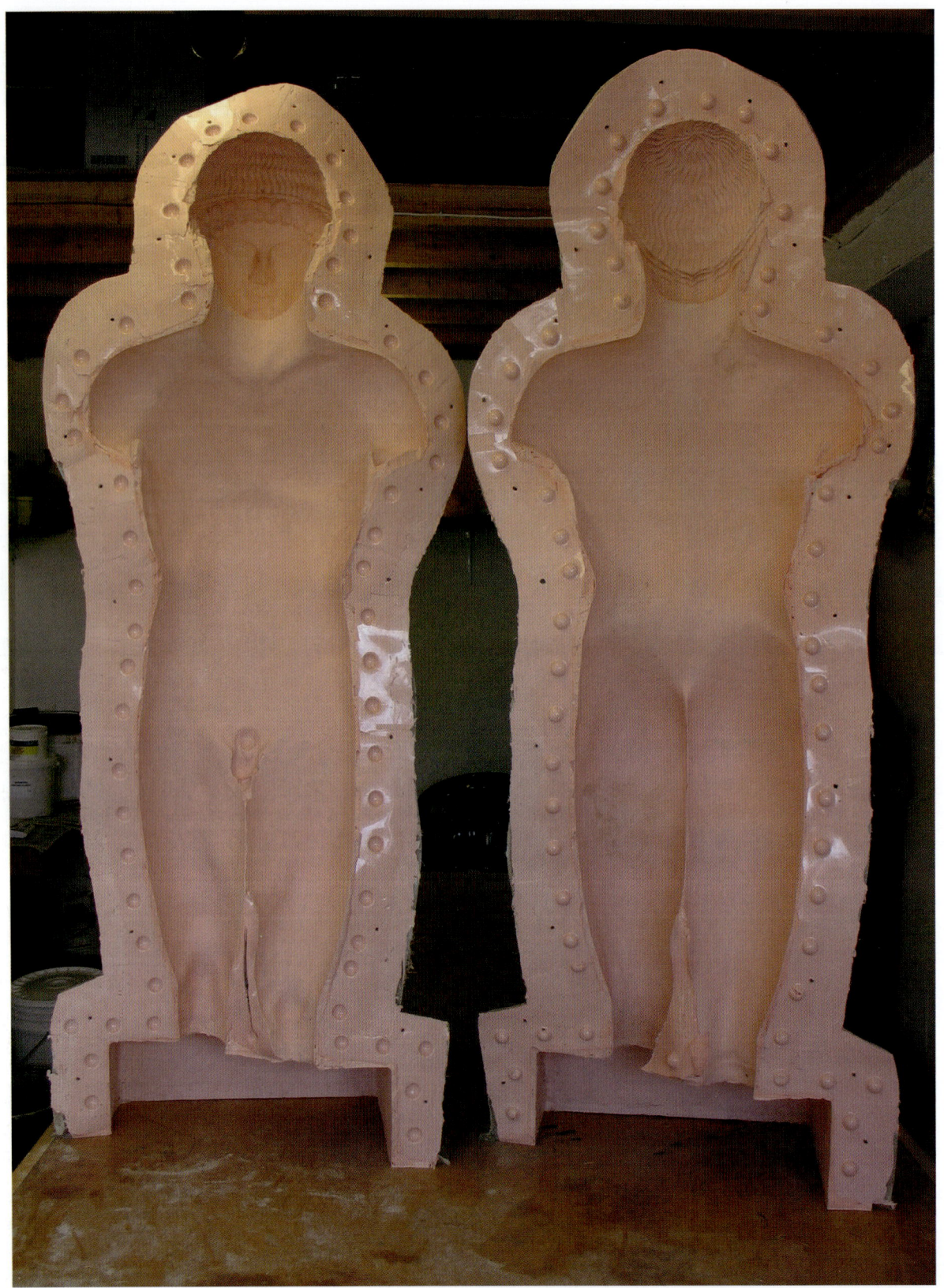

Silicone rubber mould created using 'Plas-ti-shim' system.

CHAPTER TWO

PLAS-TI-SHIM™

Developed by Andrew Sinclair in 2004 and marketed in 2008, Plas-ti-shim™ is a prefabricated plastic shim system of silicone production mouldmaking. The system has some distinct advantages over traditional silicone mouldmaking methods, namely the single application of silicone rubber in multiple-piece mould production. As Sinclair explains in his technical information leaflet on Plas-ti-shim, 'The main motivation behind it was the obvious disadvantages and shortcomings of clay walls which to me as a commercial moulder were so frustrating especially on large or complicated moulds.'

Technical Description and Specifications

The Plas-ti-shim system comprises a set of prefabricated thin plastic shim walls with vacuum-formed registration bubbles set at regular intervals along them and a set of prefabricated plaster registration buttons (Little Buddie™).

The Plasti-shim walls, available in various sizes, are used to create mould division walls traditionally created with clay walls or beds. However, unlike traditional methods of multiple-piece mouldmaking the application of silicone rubber is performed in one operation and the separation of the pieces is carried out at the last stage of production. This system clearly has advantages, particularly with dramatic time savings on production.

The 'Little Buddies' are pre-made plaster buttons that are used to produce registration pockets for the case material. The Plas-ti-shim walls and Little Buddies can be used over and

over again, with obvious cost-cutting advantages over clay wall systems.

The first stage of production is an application of a single coat of catalyzed silicone rubber over the entire original or pattern to be moulded. This coat is allowed to set and captures all original detail in one operation. Mould divisions are then determined and set out using a piped raised bead of very thixotropic silicone on top of the first coat. The piping process is carried out using a bag in the same way as for cake decorating. While the bead is still unset, Plas-ti-shim walls are set into it to form the mould divisions. The rest of the mould is then produced on either side of the shims as usual, using thixotropic silicone layers and backed up with a rigid case. On demoulding of the silicone the Plas-ti-shims are removed and the silicone is cut to separate the individual mould pieces.

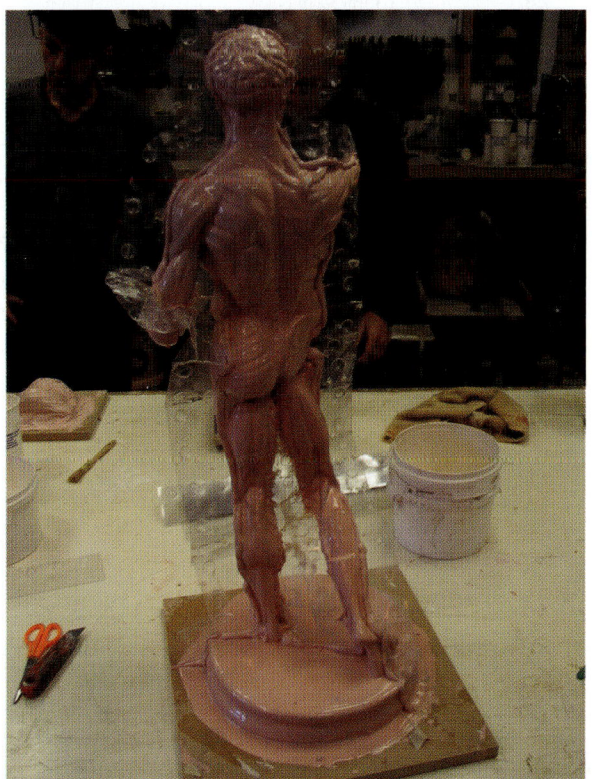

The first stages of a Plas-ti-shim moulding a figure (H: 800mm).

PROJECT

Specification

A two-piece silicone rubber and polyester resin and fibre-glass case mould. Taken from a plaster copy of the *Kouros of Anaphe* (510–50BC). Size: 1010mm (H) and 390mm (W).

Time Required

Allowing for setting times this project can be carried out over approximately two and a half days.

Materials

- Plas-ti-shim (large);
- Little Buddies;
- magic tape;
- Silastic™ 3495 condensation cure silicone rubber (supplied by Notcutt Ltd);
- polyester resin gelcoat;
- general-purpose polyester resin;
- fibreglass mat (supplied by Alec Tiranti Ltd);
- Fillite®;
- spray wax release agent;
- acetone;
- white spirit;
- reinforcing bars; and
- M6 × 30mm roofing bolts with wing nuts.

Tools

- Mixing beakers;
- digital scales;
- brushes;
- a palette knife;
- scissors;
- a craft knife;
- a drill; and
- disposable gloves.

Method

SET-UP AND PREPARATION

As with any project, careful preparation before the start of the job is crucial. Knowing the material quantities and tools needed, undertaking repairs to the original and setting-up the working area will all help to complete the job accurately and efficiently. (Tip: make sure you have enough materials to complete the job before you start. Running out of material halfway through the job is at least a waste of time and, at worst, a loss of previously executed work.)

1. Ensure the original is set on a secure work surface and any surface repairs are done. In this case some minor cracks and missing pieces are filled and remodelled in clay as a temporary repair before making the mould.
2. Ensure any gap between the base of the original and the work surface is filled with clay.
3. Apply spray wax release agent all over the original and out by approximately 100mm around the base onto the work surface.

THE FIRST COAT OF SILICONE

This first coat is crucial as it is the 'capture' layer of all the original detail. With the Plas-ti-shim system this can be done in one operation from the outset of mouldmaking.

1. Mix batches of silicone and catalyst to their specifications.
2. Apply with a soft brush methodically and evenly over the whole surface of the original. Start at the bottom and work up to avoid drips. This coat will be very runny as it does not contain thixotropic additive. This allows the silicone to pick up all the detail of the original. It will probably only be about 1mm thick.
3. The coat should be allowed to set thoroughly. Use of an extra fast catalyst will allow you to proceed to the next step more quickly.

THE APPLICATION OF DIVISION LINES

1. Create a piping bag using a strong but flexible plastic bag. The plastic bag should be about A4 size and without a folded seam.
2. Cut off a corner of the bag with scissors, creating a hole approx 8mm in diameter. This will determine the size of the bead of silicone delivered, so on a smaller mould it may need to be smaller.
3. Determine where the seam lines of the mould are to run. (This is a matter of mouldmaking principles as explained in the precursor to this book, *Mouldmaking and Casting*.) The lines can either be drawn onto the set silicone first coat with a water-based marker for guidance or committed to memory.

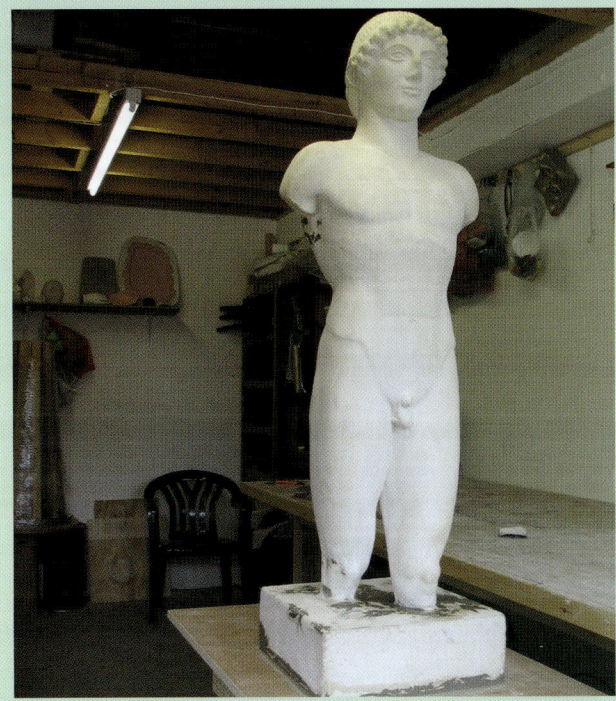

The original is cleaned and surface repairs done, ready for moulding.

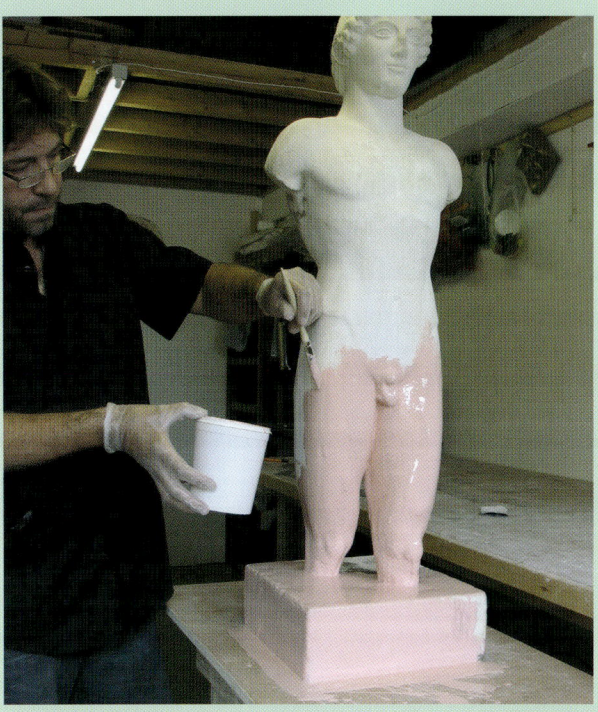

The first layer of silicone is applied, bottom to top.

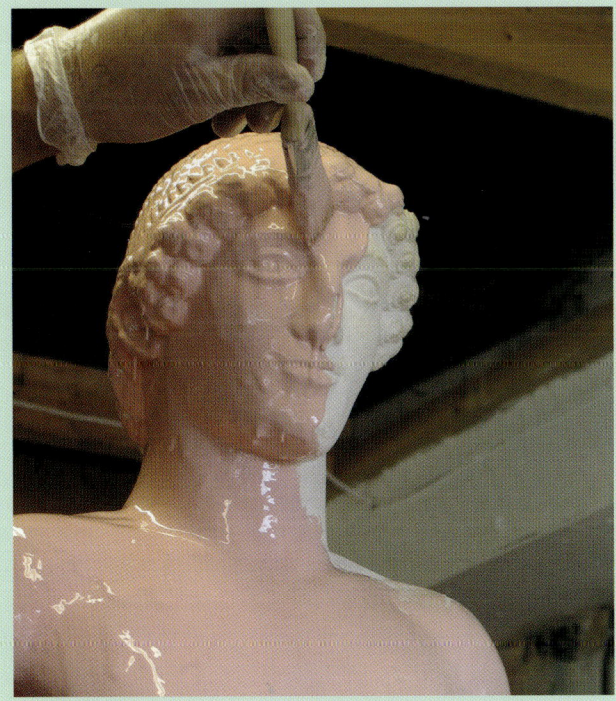

The first coat will necessarily be thin and capture the detail of the original.

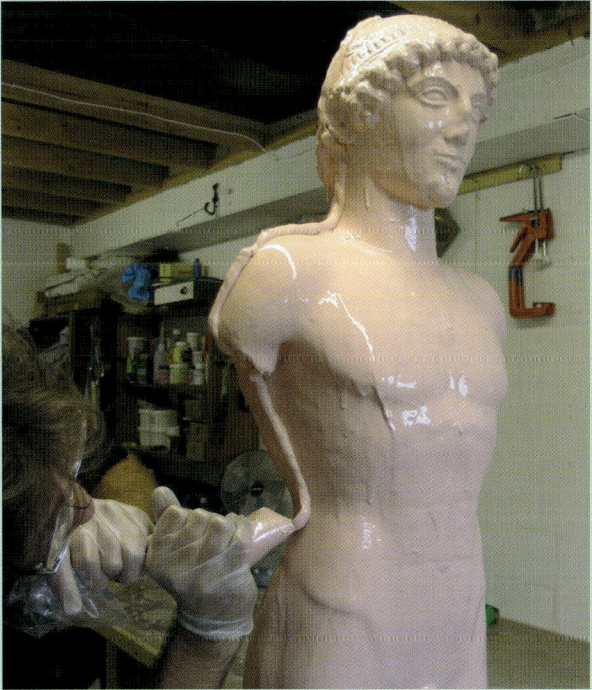

A thixotropic bead of silicone is piped along the division line of the mould.

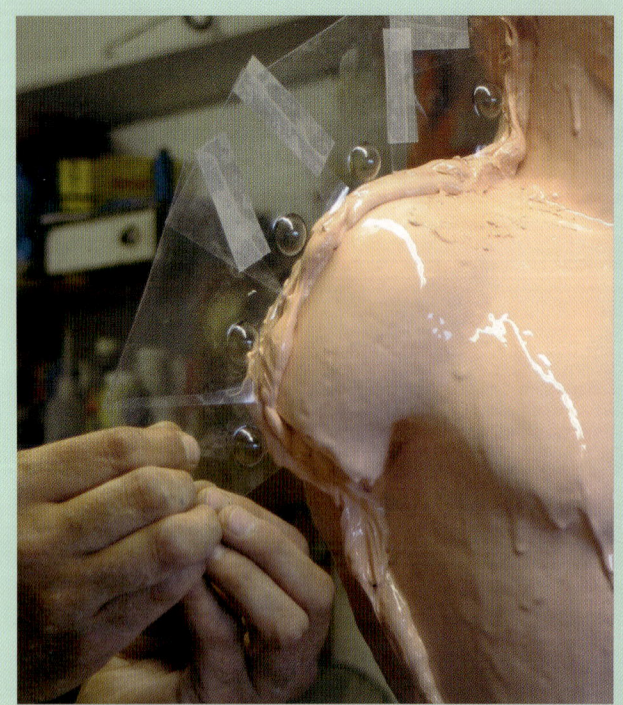

Plas-ti-shim is set into the bead of silicone while still unset. Tape is used to join overlapping pieces.

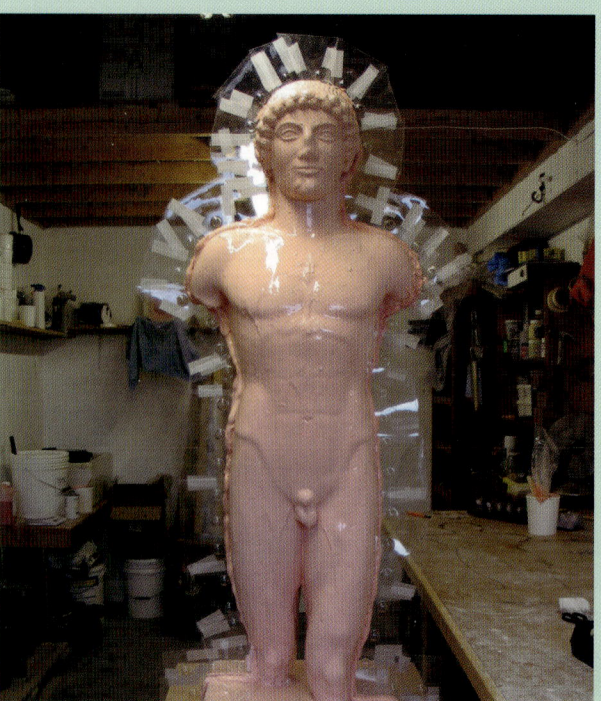

The Plas-ti-shim wall is complete.

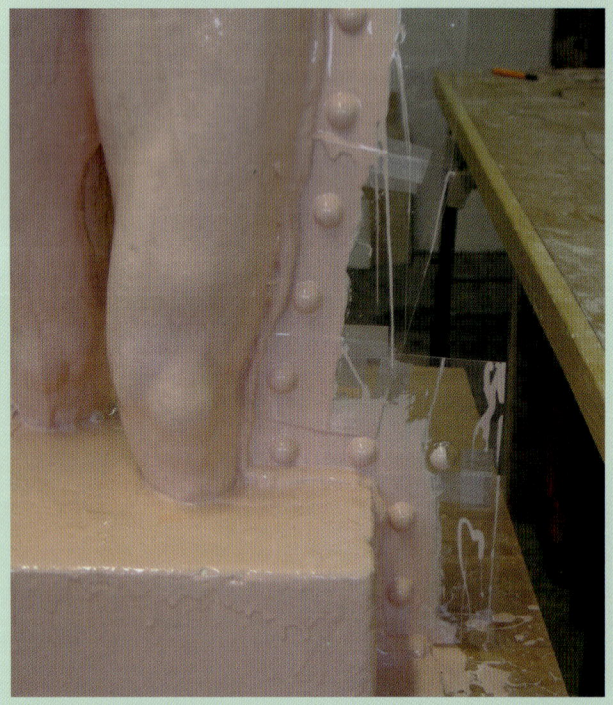

A layer of silicone is applied over the shim and bead.

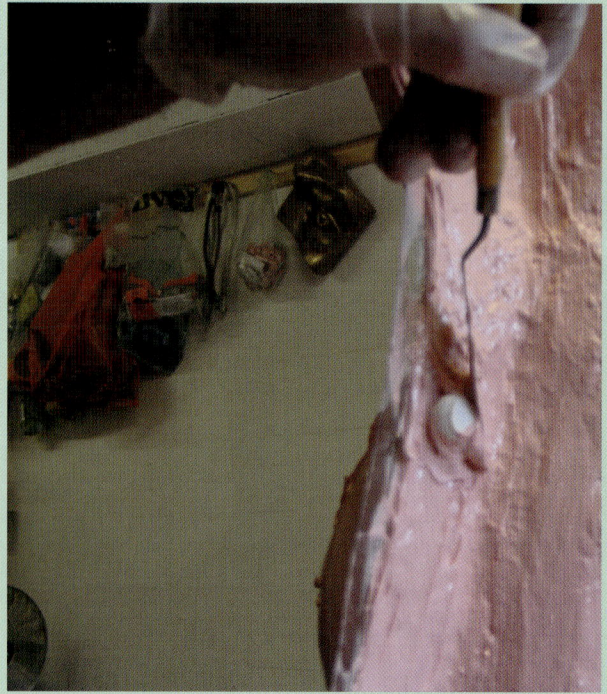

Thixotropic silicone is applied around the set Little Buddy.

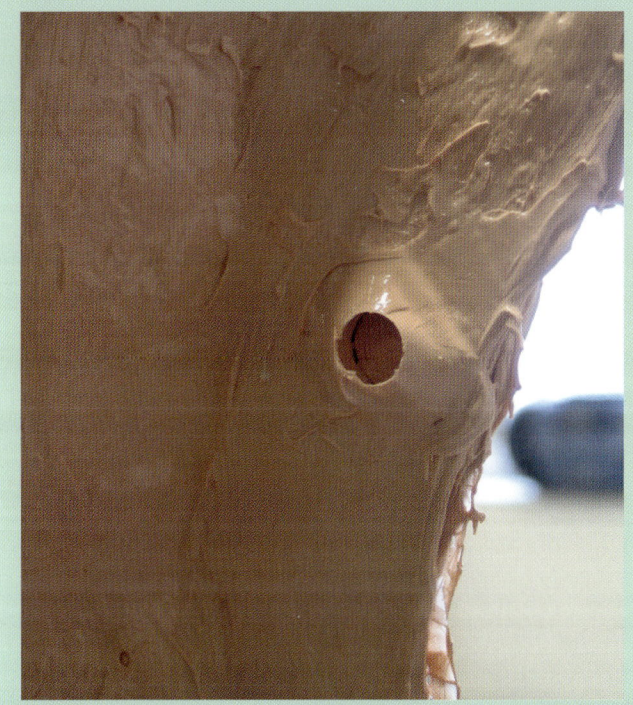

Little Buddies are removed to produce registration holes into which the mould case can locate.

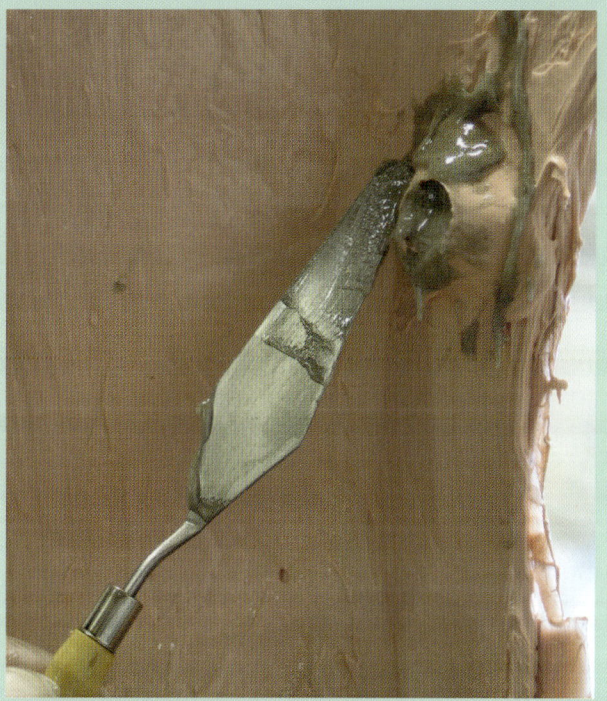

The Little Buddy holes are filled with thixotropic polyester resin.

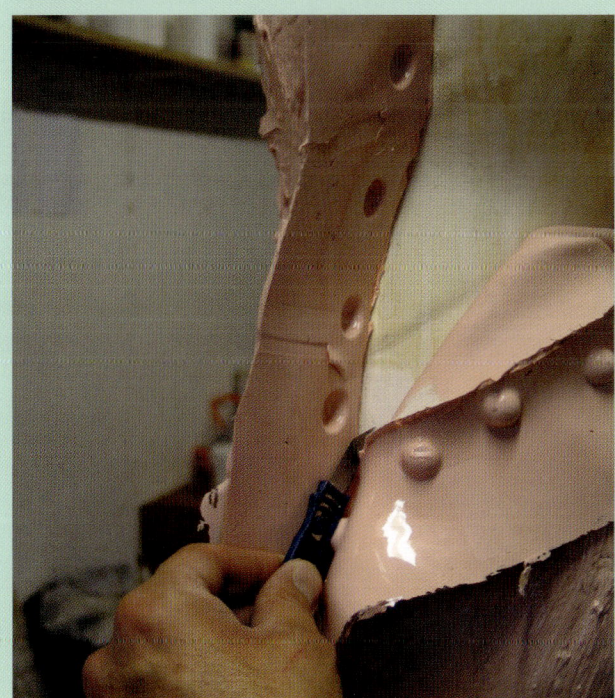

The last millimetre of silicone between the two silicone flanges is cut to separate the two mould pieces.

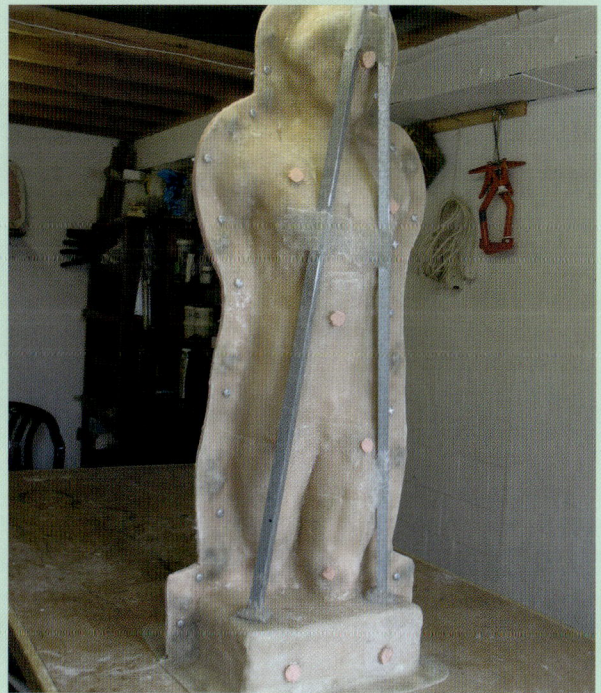

Reinforcing metal splints for added strength are built into the case.

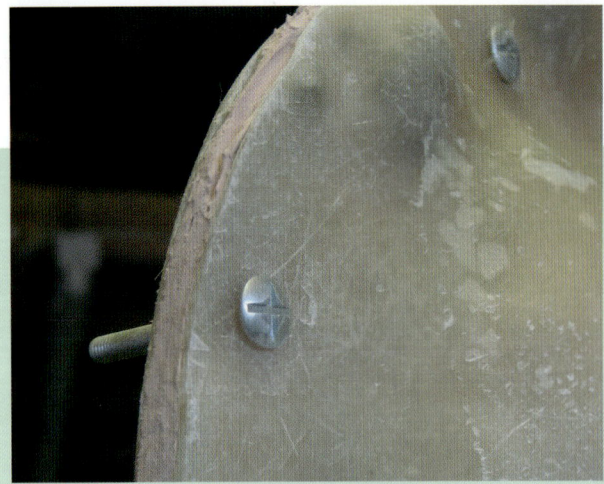

LEFT: The mould is trimmed, sanded and nuts and bolts are set to secure the mould pieces together.

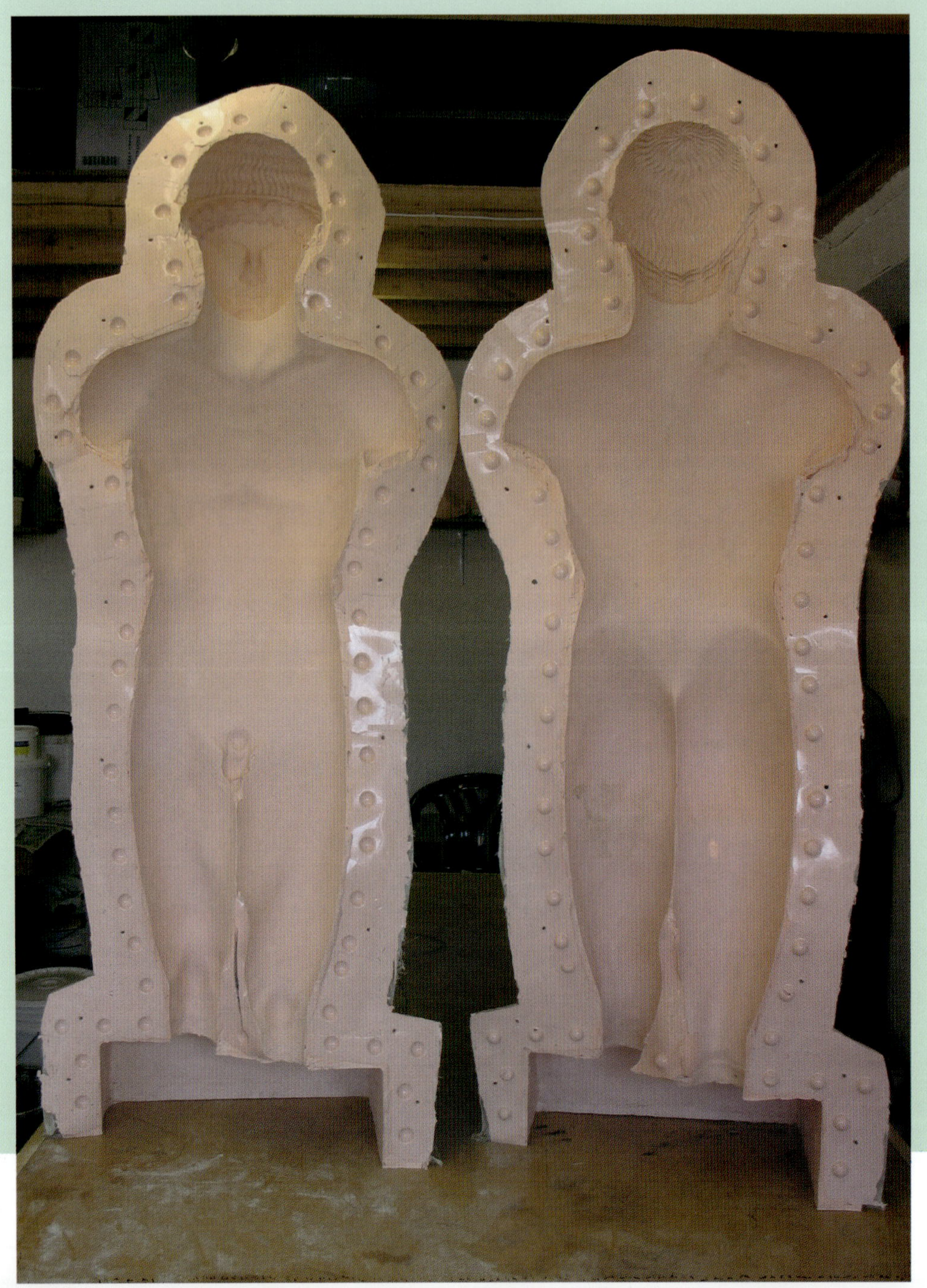

LEFT: The two-piece silicone rubber and fibreglass case mould.

4. Mix a batch of silicone with catalyst and a very high percentage of thixotropic additive. The silicone bead needs to support the Plas-ti-shim wall so it needs to be very thixotropic.

5. Half fill the bag and twist up the top to work the silicone down into the corner of it and out of the hole.

6. Keeping pressure on the bag by squeezing it evenly, deliver a regular bead of silicone along all the seam division lines.

APPLICATION OF THE PLAS-TI-SHIM WALLS

Once the division beads have been created the Plas-ti-shim walls need to be applied while the silicone is still wet.

1. Cut the Plas-ti-shim wall with scissors approximately to fit the profiled contours of the division lines. Long flat sections of Plas-ti-shim can be cut in one piece. Tight curves can be made up of small overlapped sections. The Plas-ti-shim can be bent along curves of division lines.

2. Push the shim into the bead of silicone as far as it will go, working along the lines and overlapping adjoining pieces by approximately 20mm.

3. Magic tape should be applied neatly to join sections. When cutting the shim enough room should be left between the registration bubbles to allow for the tape.

4. Tape one side as you go and then tape the other side when complete.

5. Allow the silicone bead with the embedded Plas-ti-shim wall to set thoroughly.

FLANGES

Once the bead has set it will hold the Plas-ti-shim wall in place but it needs to be reinforced to secure it thoroughly before the rest of the mould can be built up with thixotropic silicone. This will create the flanges around all the mould pieces.

1. Mix a batch of silicone and catalyst and coat evenly over both sides of the Plas-ti-shim wall and silicone bead to create the mould flange.

2. Allow to set thoroughly.

THE THIXOTROPIC COAT

This layer will build up the silicone to the full thickness required.

1. Apply thixotropic addition silicone on top of the existing silicone over the surface of the mould, up to approx 5–8mm thick.

2. Cover both sides of the shim walls as well.

SET LITTLE BUDDIES

The Little Buddies provide a method of registering and securing the silicone into the case of the mould.

1. While the thixotropic coat is still wet, gently place Little Buddies at 100mm intervals just above the registration bubbles along the flange, and push them a little way into the silicone.

2. With another batch of thixotropic silicone completely cover the Little Buddies, building up a thick collar around them and a thin layer over the top.

3. Pre-made blocks of set silicone can be placed over the body of the silicone to register into the mould case. Case registration 'buttons' can be made at a later stage if necessary when the mould is complete (see end of chapter).

4. Allow the silicone to set thoroughly.

REMOVE LITTLE BUDDIES

1. With a craft knife carefully trim off the thin skin of silicone covering the Little Buddies.

2. Remove the Little Buddies.

3. Make up a thixotropic mix of the case-making material (plaster, polyester resin or Jesmonite) and pack out the void left by the Little Buddies. This will create a registration 'button' that will locate and hold the silicone mould pieces into the case.

CASE MAKING

A rigid case needs to be created to support the silicone rubber. Case pieces should extend out to the edges of the mould wall flanges on either side, sandwiching the silicone between them.

1. Complete the case making in your chosen material as normal, covering all areas with silicone right out to the edge of the mould flanges.

2. Allow to set thoroughly.

MOULD TRIMMING

Before removing the mould from the original it needs to be trimmed for ease of handling when in use.

1. Trim all the mould flange edges by approximately 10mm until it is back to a good edge.
2. Sand the case body to make it safe to handle.
3. Drill 6.5mm holes at 100mm intervals around the mould flanges, approximately 40mm out from the original inside. These will accommodate nuts and bolts to secure the mould pieces together; M6 roofing bolts and wing nuts are good for this. It is important to drill the holes before removing the mould from the original to ensure the accurate relocation of the mould pieces.

SEPARATING SILICONE MOULD PIECES

1. Remove all case pieces. It may be necessary to introduce a strong-bladed knife between the case and the silicone flanges to ease the case pieces away.
2. Carefully fold open both parts of the silicone flange and cut through the last millimetre of silicone with a craft knife. It is important to do this as neatly as possible in one even cut rather than with a sawing action to ensure as tight a seam as possible.
3. With all the mould and case pieces separated, wash, dry and reassemble them ready for use.

Note: Nuts and bolts should be secured finger-firm for storage and tightened in opposite pairs a little at a time until tight for casting.

CREATING CASE REGISTRATION BUTTONS AFTER MOULD PRODUCTION

If the silicone rubber of a mould needs more registration into the case it is possible to make registration buttons after mould production. Sometimes this is necessary if the silicone rubber is not holding firmly into the case. The following explains how to create silicone buttons to anchor the mould.

1. Drill 20mm holes at the points on the case where buttons are required.
2. Sand inside the edges of the holes.
3. Register the silicone rubber back onto the original.

4. Register the case back onto the silicone.
5. Create a collar of clay, 20mm high, around the holes. The collar should be slightly narrower at the base than the top.
6. Clean any release agent off the exposed surface of the silicone within the collar.
7. Pour silicone into the collar to the top.
8. Allow to set.
9. Remove clay collar.

A hole is drilled through the case and the clay collar fitted around it

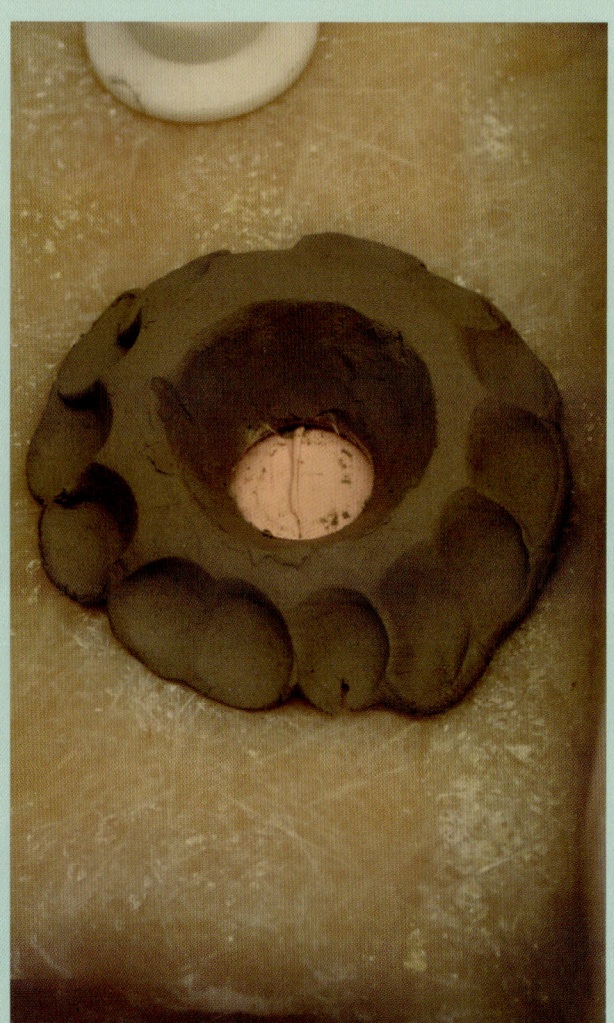

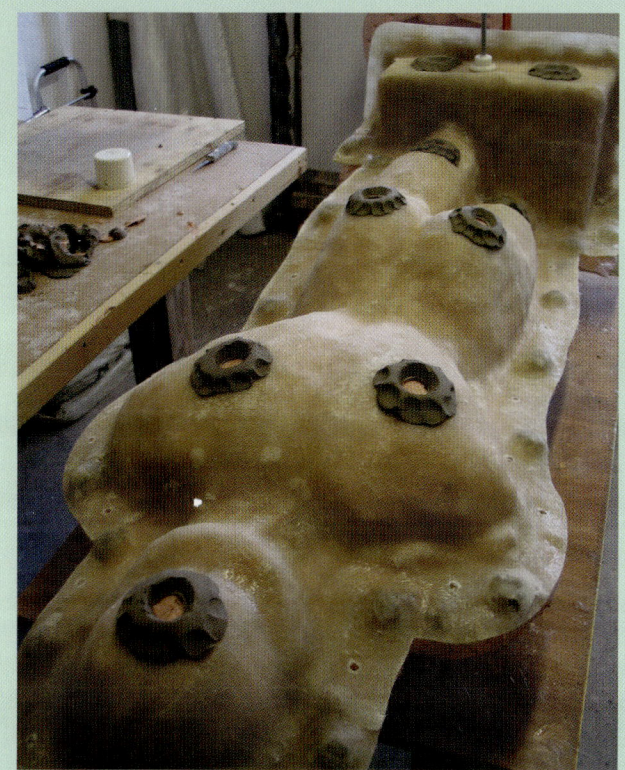

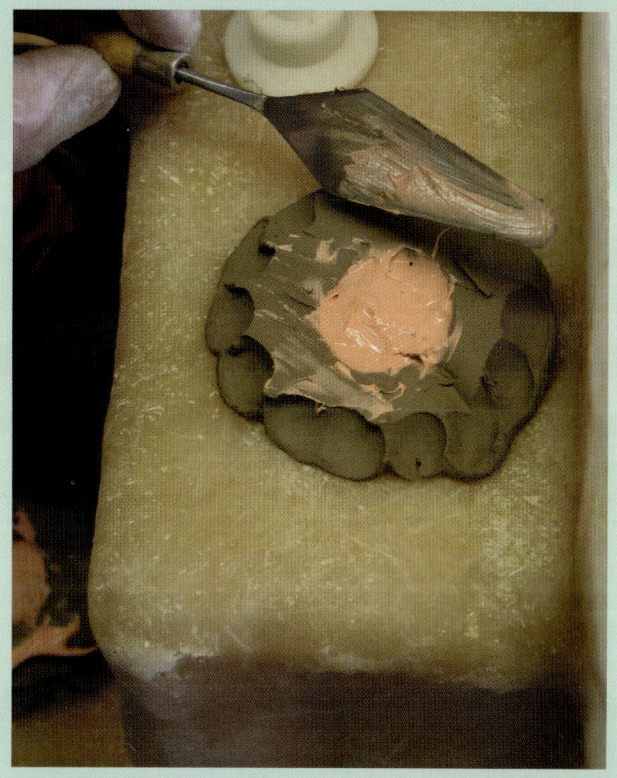

TOP LEFT: There are several strategic button points across the case surface.

TOP RIGHT: The clay collar is filled with silicone.

RIGHT: The collars are removed, revealing the set buttons that anchor the silicone into the case.

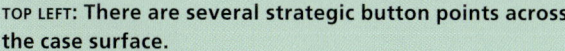

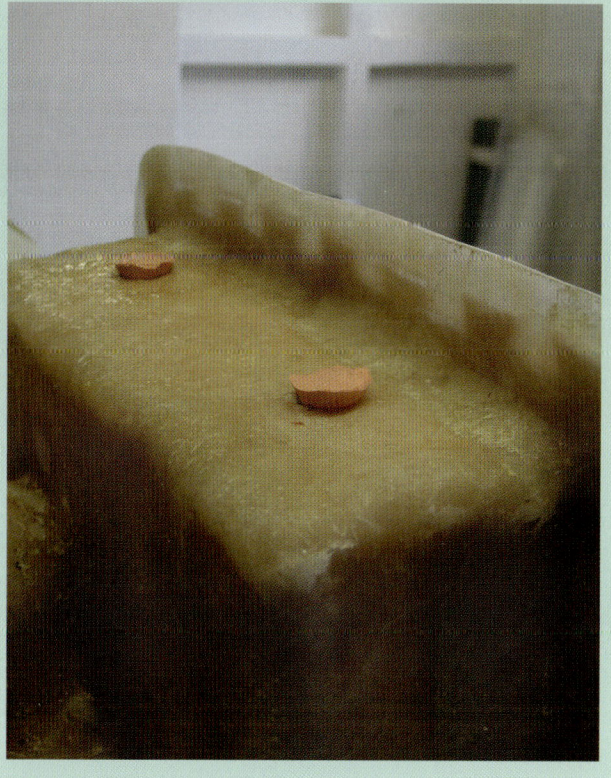

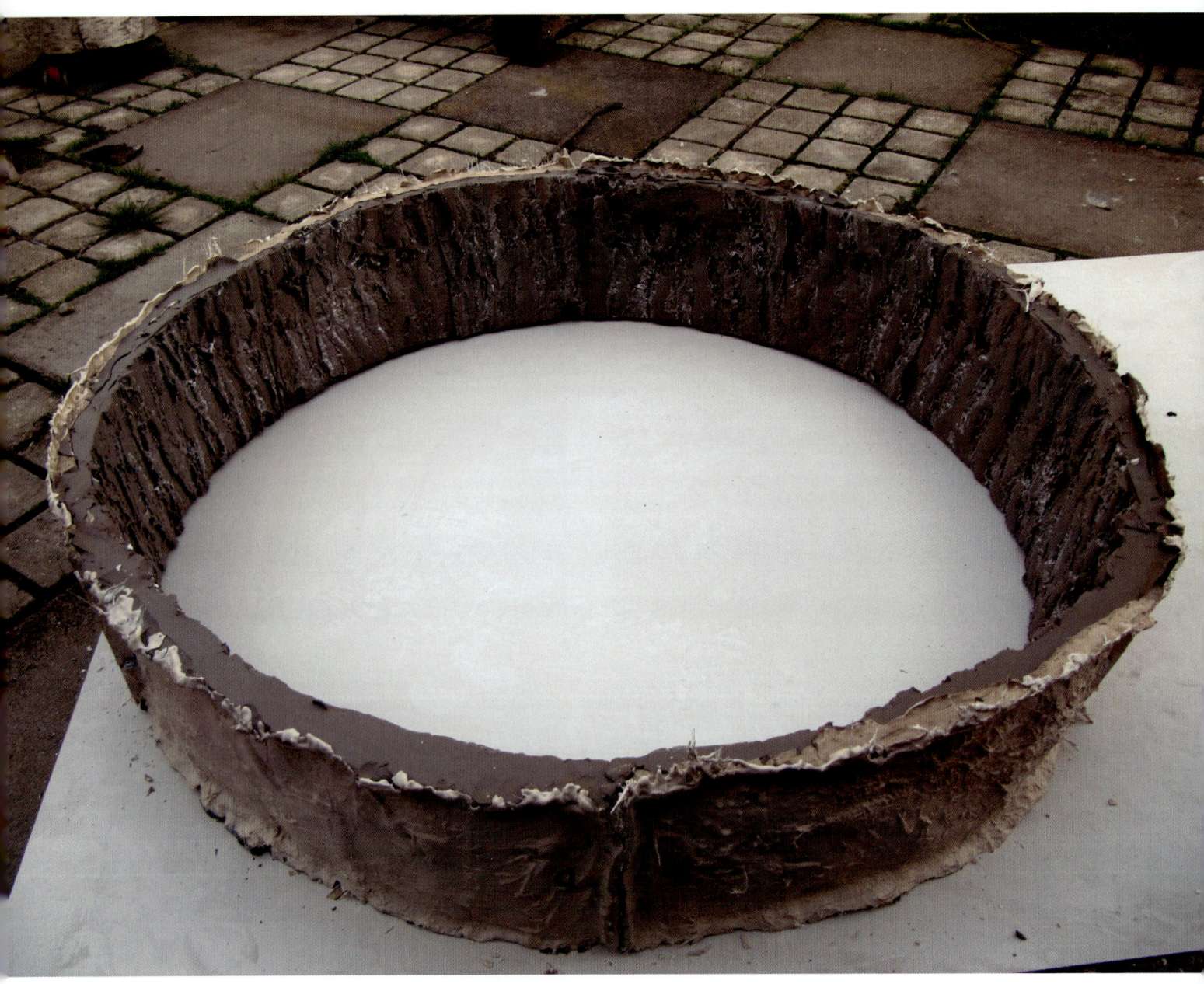

Large scale 'site' clay press mould.

CHAPTER THREE

LARGE-SCALE PRESS MOULDING ON SITE

Press moulding can be an economical and surprisingly accurate method of mould production. Clay press moulding is probably the most fundamental method of mouldmaking. That is, it encompasses the most basic of mouldmaking principles, taking a 'negative from a positive', by the most fundamental of methods: using wet clay to produce a mould from an original. This is mouldmaking at its most basic, the use of wet clay pressed onto the surface of an original or the pressing of a pattern into the clay to create an impression (the mould) and then casting directly into that clay.

The use of clay as a moulding material can be considered as similar to the synthetic moulding materials (such as silicone or gelflex), in that to a certain extent it can be bent around undercutting and then retain its pattern shape. Any sort of clay can be used but bear in mind that red clays may colour the casting (which can be interesting). The consistency of the clay used is important, however. Too soft and the clay will break up and smear when released from the pattern; too hard and a good impression will not be achieved.

Generally plaster is used to create the casting from the clay mould because it can be produced quickly before the clay starts to dry out and no release agents are required. It is usually the case that a one-off mould is created, which is destroyed upon the removal of the first casting.

This mouldmaking method by no means has 100 per cent accuracy compared to the more high-tech moulding processes, and there are certain restrictions in terms of the amount of undercutting and detail that it will accommodate. However, these imperfections can produce unique and interesting castings. It is amazing just how much detail can be achieved with such a basic method of mouldmaking.

On a large scale, case-supported methods of press moulding should be employed. This is a method suitable for large-scale 'site' moulds, where the subject to be moulded cannot be moved and mouldmaking needs to be carried out 'on site'. Slabs of clay are prepared and applied to the original to be moulded and backed up with a rigid plaster case. Moulds in multiple pieces can be created in this way.

PROJECT

Specification

A six-piece clay press mould with a six-piece plaster case from an oak tree. Circumference 3330mm, a section 200mm deep.

Time Required

Due to the nature of the process, press moulding on a large scale should be carried out in one operation, which in practice means completing the project on the same day. This needs to be considered when deciding on the scale of a project.

Materials

- Grey clay (red clays tend to stain castings);
- alpha casting plaster;
- a water source (if not available you will need large tubs of water or jerry cans);
- a heavy fibreglass mat;
- talcum powder;
- plastic sheeting;
- string;
- petroleum jelly; and
- chalk.

Tools

- A sturdy collapsible table;
- a clay harp;
- a plaster mixing bowl;
- 2in brushes;
- scissors;
- a builder's bucket; and
- a permanent marker.

Method

SET-UP AND PREPARATION

As with any project, careful preparation before the start of the job is crucial. Knowing the material quantities and tools needed, undertaking repairs to the original and setting-up the working area will all help to complete the job accurately and efficiently. (Tip: make sure you have enough materials to complete the job before you start. Running out of material halfway through the job is at least a waste of time and, at worst, a loss of previously executed work.)

In the case of large-scale press mould production careful preparation is of particular importance because of the nature of the process. The project needs to be completed efficiently and quickly because clay moulds will dry out, shrink and distort if not cast into immediately after completion.

1. Put up a sturdy collapsible table near the project site to prepare materials. Ensure your water source and bucket for washing tools and equipment are accessible.
2. The area to be moulded should be defined with a chalk line, or in this case a string line.
3. Protect areas not to be moulded using plastic sheeting or heavy-duty dustbin liners.
4. Prepare the clay slabs for the first section. These should be of a size appropriate to the job. Their thickness will depend on the depth of detail to be captured, although they should be thick enough not to break through when pressed into detail. In this example the size of the slabs are 550mm × 200mm × 30mm, and they are applied two at a time by two people.

THE APPLICATION OF RELEASE AGENT

1. With a soft brush apply a liberal amount of talcum powder to the whole area to be moulded.
2. Brush off any excess talcum powder, leaving a fine coating of powder on the surface.

APPLY THE FIRST TWO SLABS

The first two slabs in this project are applied on opposite sides of the tree.

1. Press your pre-prepared slabs firmly to the surface of the tree. Use the heel of your hand to methodically press over the surface of the slab to push it into the detail.
2. If necessary apply the slab in sections butted up against one another. This is usually necessary with large pieces where it may be difficult to apply a section of the mould in one piece because of its size.
3. Create a neat clay wall around the outside edge of the slab. This is to retain the plaster when case making. The wall should be 15mm high along the top and bottom edge of the slab. It should be approximately 50mm high at either end of the slab to create a flanged wall to the case section that will join it to the next section of the mould.
4. Pinch the bottom outside edge of the wall onto the surface of the tree to keep it in place.

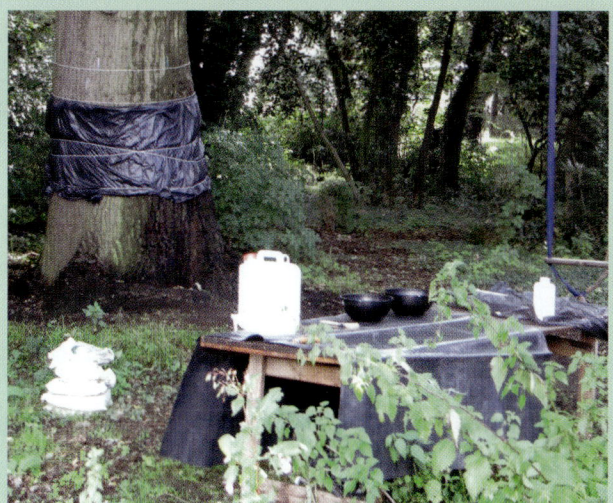

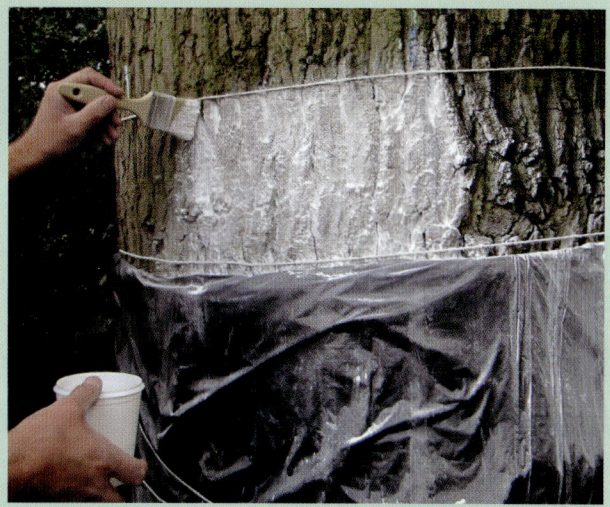

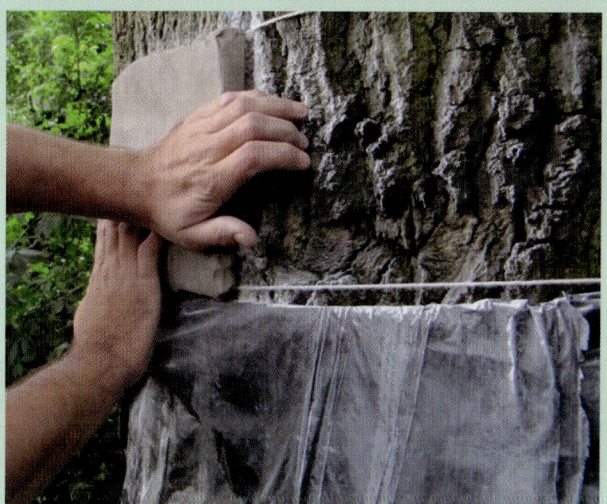

TOP LEFT: Site preparation and bench set-up.

TOP RIGHT: Talcum powder is dusted on the area to be moulded.

RIGHT: The first clay slab is pressed onto the first section to be moulded.

BOTTOM LEFT: A second slab is pressed up against the first to create the first mould section.

BOTTOM MIDDLE: A wall is created around the slab to retain the plaster case.

BOTTOM RIGHT: A first layer of plaster is applied to create the case supporting the slab.

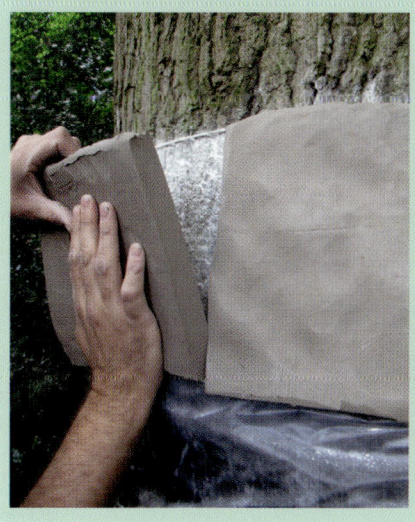

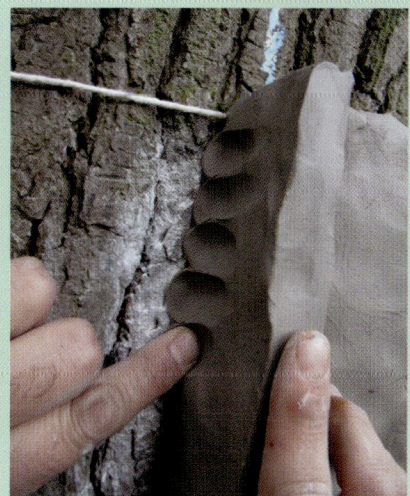

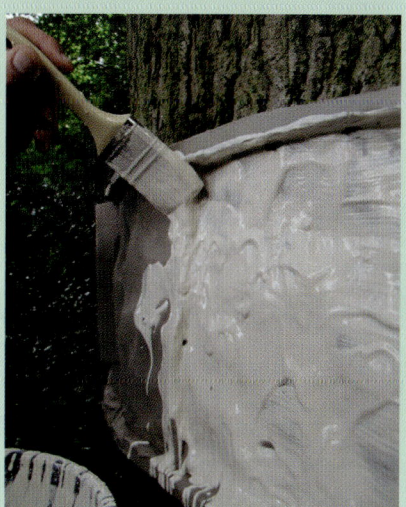

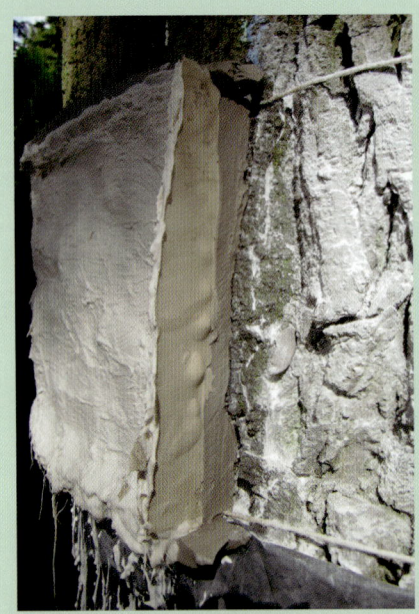

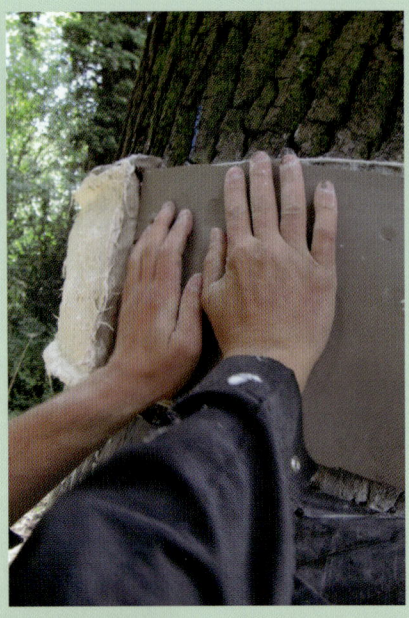

FAR LEFT: With the first mould piece complete, the end retaining clay wall is removed and release agent applied to the case flange.

LEFT: The second mould slab is butted up against the exposed edge of the first.

MIDDLE LEFT: Working on opposite sides of the site to create two mould pieces at the same time.

MIDDLE RIGHT: The last two mould pieces are created between the previously made pieces to complete the mould.

BOTTOM LEFT: Holes are drilled through flanges to accommodate nuts and bolts to secure them upon reassembly.

BOTTOM RIGHT: The mould pieces are removed.

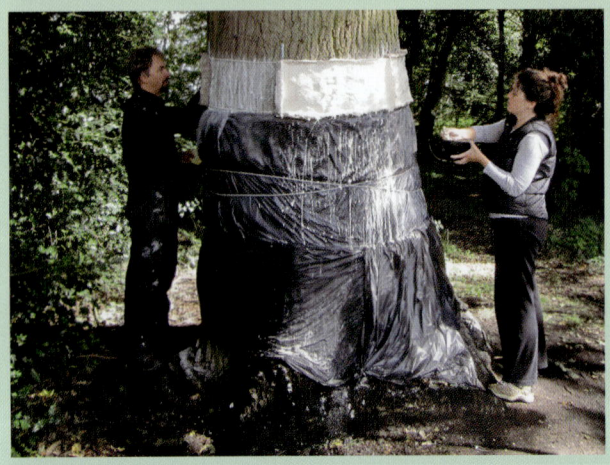

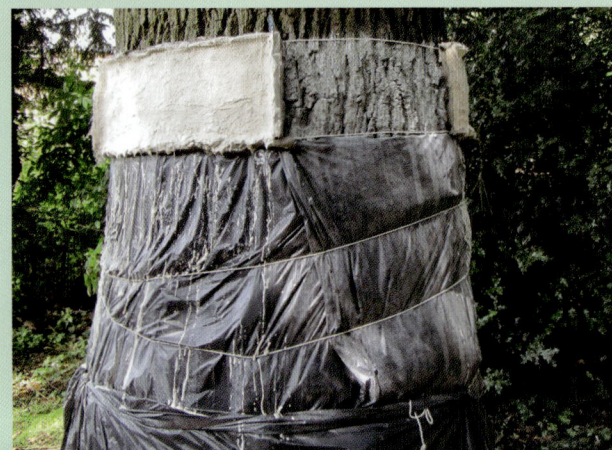

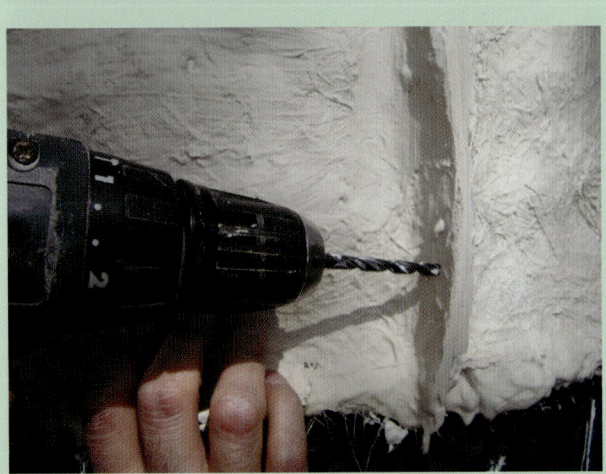

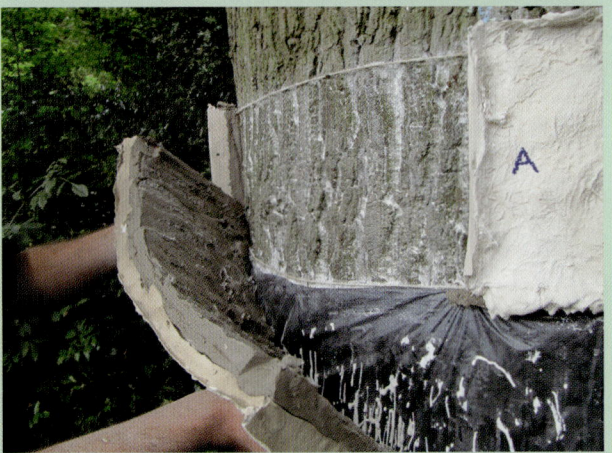

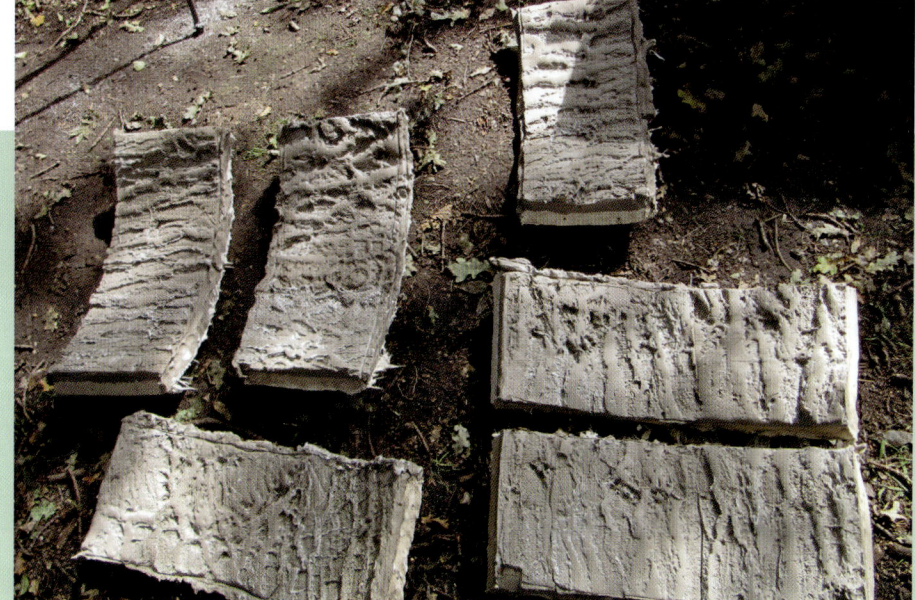

The six mould pieces, ready for reassembly.

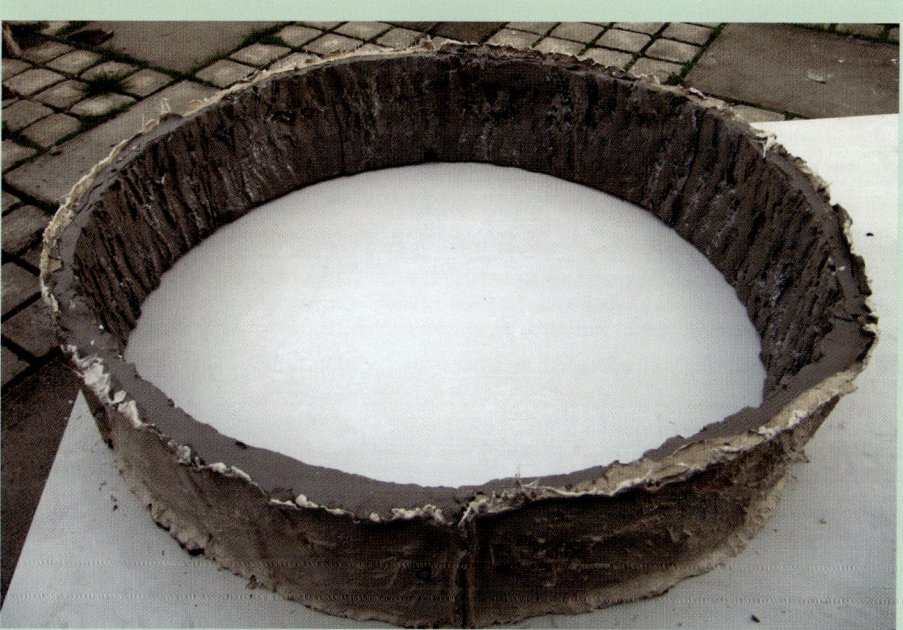

The mould reassembled, ready for casting.

CASE MAKING

The clay slab will have picked up the detail and shape of the tree section but when it is removed it will distort so a rigid case is needed to enable it to hold its shape. The quickest way to do this is with casting plaster.

1. Prepare strips of heavy fibreglass mat. There should be enough to cover the slabbed section once.
2. Apply a layer of plaster 2–3mm thick to the surface of the clay slab. This will pick up detail of the clay slab. Apply plaster to the inside surfaces of the clay walls as well.
3. Allow it to set until it is not depositing onto your finger when touched lightly.
4. Apply a second coat to the first and allow this to set.
5. Dip strips of the fibreglass mat into a mix of plaster and lay them on top of the plaster you have already applied. Ensure a good lamination by pressing lightly over the surface to push out any air bubbles.
6. Apply a thick mix of plaster over the mat layer to complete the case.
7. Allow the casing to set hard.

THE NEXT TWO SECTIONS

With the first two sections of the mould complete, the next two sections can be created. These will be formed directly against the first two sections.

1. Carefully remove the clay walls at either end of the first mould section, revealing the flange wall of the case and the edge of clay mould.
2. Apply petroleum jelly to the exposed flange wall of the plaster case.
3. Prepare the clay slabs to create the next section.
4. Butt up the first strip tightly to the exposed clay edge of the first mould section and then continue the slabbing process in the same way as for the first section.
5. Create a 50mm clay wall at the free end of this slabbed section.
6. Create the clay retaining wall along the top and bottom edges of the second slabbed section. These walls should connect to the exposed edge of the adjoining first plaster case flange.
7. Create a plaster case as before, applying plaster directly against the exposed case flange of the first mould section.
8. Allow the casing to set hard.

THE LAST TWO SECTIONS

Next the last two sections of the mould will be created between the finished previously created mould pieces.

1. Apply petroleum jelly to the two exposed case flanges of the previously made mould pieces.
2. Create the final mould pieces using clay slabs as before, butting up the clay directly against the clay edge of the adjoining mould pieces.
3. Create the last two plaster case pieces as before, applying plaster directly against the flange wall of the previously made case pieces.
4. Allow the casing to set hard.

REMOVING THE MOULD

Once the mould is complete it can be removed from the tree section by section.

1. Before removing any sections, drill two 6.5mm holes through the two adjoining plaster case flanges between each section of the mould. These will accommodate M6 roofing bolts and wing nuts to hold the mould sections together when casting.
2. With a surform tool take back the top edges of the adjoining case flanges to expose the seam line between them.
3. Number or letter each section of the mould to aid reassembly. Also mark an arrow to indicate which way up each section should be when reassembled.
4. Carefully remove the mould sections one piece at a time from the surface of the tree. When doing this be careful not to smear the clay as it comes off. If while removing the sections the plaster case comes away from the clay slabs, carefully lay the empty case on a surface, remove the slabs separately and lay them directly back into the case. This can also be a good way to remove moulds that are deeply undercut, allowing the clay slabs to be bent past any undercutting.
5. Carefully lay each mould piece down on a surface as they come off.
6. When all the mould pieces have been removed reassemble them in order, a section at a time, tightly fastening the sections together with nuts and bolts.
7. Once the mould is reassembled it should be cast immediately to prevent shrinkage of the clay as it dries.
8. For the casting process, laminate the mould with alpha casting plaster and heavy fibreglass mat directly against the wet clay surface.
9. Demould the casting by removing the case pieces and peeling the clay slabs away from the casting.
10. Clean up the site and remove any rubbish and waste.

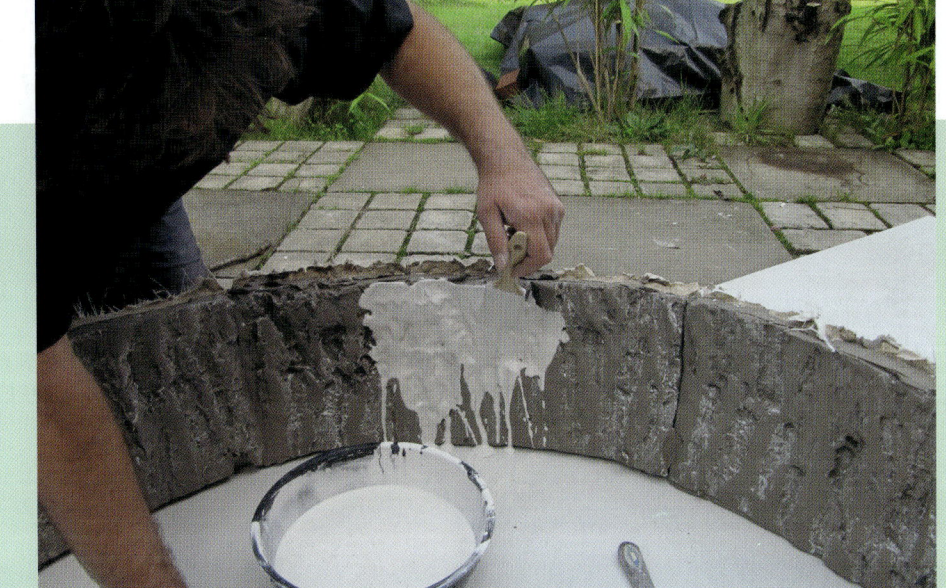

Alpha plaster is applied directly to the clay mould to create a laminated cast.

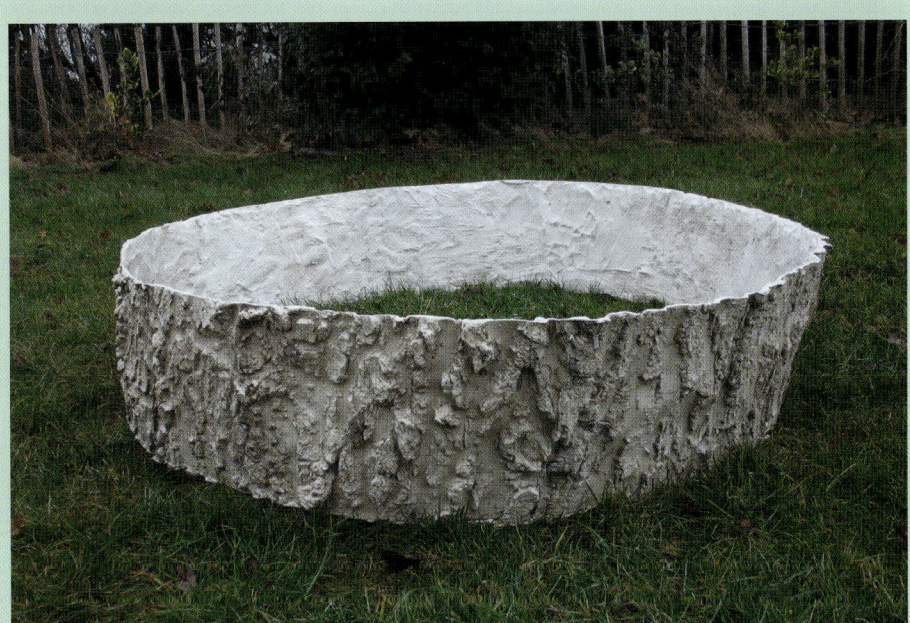

The demoulded cast.

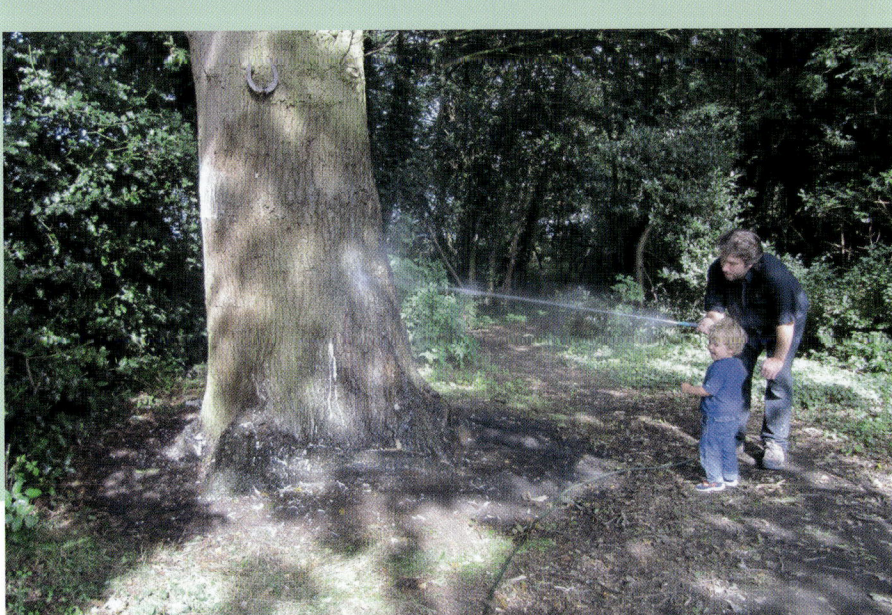

Cleaning up the site.

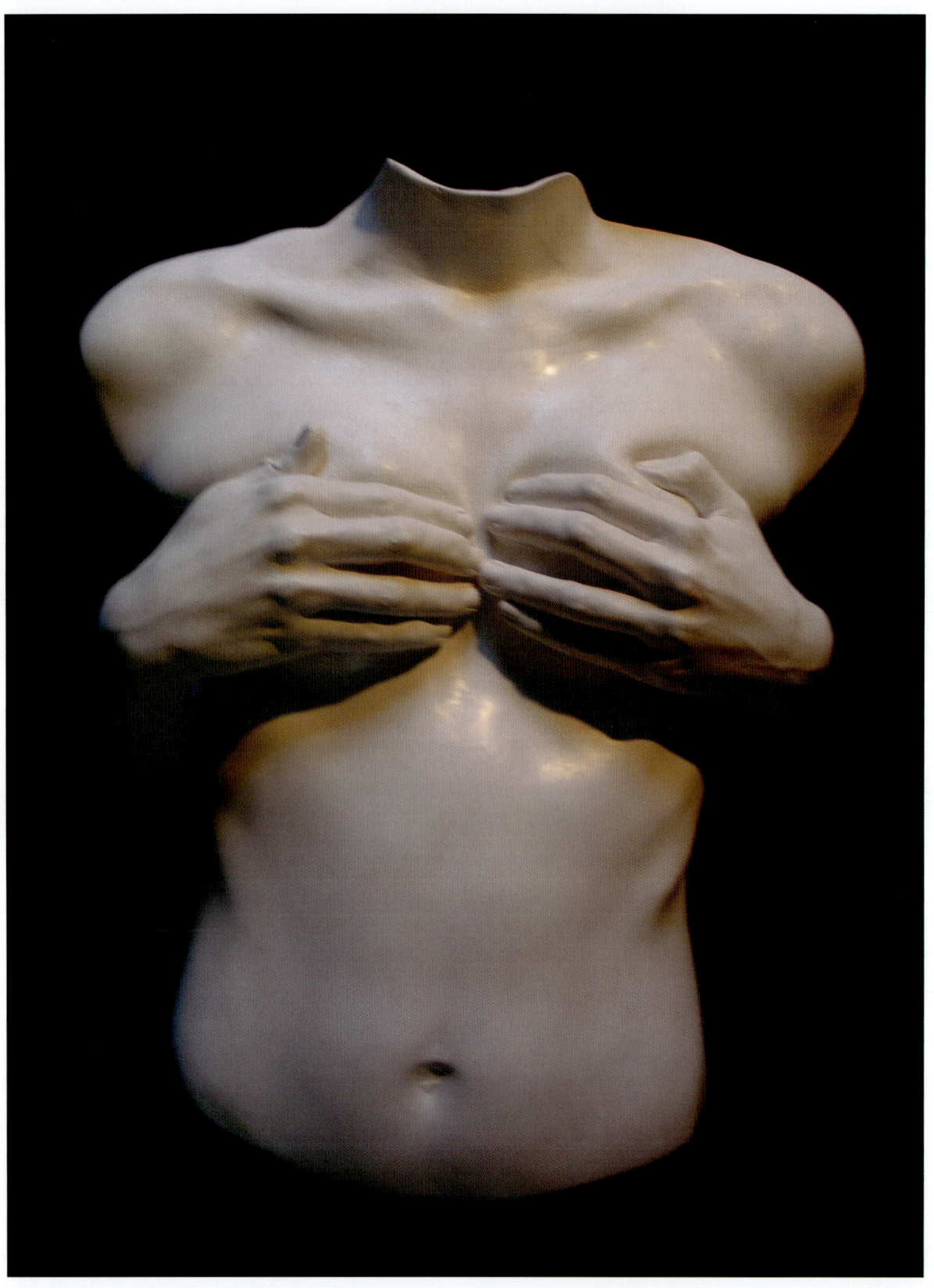

Alpha plaster cast produced from a life-moulding silicone mould (by Angharad Bailey).

CHAPTER FOUR

LIFE MOULDING SILICONE

Developed in the last ten years, life moulding silicone has revolutionized the production of life moulding methods from the human body. Commercially available on the professional and domestic market in the last seven years, the system enables the mouldmaker to produce production moulds directly from the body in one operation.

Traditional life moulding systems, including alginate and plaster bandage, have the major drawback of being effectively waste moulds, in that the moulds produced using these systems can only be used once. These systems also provide a limited timescale in which the moulds can be cast effectively. Alginate moulds are fragile and will dry out and become ineffective in a relatively short time. Similarly, plaster bandage moulds are not durable and are relatively inaccurate.

With the limitations of single-use and short-life moulding systems multiple-cast production is clearly not an option. In order to produce multiple castings from life the mouldmaker is required to remould from the life cast to produce a production mould capable of producing multiple castings. The options for casting material for these systems are also limited. Casting materials sensitive to water cannot be cast in alginate moulds and materials that are time-consuming to produce can also be problematic.

Life-casting silicone enables the mouldmaker to create a production mould capable of multiple castings of multiple types in one operation, directly from the body. The principal method consists of application, by brush, of silicone rubber directly to the skin, which is then backed up with a plaster bandage case to support it.

A polished Alpha plaster life cast.

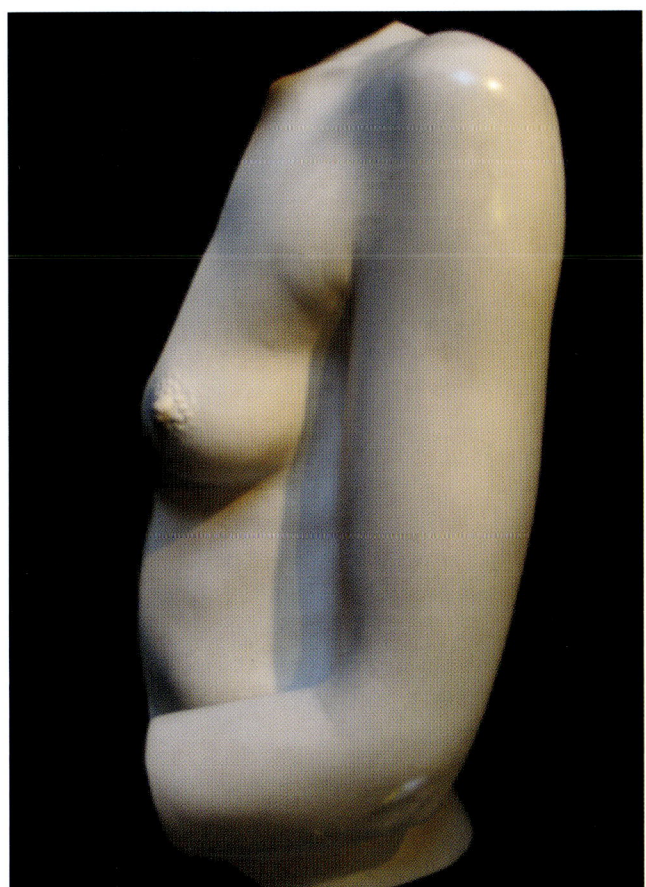

The Material

Life-moulding silicones are two-part platinum cure silicone rubber moulding systems that are safe (hypoallergenic) to use on the human body. They are available in a self-mixing cartridge or as a hand-mixable system.

- **Cartridge** A twin cartridge that contains the two parts of the silicone system. The cartridge is loaded into a twin mastic gun that when activated mixes the two components.

◼ **Hand mix**   A twin container system that can be mixed by hand in small batches.

◼ **Pot life and demould time**   Pot life is the working time of the silicone before it becomes too thick to use and pick up detail. Demould time is the amount of time before the silicone is set enough to remove from the body. There are two speeds available, *Standard* (pot life 6 minutes; demould 30 minutes) and *Fast* (pot life 90 seconds; demould 5 minutes). Setting times are affected by ambient temperature; warm temperatures will decrease both pot life and demould times. It should be noted that the demould times do not include application and setting times of the plaster bandage case.

◼ **Storage and shelf life**   Room temperature. Materials have a short shelf life and should be used soon after purchase. High temperatures will decrease shelf life.

Release Agents and Protection

Life-casting silicone will not adhere to the skin but will bond mechanically to hair. Caution should be employed to prevent the material getting into hair as it can be extremely uncomfortable to remove.

It is not possible to take moulds from large amounts of hair on the head and these should be masked completely with a tight-fitting bathing cap or tightly wound kitchen cling film. Other not-so-hairy bits should be applied liberally with release agent. Particular attention should be applied to eyelashes and brows. It is a good idea to apply release agent to hairless skin as well, to help in the removal of the mould.

◼ **Proprietary release cream**   These are specially formulated release creams for life moulding manufactured by the silicone suppliers. They are generally quite thick and greasy and very efficient.

◼ **Petroleum jelly**   This is good for hairless skin but can also be used liberally on hairy bits.

◼ **Baby oil**   As above.

◼ **Clothes protection**   It is extremely difficult to remove set silicone from clothing and so ensure clothes are covered with overalls, plastic aprons or black bin liners.

Tools

◼ **A dispensing gun**   This is necessary to dispense silicone using the twin-cartridge system. There are hand-pumped and electric guns available. The electric version automatically dispenses the mixed silicone and can take a lot of work out of the silicone application.

◼ **Mixing nozzles**   These are screwed onto the opened cartridge and mix the two components of the silicone as a spiral. There are several sizes available to allow for different rates of application. The narrower diameter nozzles dispense more slowly than the wider ones. Once the required amount of silicone has been dispensed the nozzle can be disposed of and the cartridge resealed for later use with a new nozzle.

◼ **Brushes**   Brushes are needed for spreading the silicone across the skin. These should be of good quality and fairly soft. Sizes appropriate to the area of the body being moulded should be used, such as 12–25mm for the face and 25–50mm for larger body areas.

◼ **Plastic beakers and wooden/plastic spatulas**   These are used for dispensing and mixing hand-mixed silicone systems.

◼ **Scissors**   These are necessary for trimming excess set silicone and cutting lengths of plaster bandage to size. Only round-ended or medical crooked bandage scissors should be used near the body.

◼ **A plaster mixing bowl**   For dipping lengths of plaster bandage.

Principal Methods

The principal method comprises the application of silicone to the skin, which is then back up with a plaster bandage case. Preparation is all-important when life moulding. The working area, materials and tools should be prepared before the execution of the project.

Life moulding by its nature is a rapid process, enabling the mouldmaker to create a mould quickly from a posed life model. Because of the speed of the process it is essential to have two or three people involved in its application. Materials set quickly and need to be applied rapidly and efficiently to produce accurate moulds and create minimum discomfort and maximum safety for the model. Ideally one person should dispense the silicone, another apply it to the skin and another observe model safety.

From the model's perspective life casting can be a strange experience, particularly for the uninitiated, and they should be comfortable and secure in the knowledge that they are in capable hands. This is particularly the case when moulding the face. All materials and mouldmaking procedures should be fully understood and practised on easy parts of the body before embarking on a face.

Novice models should be briefed fully in the whole process of life moulding beforehand. Agree on hand signals to be used by the model to indicate requests such as, 'Slow down', 'Stop for a break', 'Clear airway' or 'Abort process'. Explain when and how they can help. Make the model feel involved.

Moulds will need to be broken down into pieces when doing whole body sections in order to remove the mould from the body. An approximate breakdown of the mould pieces required for a whole body, standing with arms and legs straight and palms facing back, would include:

- ▓ **Head, face and back** The seam line should run behind the ear and over the top of the head.
- ▓ **Arms and hands** Top and bottom pieces will be created, with the seam line running along the length of the arm.
- ▓ **Legs and feet** Front and back pieces will be created, with the seam line running down the inside and outside of the leg.
- ▓ **Torso and pelvis** Front and back pieces will be created, with the seam line running down the sides of the body.

Of course, different poses will require different mould breakdown sequences.

1. Enough materials should be prepared prior to beginning the task. Ensure there is adequate silicone for the job. Cut lengths of plaster bandage in advance, to cover the applied silicone area, and lay them out in the sequence of application.
2. Cover the model's head hair and protect their and your clothing.
3. Apply release agent to skin. It may be appropriate and more comfortable for the model to do this. Take particular care with 'hairy bits'.

4. Dispense silicone from the gun or container in small amounts and then spread over the skin to a thickness of 2–10mm by brush. Care should be taken not to trap air when brushing out the silicone, particularly in difficult-to-access area like the corners of the eyes or ears.
5. It is some times a good idea on larger areas of the body to apply a layer of hessian scrim on top of the layer of silicone to provide registration for the plaster bandage case.
6. Allow the silicone to set.
7. Apply a plaster bandage case appropriate to the mould size. A face may need just two or three layers of plaster bandage, larger body areas will need more. Reinforce cases for larger body areas with wooden splints built into the plaster bandage.
8. Allow the plaster bandage to harden.
9. If doing multiple-piece moulds adjoining pieces should be created against the previously made pieces while in situ, to ensure tight registration between pieces. This is of course not possible if creating a whole-body mould, as the model will need to rest periodically. In this case remove the mould pieces, allow the model to rest and then replace the piece that needs to be worked against before starting again.
10. Apply petroleum jelly release agent between mould pieces. Ensure the exposed mould flange of silicone and plaster bandage between mould pieces is covered.
11. When the mould is complete it can be removed. This is done in conjunction with the model. The model should flex and move gently within the mould to allow the mouldmakers to remove the mould. Do not rush this process; allow the model to determine the speed of removal. With a face or head mould it may be preferable to allow the model to remove the mould.
12. Once removed the silicone part of the mould can be washed and dried before casting.
13. Plaster bandage mould cases are not very durable and a case can be remade in a more durable material at a later date if required. Do this before demoulding a casting (preferably in a hard material) so the silicone retains its correct shape while the new case is being made.

PROJECT

Specification

A two-piece mould and cast from the head. Two people (first and second assistant) were employed to produce the mould and a third person (third assistant) was employed to keep the airways of the model clear during production.

Materials

- EZ 20 Silicone cartridge 400ml × 2 (supplied by Notcutt Ltd);
- Gypsona® plaster bandage (supplied by Alec Tiranti Ltd);
- release cream;
- petroleum jelly;
- kitchen cling film; and
- Crystacal R. Alpha casting plaster (for the cast).

Tools

- A dispensing gun (hand pumped);
- medium-flow mixing nozzles × 2
- a cosmetic eyebrow pencil;
- round-ended scissors;
- a Stanley knife; and
- a plaster mixing bowl.

Method

PREPARATION OF MODEL AND MATERIALS

1. Make the model comfortable and protect clothing.
2. Wrap cling film tightly over the head to cover the hair just over the hair line.
3. Allow the model to apply release agent to skin, eyebrows and lashes.
4. Draw a line with an eyebrow pencil to define the two halves of the mould.
5. Cut enough lengths of plaster bandage to cover the two halves of the head separately.

FIRST HALF SILICONE (BACK)

First assistant

1. Cut the seal on the silicone cartridge with a Stanley knife and screw on the mixing nozzle.
2. Cut the end off the nozzle. The ends of the nozzles are usually graduated to regulate flow. Start by cutting the smallest graduation end and increase the size if necessary.
3. Insert the cartridge into the dispensing gun. Ensure it is securely located into any registration system incorporated in the gun.
4. Pump up the gun to allow the two silicone parts to flow into the mixing nozzle. As the mixed silicone approaches the end of the mixing nozzle move into position for the first application.
5. Dispense a bead of silicone along the mould division line pre-marked on the model.
6. Dispense a small mound of silicone to an area at the top of the head.

Second assistant

1. With a brush spread the mound of silicone down over the back of the head.
2. The silicone will flow slowly but it needs to be spread with a brush to a thickness of approximately 5mm.
3. Once a layer of 5mm has been applied dispense another bead of silicone on top, 10mm away from the seam line. Leave this raised and intact to set. This will provide registration into the case.

First and second assistant together

1. Working in unison the first and second assistants cover the whole of the back of the head in this way, working away from the dispensed line of silicone at the division line. The first assistant should dispense small mounds of silicone on demand from the second assistant, when and where they need it. The division line of silicone should remain intact to create a flange that will connect up to the front half of the mould.
2. Once the whole of the back of the head is covered, the silicone should be allowed to set. It should not pick up on a finger when touched lightly.

FIRST HALF PLASTER BANDAGE

First and second assistant

A plaster bandage case should be created jointly by first and second assistants working with alternating strips for speed of production.

1. Ensure the bandage is thoroughly squeezed out to eliminate excess water before application. This will allow a quicker setting time to proceed to the next stage.

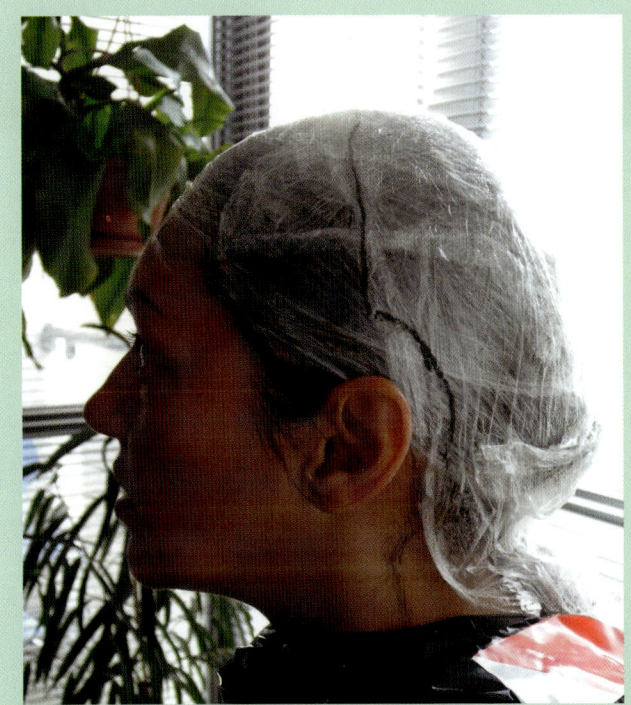

The model's hair is protected and the mould division line drawn.

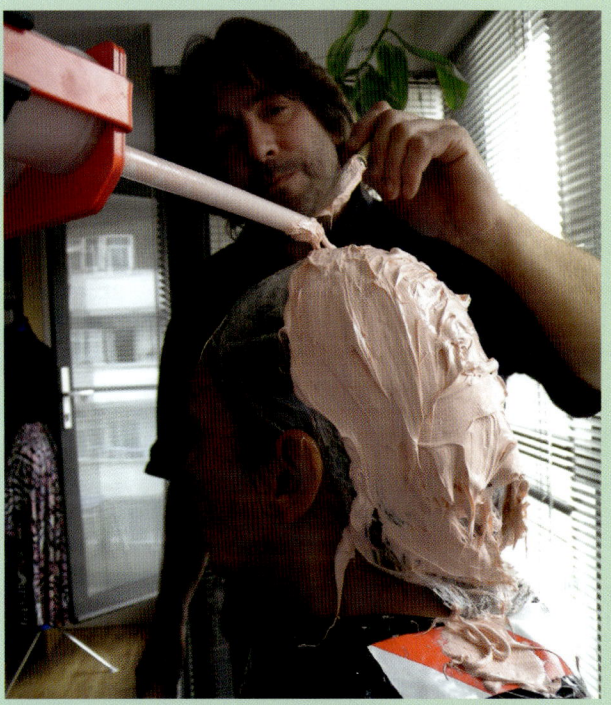

The first half of silicone is applied and brushed over the back of the head.

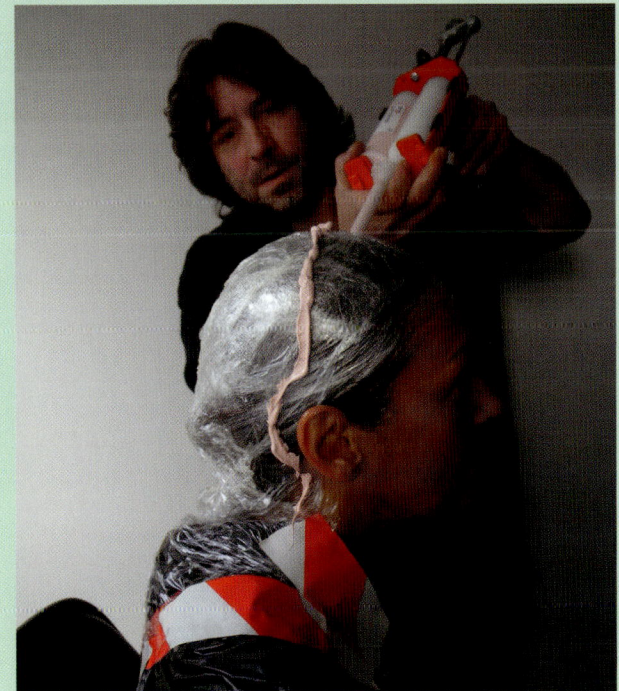

A bead of silicone is applied at the division line.

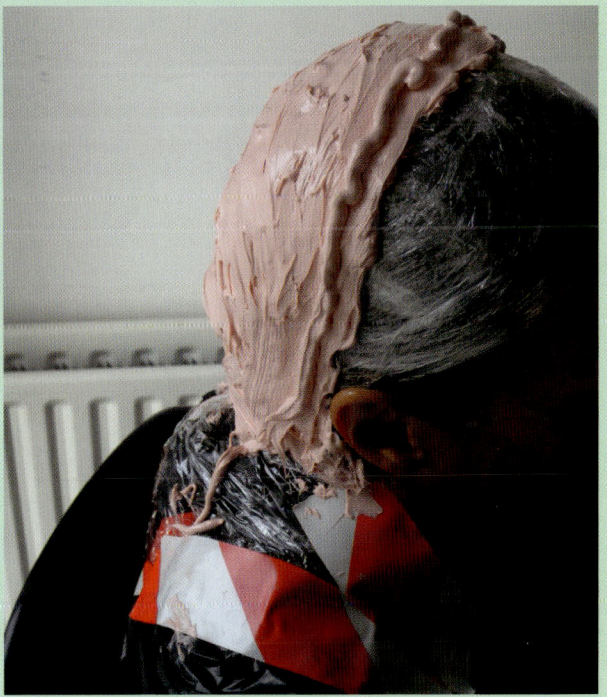

A case registration bead is applied near the division line.

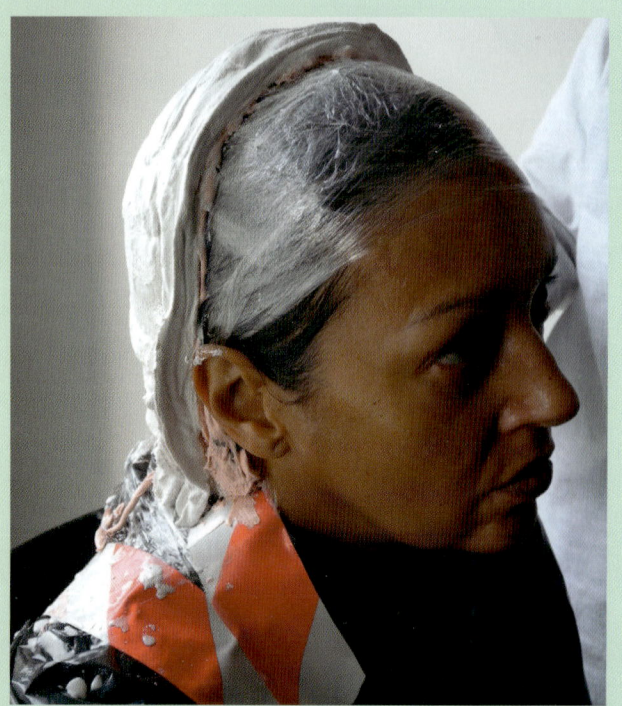

The plaster bandage case is created with a flange at the division line.

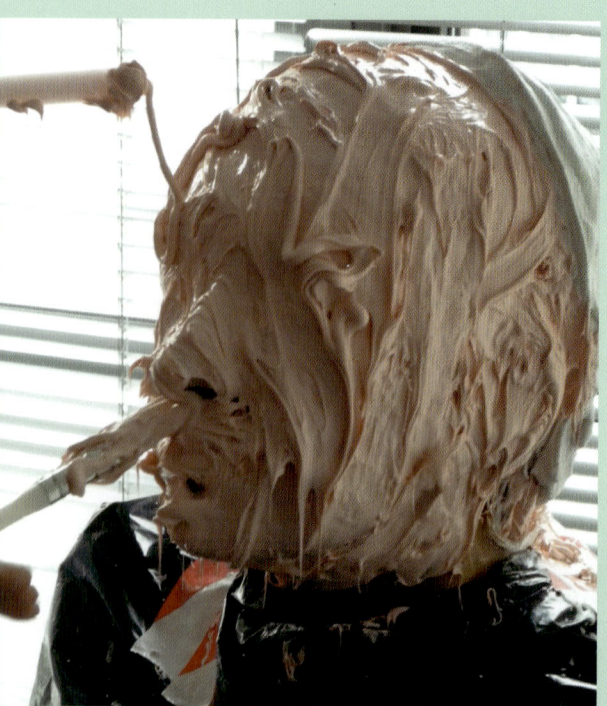

Silicone is applied around the nostrils last.

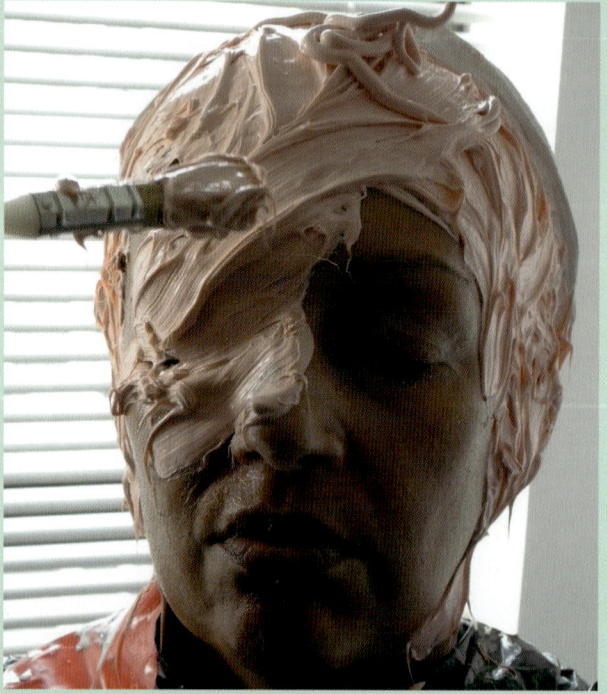

The second half of the silicone is applied.

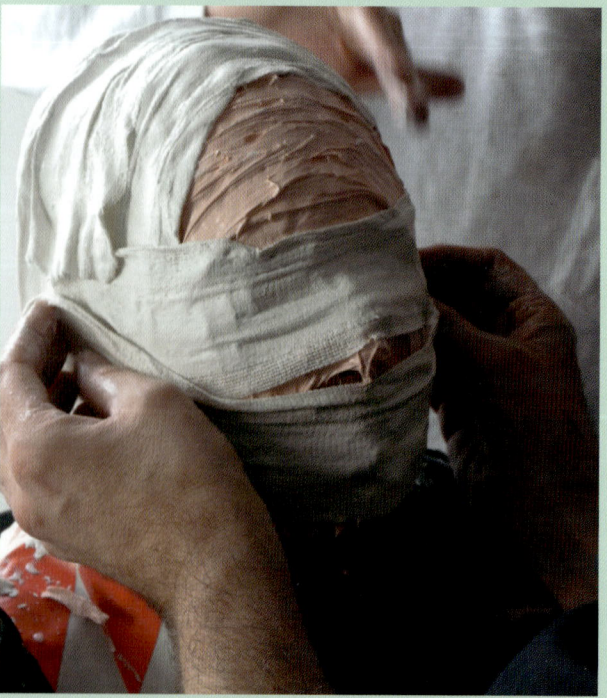

The second half of the case is applied.

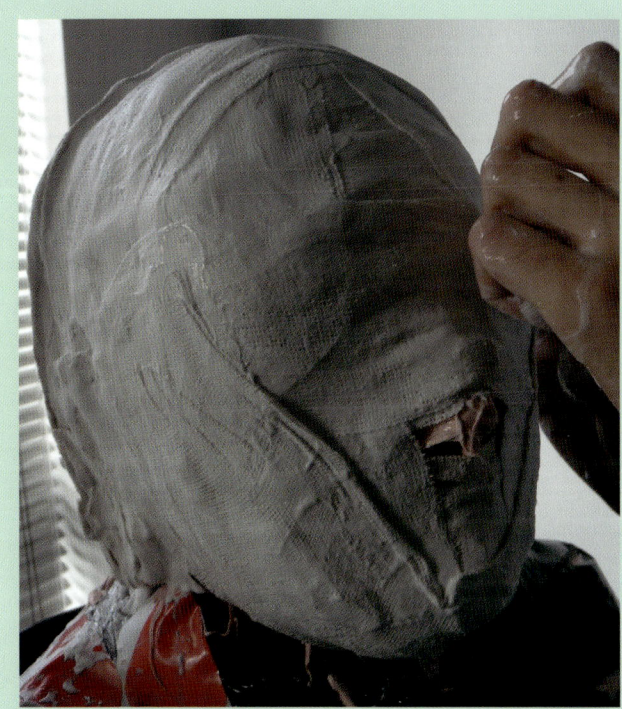

Ensure nostrils are kept clear.

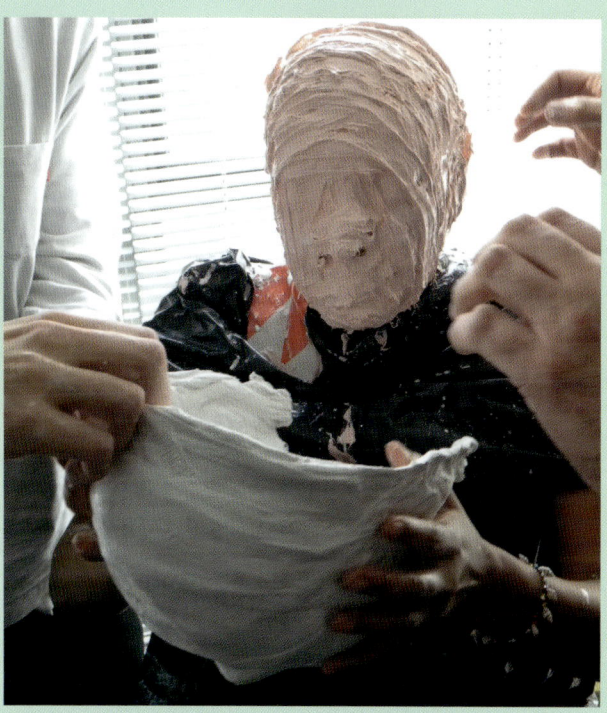

The front case half is removed.

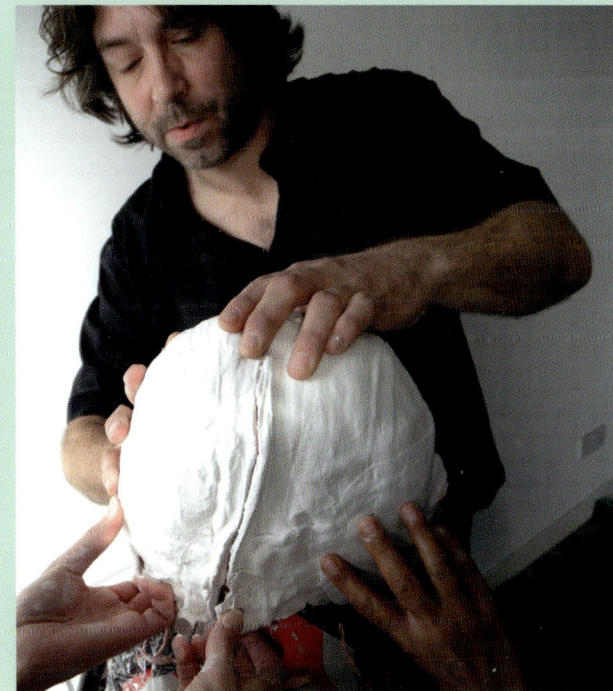

The case is removed gently from the back of the head.

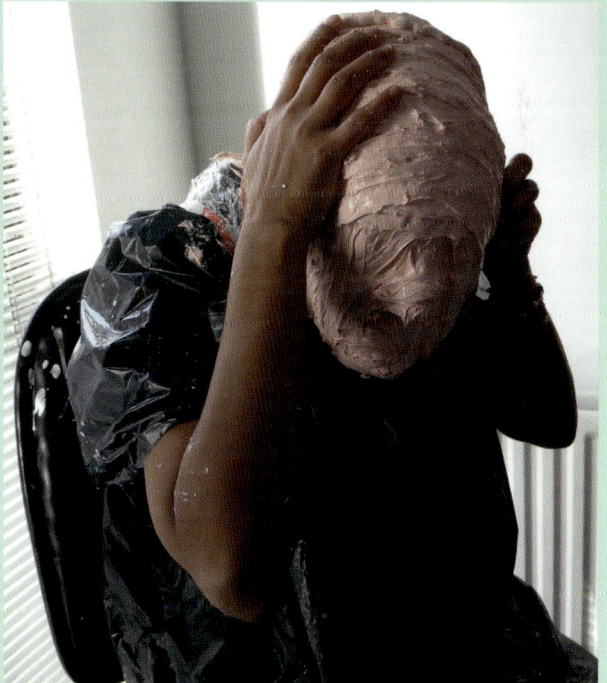

The model begins to the release the silicone from her face.

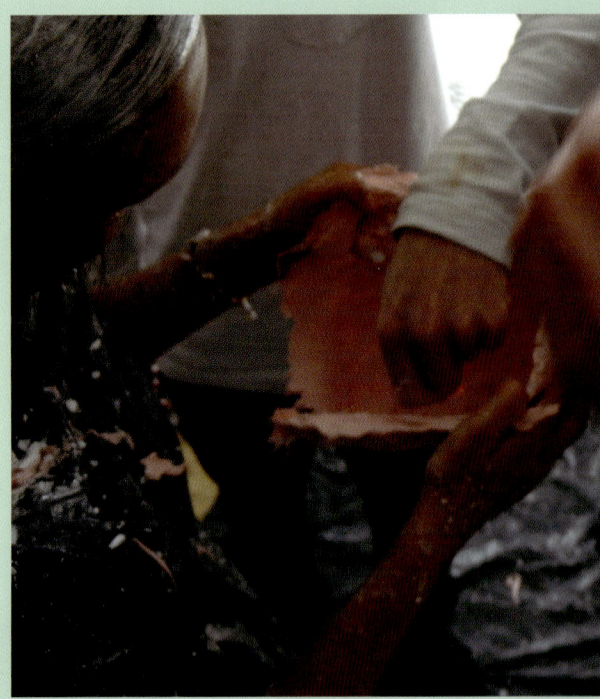

The silicone is removed from the face.

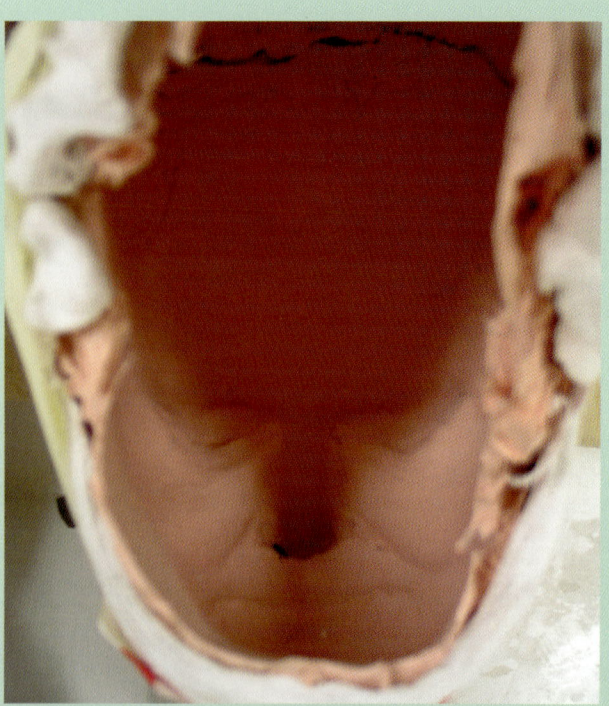

The two-piece silicone mould is reassembled and allowed to harden.

2. Ensure air bubbles are rubbed out of applied bandage strips to ensure an accurate registration between silicone and case.

3. A raised flange should be created at the seam line by squeezing bunched-up bandage between forefinger and thumb. This is important to achieve accurate registration between the mould pieces.

4. Layers of bandage should be laid in strips, and overlapped by 5mm, to a thickness of approximately 5mm.

5. Raised reinforcing strips can be made by folding over strips of bandage several times, placing them at strategic points on the surface and pinching to a point with forefinger and thumb.

6. Allow the plaster bandage case to harden. It should be firm to the touch.

SECOND HALF SILICONE

1. Carefully trim any excess silicone back to the seam flanges of the first half of silicone and the plaster bandage mould half. The silicone and case flanges should be flush.

2. Apply petroleum jelly release agent to the silicone and plaster bandage mould flanges.

3. Use damp cotton wool balls to plug the model's ears to prevent silicone entering the ear. Allow the model to apply these to a depth that feels comfortable and safe.

4. Starting at the top of the head, the first and second assistants should create the second half of the silicone mould in the same way as the first.

5. Work the silicone up to and cover the first silicone mould flange.

6. Ensure the silicone covers, without trapping air, difficult-to-access areas such as the corners of the eyes and the ears. This is where the thickness of silicone may exceed 5mm up to approximately 10mm to allow good coverage.

7. Throughout the production of the second mould half the third assistant should be employed to check that airways (nostrils) are kept clear. This is probably the most important job!

8. The area just below and around the nostrils should be left until the last stages of silicone application. A small brush should be employed at this stage to

gently touch in around the nostrils. Note: Do not use straws to allow ventilation to airways, they just get in the way!

SECOND HALF PLASTER BANDAGE

The second half of the plaster bandage case should now be created, as for the first half.

1. Work the plaster bandage up against the first half flange of the mould case to ensure a tight registration between the two halves.
2. Ensure the airways are kept open when creating the second half of the plaster bandage case.
3. Allow the plaster bandage case to harden. It should give a wooden-sounding knock when tapped lightly.

MOULD REMOVAL

The mould complete, it can be removed from the model. Do not rush this process!

The mouldmakers will be keen to see the results of the mould, and the model will be even keener to be rid of it, but it is important not to rush the removal so as not to cause discomfort to the model and not to damage the mould. It can be much more comfortable to allow the model to take control over the removal of the mould, so always allow them to dictate the process.

1. Begin by carefully separating the two pieces of the plaster bandage case. It may be necessary to insert a blunt wooden clay tool or plastic spatula between the mould piece seam.
2. Sometimes the plaster bandage case with the silicone piece inside will come away in one (this usually happens with the back section of the head), other times the case may come away from the silicone separately. If the case comes away separately, remove it and put it to one side.
3. Carefully insert your fingertips under the seam line a little at a time, working all the way around the seam from the top of the head.
4. Start to peel the silicone away from the model.

5. Once the first silicone piece has been removed, replace it into the plaster bandage case directly.
6. Repeat as above for the second half of the mould. Be particularly careful with the face half of the mould. Allow the model to remove it if preferable.
7. Once the mould pieces are removed check the condition of the model first. It can be extremely disconcerting for the model if the mouldmakers all gather round and inspect the mould before checking the model is comfortable and safe. Words of thanks and praise to the model do not go amiss.
8. Inspect the condition of the mould briefly and then reassemble and allow the plaster bandage to harden fully before use.

CASTING

Life silicone moulds can be cast in a number of different materials (see the casting principles for 'Silicone Moulds' in Chapter 2 of *Mouldmaking and Casting*); however, it is a good idea to try a plaster cast first to see how the mould is working.

1. Excess strands of silicone should be trimmed away from mould seams.
2. Nostril holes should be blocked before the solid pouring of casting material. Hollow cast materials can be applied around the nostril holes.
3. It may be necessary to reinforce the case with more plaster bandage or regular casting plaster, to provide adequate support to the silicone.
4. Apply release agent to all seams before casting in case of leakage of the casting material.
5. Secure the mould halves together and seal with clay if you are not confident of the registration. Registration of any life mould in multiple pieces will not always be perfect due to the nature of the process.
6. Demould castings as for any silicone mould, by removing case pieces first and then peeling away the silicone from the cast.

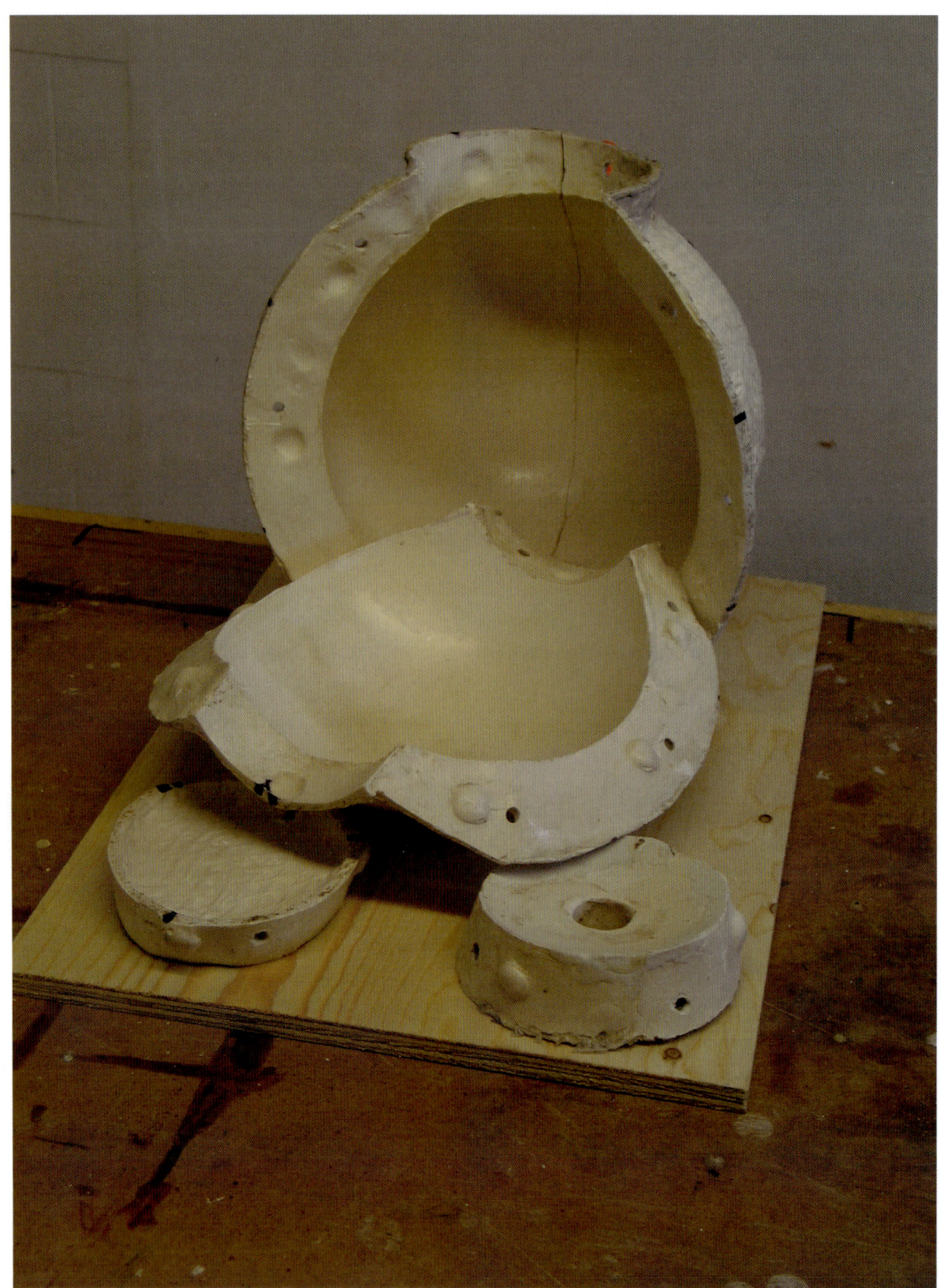

Multiple piece Jesmonite mould.

CHAPTER FIVE

JESMONITE™ MULTIPLE PIECE

Jesmonite™ composite resin systems can be utilized as very effective mouldmaking materials. Being lightweight and very durable, Jesmonite can be an attractive alternative to plaster mouldmaking. It is non-toxic and easy to clean up, so it also has many advantages over polyester resin. These factors combined with high detail capture provide an excellent mouldmaking alternative to traditional rigid systems.

Jesmonite can be used with traditional clay wall/bed techniques for mouldmaking and can be employed as an excellent case-making material for flexible mouldmaking. Wax-based release agents can be used effectively. (For full specifications on Jesmonite see Chapter 7.)

PROJECT

Specification

A five-piece laminated Jesmonite mould using clay wall mouldmaking divisions, from a plastic ball 700mm in circumference.

Time Required

Allowing for setting times this project was carried out over approximately one and a half days.

Materials

- Clay;
- Jesmonite AC100 Powder (supplied by Notcutt Ltd);
- Jesmonite AC100 Liquid;
- Jesmonite Thixotropix additive;
- spray wax release agent;
- paste wax release agent; and
- M6 × 30mm roofing bolts with wing nuts.

Tools

- Mixing beakers;
- a cordless drill fitted with a high shear mixing blade;
- brushes;
- clay tools;
- a clay harp;
- scissors;
- an electric jigsaw;
- medium-grade sandpaper; and
- a water bucket for washing tools and equipment.

Method

SET-UP AND PREPARATION

As with any project, careful preparation before the start of the job is crucial. Knowing the material quantities and tools needed, undertaking repairs to the original and setting-up the working area will all help to complete the job accurately and efficiently. (Tip: make sure you have enough materials to complete the job before you start. Running out of material halfway through the job is at least a waste of time and, at worst, a loss of previously executed work.)

1. Prepare the original. In this case a fine manufacturer's seam line on the surface of the ball was removed with very fine abrasive paper. The original was then cleaned and dried.

2. Consider the division lines of the mould. Mouldmaking and casting principles for rigid mouldmaking should be considered at this point (see *Mouldmaking and Casting*). Once determined, division lines can be drawn on the original or committed to memory.

3. Secure the original in position for production of the first mould piece. In this case a plaster mixing bowl is employed to keep the ball still and secured while placing the clay walls used to produce the mould pieces.

THE FIRST CLAY WALL

1. Using a clay harp or rolling pin, prepare clay walls of a size appropriate for the job.

2. Apply the clay wall to the first division line in one operation. Avoid repeatedly resetting clay walls to ensure a clean line.

3. Pinch the clay wall onto the surface of the original from the outside of the wall. It is important to leave the inside edge of the clay wall sharp and perpendicular to the original surface to avoid feathered edges to the mould pieces (see Chapter 2 in *Mouldmaking and Casting*).

4. Press hemispherical registration indents at 80mm intervals along the clay wall. These will create 'nipple and cup' registration points between the mould pieces.

5. Set a tapered clay cone to provide the pouring hole into the mould.

6. Apply two coats of spray wax release agent. Allow to dry between and after coats. (The type of release agent used will depend on the material of the original.)

THE FIRST MOULD PIECE

The thixotropic coat

This layer will pick up the detail of the original.

1. Make up a thixotropic addition mix of Jesmonite composite. Thixotropic additive should be added according to the specified ratios. Adjustments can be made by adding small amounts of thixotrope at a time until the required consistency is achieved. The mix should adhere to a depth of 1–2mm when applied to the surface of the

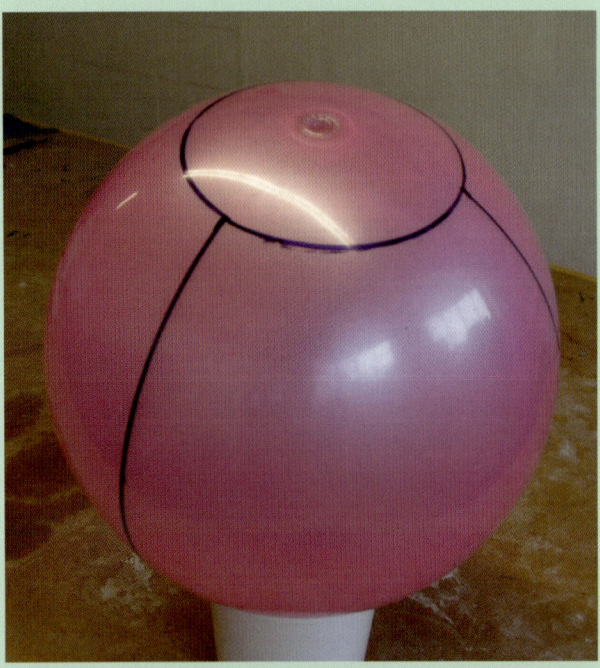

Original model.

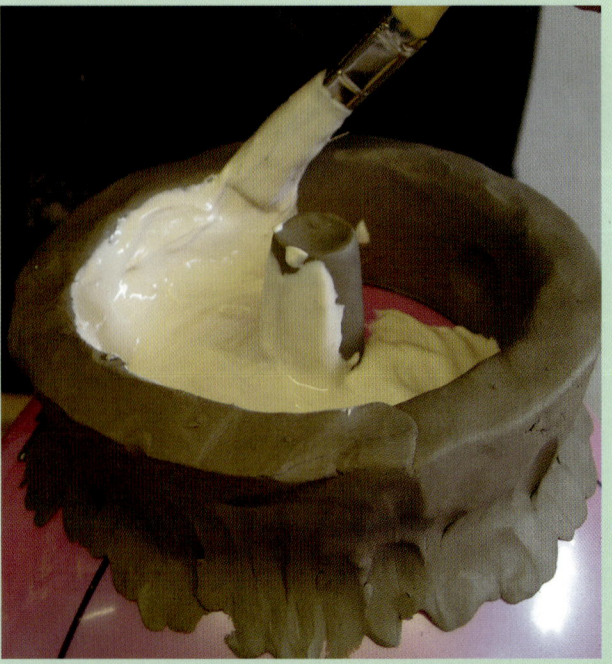

The thixotropic Jesmonite gel coat is applied.

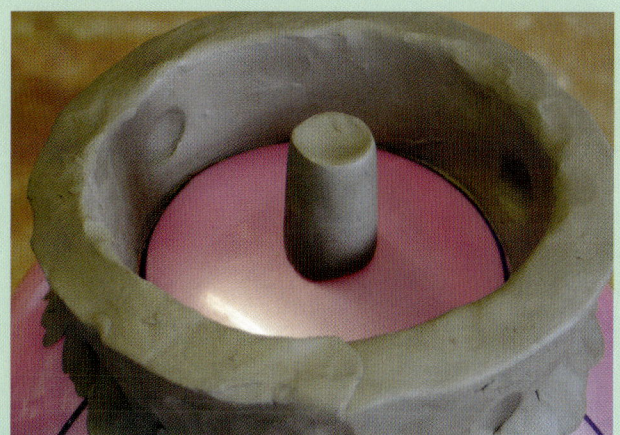

The first clay wall and pouring hole cone are created to define the first mould piece.

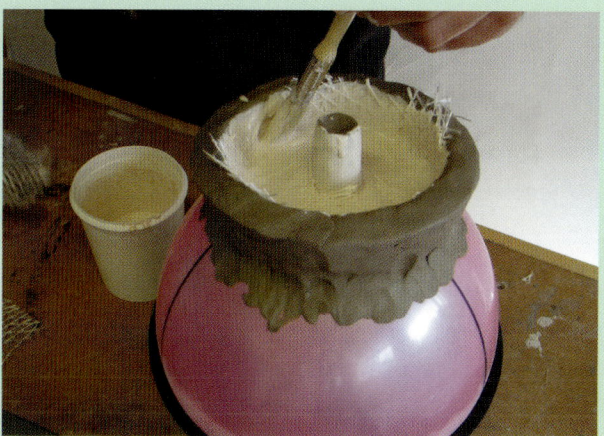

The quadaxial mat is applied to the set gel coat.

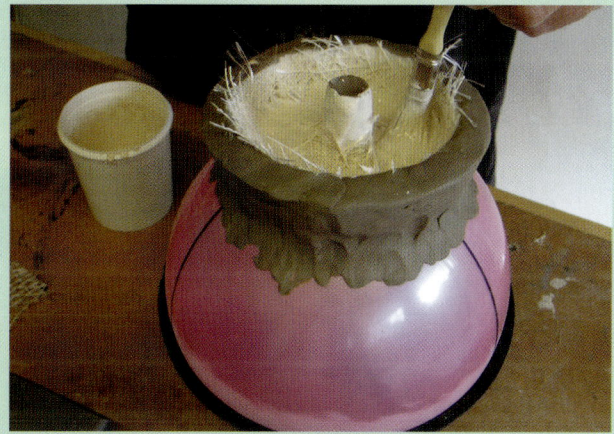

The chopped strand mix and second quadaxial layers are applied.

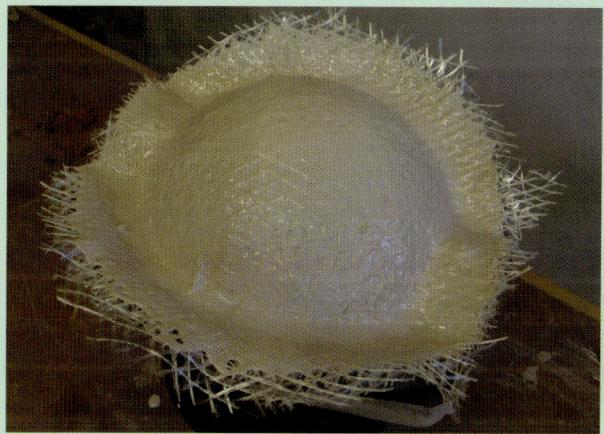

The third mould piece is created.

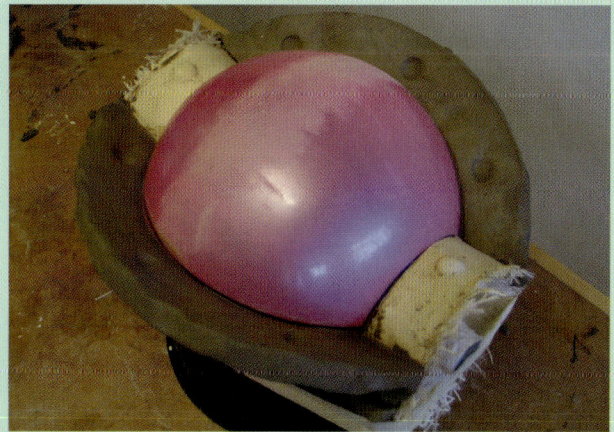

With the two end pieces created, clay walls are spanned between them to create the third mould piece.

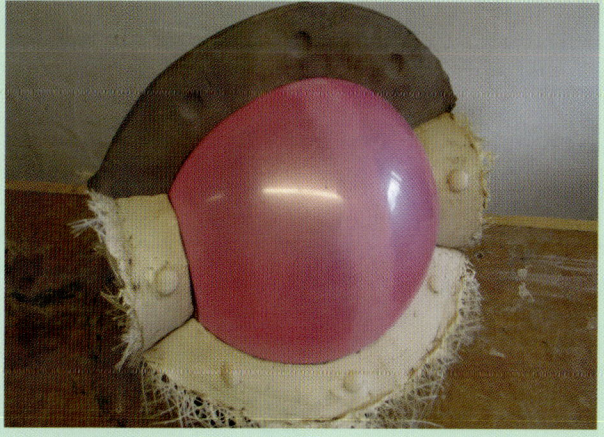

The clay wall defining the fourth mould piece.

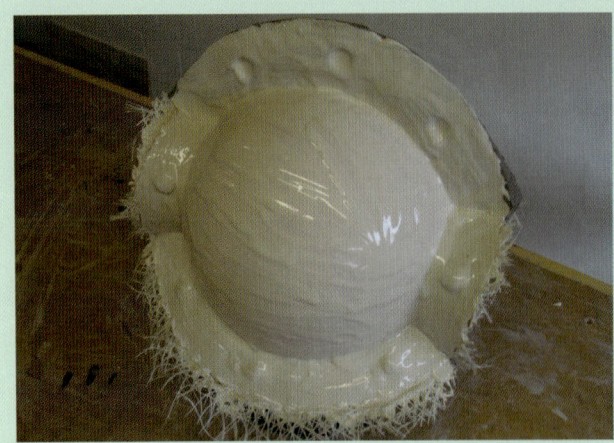

Thixotropic coat is applied for the fourth mould piece.

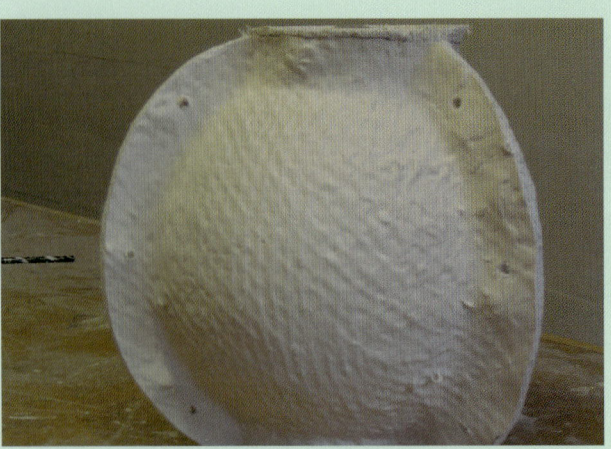

The completed mould with seams trimmed.

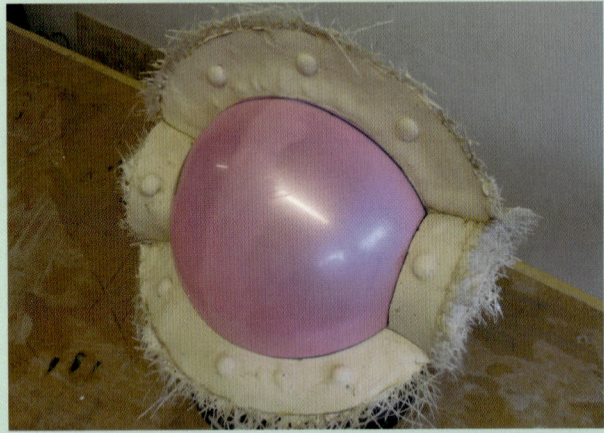

The exposed last remaining section of the original model.

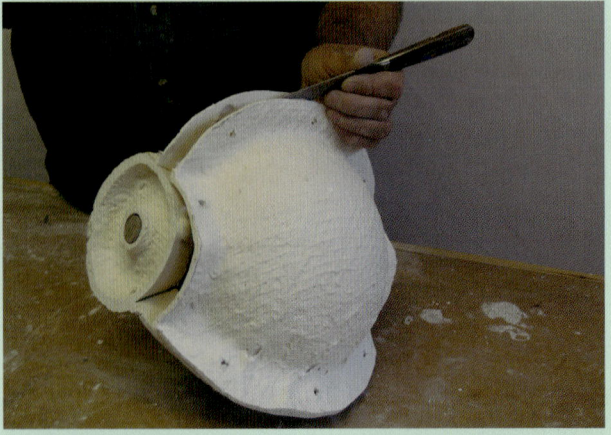

The mould pieces are carefully separated.

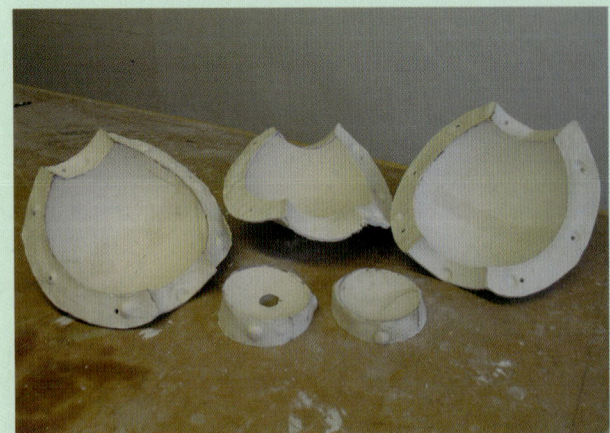

The five-piece Jesmonite mould.

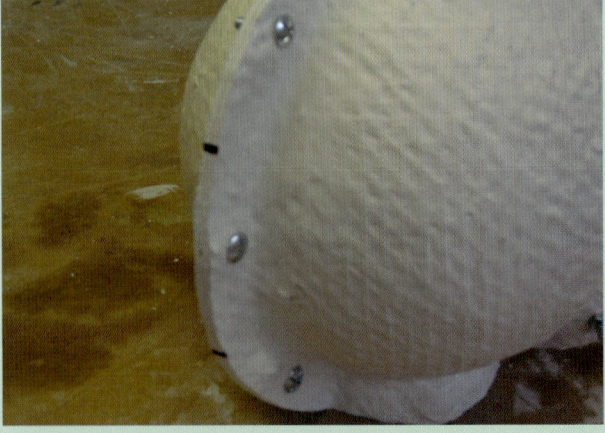

Nuts and bolts secure the mould pieces together.

original but not be so thick that it does not pick up detail.

2. Apply the thixotropic mix with a soft brush to the whole exposed surface area of the original within the clay division walls.
3. Extend the thixotropic coat up the inside of the clay walls to create a raised flange wall around the mould piece.
4. Allow it to set for 15–20 minutes, until firm to the touch and not picking up on the finger when touched lightly.

The first quadaxial layer

The gel coat layer on its own will not be strong enough and needs to be laminated to achieve the full strength of the Jesmonite system. The first stage of the laminating process is a layer of quadaxial mat.

1. Cut and prepare enough pieces of quadaxial mat to cover the surface of the applied gel coat twice. The size and shape of the pieces should be tailored to the contours of the gel-coated surface. Large open areas can be laminated with large pieces of mat; small difficult-to-access areas may need to be covered in smaller sections of mat.
2. Set out the cut mat in sequence on the work surface.
3. Prepare a mix of composite.
4. Apply the mix with a brush to the area of the gel coat to be covered with mat first.
5. Lay the mat onto the wet mix and push down gently with the brush.
6. Saturate the surface of mat with more mix. You will find that the mat softens when saturated with mix, enabling it to be laminated closely to the gel coat. Do this by gently stippling the surface of saturated mat, pushing any air entrapment out as you go. The idea is to get a tight lamination of the mat to the gel coat without any air bubbles.
7. Methodically work over the entire surface of the gel coat, overlapping mat pieces by approximately 5–10mm.

The chopped strand layer

This is a mix of composite mix and fibreglass chopped strands that is applied between the layers of quadaxial mat to give the laminate more strength. Chopped strand is added to a pre-mixed batch of composite at a rate of 1–2 per cent by weight of the mix. The consistency should be that of a thick spreadable paste.

1. Use a wooden mixing stick to mix chopped strand into the composite mix.
2. Apply it with a brush and spread out to a depth of 2–4mm.
3. Use a stick to push the mix into difficult-to-access areas.
4. Methodically work over the entire surface of the first layer of quadaxial mat.

The second layer of quadaxial mat

1. Apply a second layer of quadaxial mat, as for the first layer, over the layer of chopped strand.
2. Allow it to set for at least an hour before continuing to the next mould section.

The total laminating process will produce a mould 5–6mm thick. At this thickness the mould will have a weight of 9–11 kg/m². Increasing the thickness of the chopped strand layer will produce stronger moulds for larger subject matter.

CURING AND DRYING

As the composite starts to set an exothermic reaction takes place, producing heat between the initial and final set of approximately 30°C. After approximately one hour the chemical reaction is complete and the casting will have achieved 60 per cent of its total strength.

Full strength will be achieved dependent on drying conditions and the thickness of the mould. Thin sections will dry faster than thicker ones. Dry atmospheric conditions will increase the speed of the drying process.

THE SECOND MOULD PIECE

Subsequent mould pieces in a multiple-piece mould are usually constructed directly against the flange wall of the first mould piece. The mould is built up sequentially in pieces from the first. However, in the case of this project the first mould piece is one of a pair of capping pieces at the top and bottom of the mould. The second capping piece can therefore be created independently of the first. This is acceptable as long as the pieces are secure to the original until a third piece can be spanned between them.

Construction in this sequence makes it easier to create evenly shaped pieces in this case, but it is not necessary and may not be possible with more complex shaped moulds.

1. Remove the clay wall from the first set piece.
2. Clean off any clay from the mould piece flange wall and the surface of the original with a small sponge.
3. Construct and apply clay walls for the second mould piece as for the first.
4. Apply registration indents along clay wall as above.
5. Construct the second mould piece as for the first mould piece.
6. Allow this to set for an hour.

THE THIRD AND FOURTH MOULD PIECES

1. Remove the clay walls from the second mould piece and sponge clean, as above.
2. Construct and apply two clay walls that span between the two capping pieces. The walls should be the same height as the flange walls on the first two pieces.
3. Apply registration indents along clay walls, as above.
4. The two exposed sections of flange wall on the two capping pieces need to be applied with a wax paste release agent so the third piece does not stick to them.
5. Construct the third mould piece between the first two pieces and allow it to set.
6. Remove the clay walls from third mould piece and clean, as above.
7. Construct the clay wall for the fourth mould piece (it only needs one as its other walls are provided by the walls from the other three pieces).
8. Apply registration indents along the clay wall, as above.
9. Apply wax paste release agent to the exposed flange walls of previously made mould pieces.

10. Construct the fourth mould piece directly against the flange walls of the previous three mould pieces.
11. Allow to set for an hour.

THE FIFTH MOULD PIECE

1. Remove the clay wall and clean the flange wall of the fourth mould piece.
2. The fifth and last mould piece will require no new clay walls as they are all provided by the flange walls of the other mould pieces. This last piece completes the mould over the original.
3. Apply release agent to all exposed flange walls.
4. Construct the final mould piece as above.
5. Allow it to fully cure and air dry until hard (this can take up to twenty-four hours at room temperature).

OPENING, TRIMMING AND CLEANING

1. Trim all the doubled flange mould walls with a hacksaw blade or electric jigsaw.
2. Before opening the mould 6.5mm holes should be drilled at 80mm intervals along the doubled flange walls of the mould to accommodate M6 bolts to secure the mould pieces together when casting.
3. Open the mould piece by piece using a wide strong-bladed knife. Small wooden wedges can be useful to push into seams, to keep them apart as they are opened.
4. Once apart, mould pieces should be sanded of any rough edges, washed, dried and reassembled ready for use. Nuts and bolts should be secured finger-firm for storage and tightened in opposite pairs a little at a time until tight for casting.

Jesmonite as a Case-Making Material for Flexible Moulds

As well as being a versatile casting material Jesmonite can be used as an effective case-making material for flexible moulds. Being lightweight and extremely durable it can be used to produce a very viable alternative to traditional case-making materials. As an alternative to fibreglass cases it also has the obvious advantages of being non-toxic and easy to clean up.

AC100 is probably the best system to use, being very durable and designed for laminating. The process is effectively the same as for a laminated cast but it can be used on the cured surface of a thixotropic-applied silicone mould. The first layer of Jesmonite needs either an addition of thixotropic additive or inert filler to make it thixotropic and it is capable of being brushed onto the surface of the silicone as a gel coat. This is then laminated in the same way as for casting or mouldmaking to create a case.

Note that Jesmonite cases can also be used with vinyl mouldmaking methods. The case would be produced after the clay slab stage in vinyl case mouldmaking.

Method

1. Apply silicone to the original subject matter using the brushable thixotropic method. Allow it to set and cut registration dovetails.
2. Mix a batch of Jesmonite AC100 with thixotropic addition.
3. Paint a layer of this 2–3mm thick onto the silicone and allow to set.
4. Cut enough quadaxial mat to cover the gel-coated layer twice.
5. Mix a batch of Jesmonite and apply it to the set gel coat.
6. Lay the first layer of mat and thoroughly saturate with more mix. This can be done in one piece of mat if the size and shape of the mould allows or it can be laid in overlapping strips.
7. Stipple out any air bubbles from between the gel coat and mat.
8. Mix a batch of Jesmonite with an addition of fibreglass chopped strand to make a thick paste.
9. Apply the chopped strand paste to the previously applied quadaxial layer and spread it out to 2–4mm thick.
10. Apply a second layer of quadaxial mat, as for the first.
11. Allow this to set and cure fully before trimming with an electric jigsaw or hacksaw blade.
12. Demould.

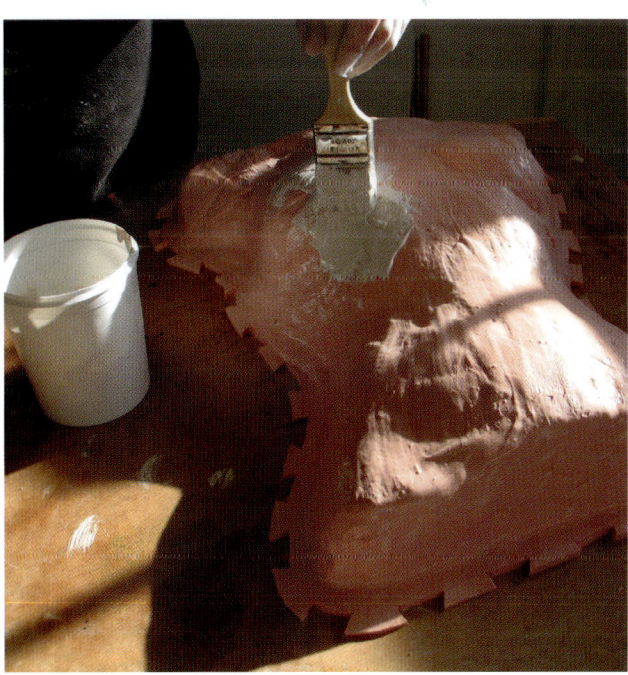

The silicone rubber mould.

The application of the thixotropic Jesmonite layer.

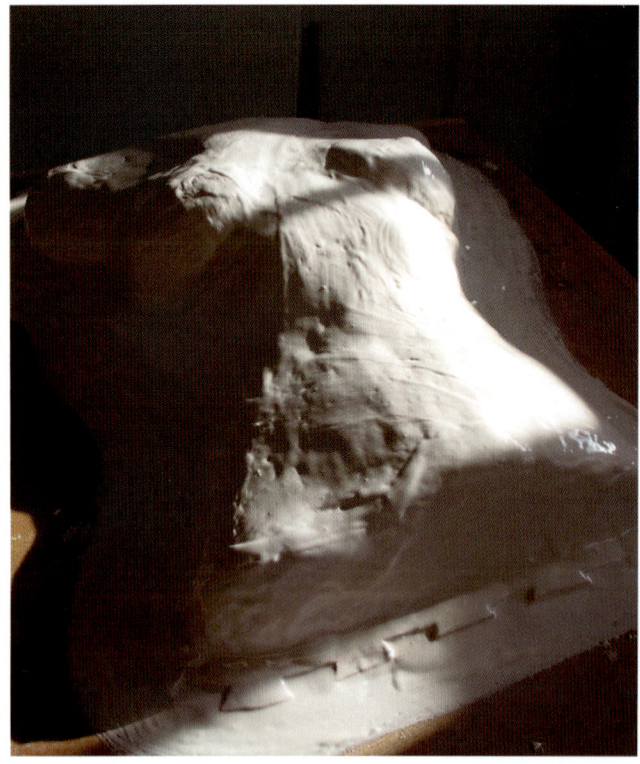

The thixotropic layer is allowed to set.

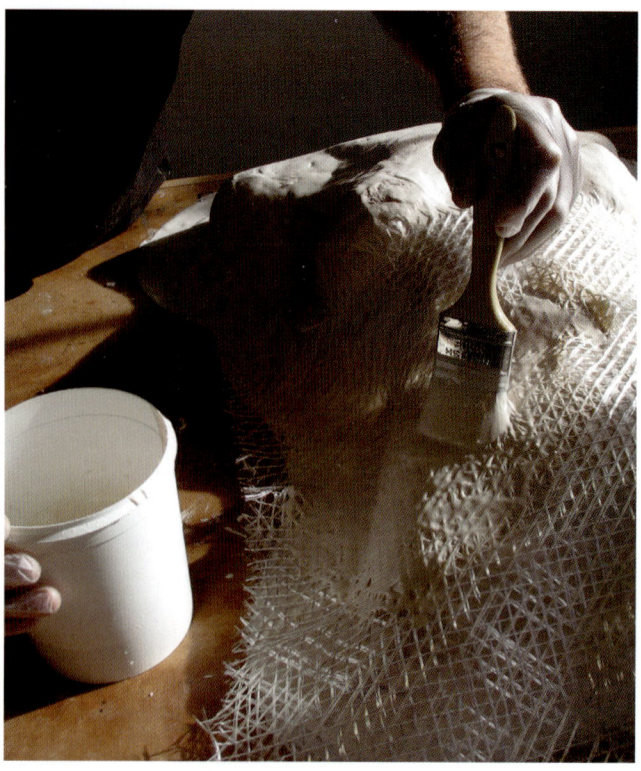

The first quadaxial mat layer.

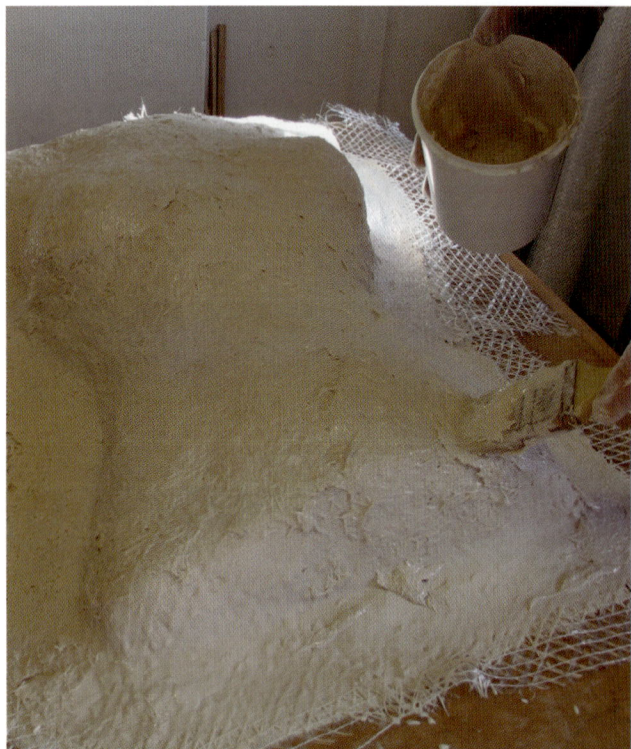

The chopped strand layer.

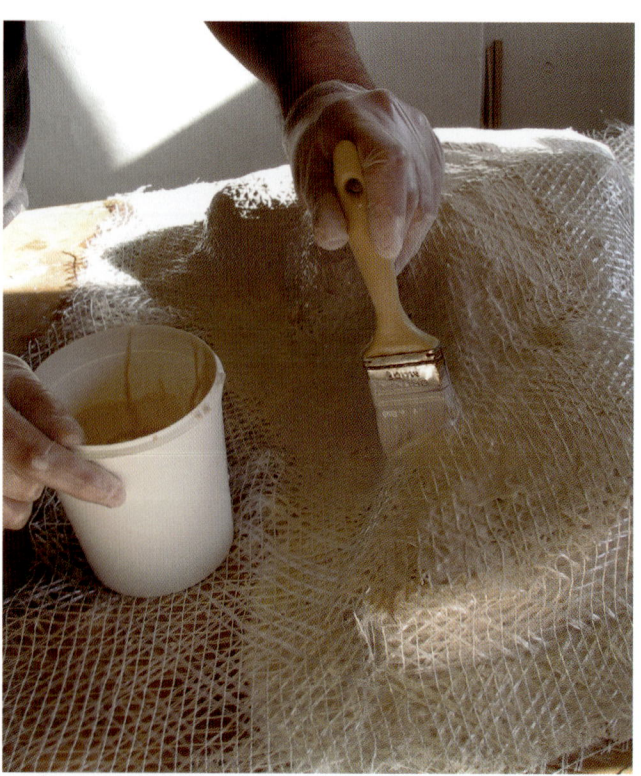

The second quadaxial mat layer.

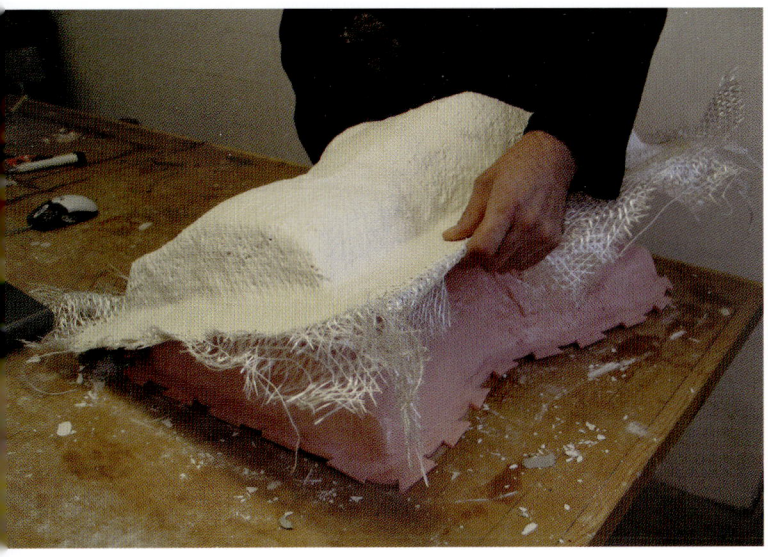

Removing the set and hardened case from the silicone mould.

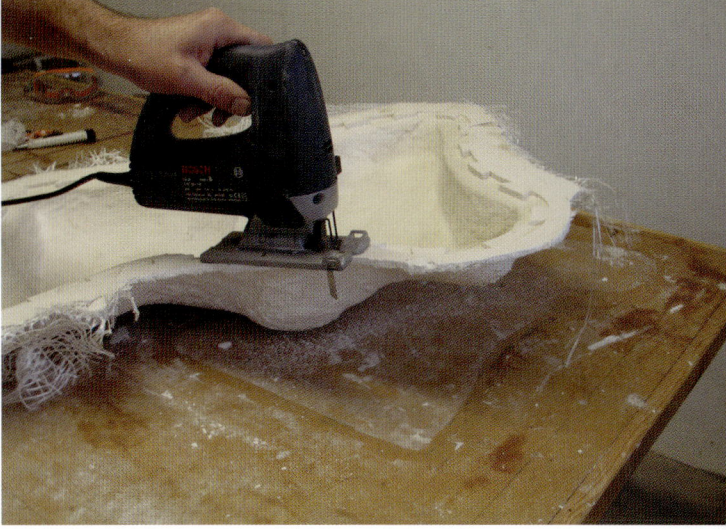

Trimming the case.

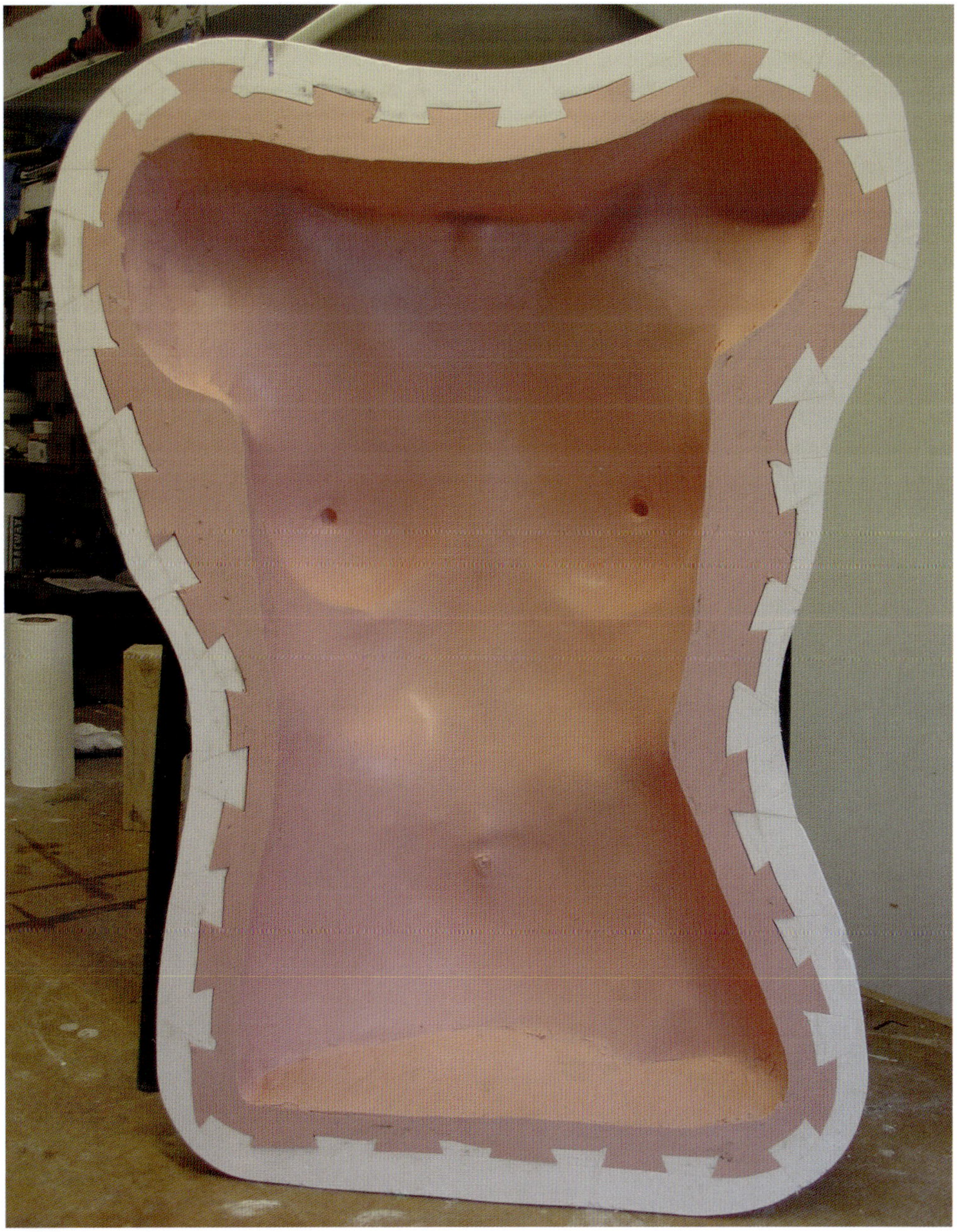

The silicone rubber mould
and Jesmonite case.

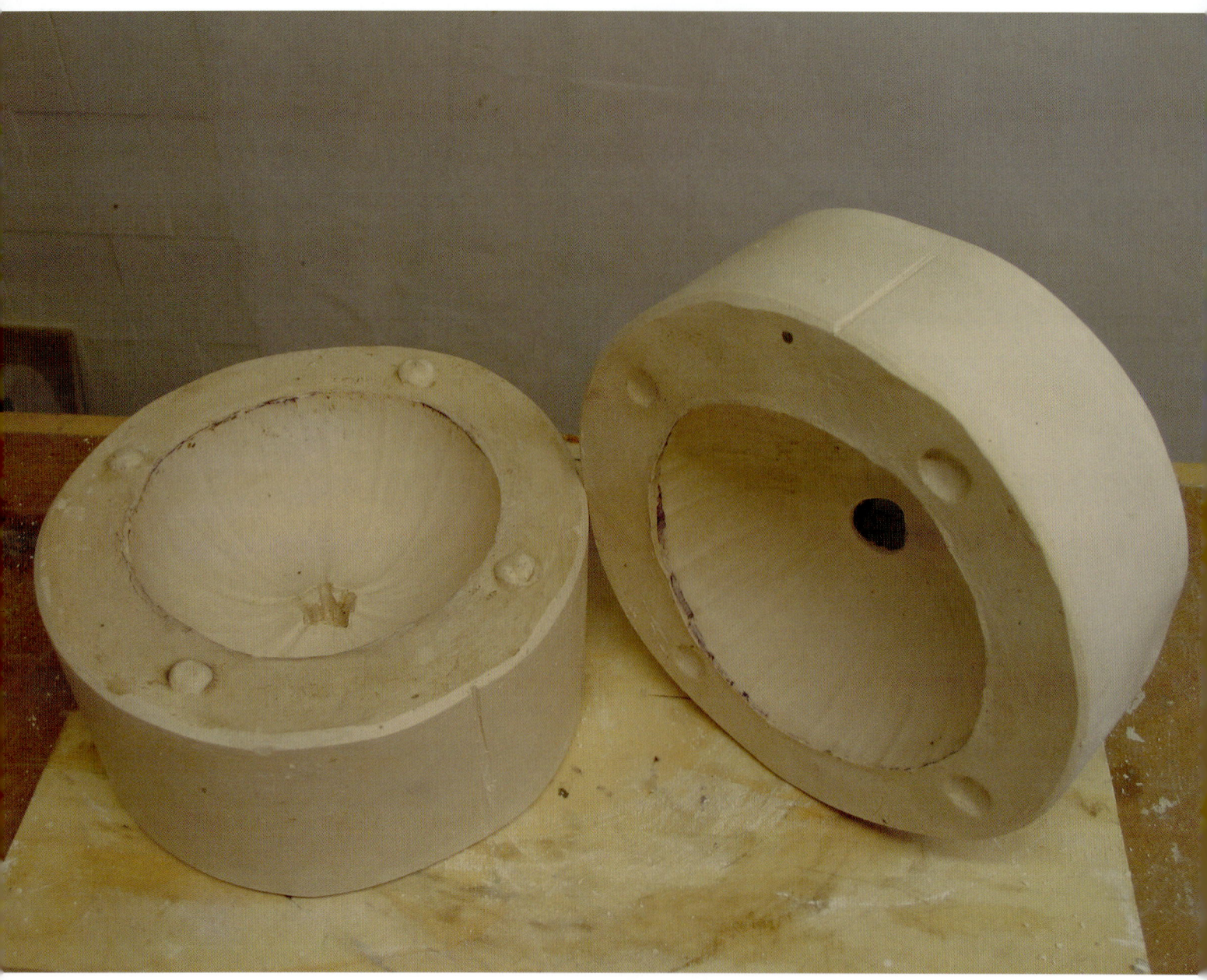

Clay slip mould.

CHAPTER SIX

CLAY SLIP MOULDING AND CASTING

The use of liquid clay slip cast in a mould to form an object and the possibilities of clay as a creative medium are manifold and have informed and inspired artists and craftspeople for thousands of years. Casting clay from a mould has advantages of multiple-piece reproduction and time-savings over one-off modelling in clay.

Clay slip is a liquid form of clay that when poured into a plaster mould deposits a layer of plastic clay onto the surface (*see* 'Moulds' section below). Once set, the object is removed from the mould and fired in a kiln to harden. Owing to the liquid nature of clay slip objects of great complexity can be reproduced easily from moulds where plastic clay may not be able to capture the detail.

Clay Slip

Most plastic clay can be made into a liquid slip and used for casting. Clay slip, although liquid, is not just a mixture of clay and water. Although the addition of water to any plastic clay would have the effect of liquefying it the process of slip casting requires a few other criteria to be available to the liquid clay. To understand this a little chemical analysis is required.

Clay is made up of minute particles that have an electrical attraction and will naturally gather together to form clumps, or flocks. It requires relatively large amounts of water to break up these flocks into a suspension and to allow the clay to become liquid and free-flowing. Many clays will require an equal amount of water by weight in order to liquefy them. Even when large amounts of water are added, clay will still have a tendency to flock, with the clay particles gathering together at the bottom of a volume of liquid clay.

The propensity of clay to flock has disadvantages in the casting process. In order for the liquid clay to adhere in an even coat to the surface of a mould requires the clay particles to be individually freely suspended in liquid. If the particles gather together in flocks castings of an uneven thickness will be produced with very sticky areas that will not demould properly. So we can see that a casting slip needs to be liquid but with a minimal addition of water.

Clays for making casting slips require an addition of water of only about a quarter of their weight to create a liquid clay. This is achieved by the addition of an electrolyte. The addition of an electrolyte to a plastic clay allows it to become 'deflocculated', dispersing the particles evenly throughout slip with minimal addition of water. A less than 1 per cent addition of deflocculant such as sodium silicate or soda ash will usually be enough to create a deflocculated slip.

A plastic clay will normally require the addition of only 35 to 50 parts water to 100 parts clay in order to liquefy it with the addition of one third of 1 per cent of deflocculant.

There is a wide range of pre-made clay casting slips available commercially. It is also quite possible to create your own slips from plastic clay, but careful research into recipes and testing are recommended. Note that some clays cannot be deflocculated and are not suitable for casting.

Moulds

In order to cast with clay slip a mould is required. The casting process involves pouring the liquid clay slip into a porous plaster mould. The porous plaster absorbs the water from the liquid clay, depositing plastic clay onto the surface of a mould.

When creating slip moulds the porosity of the plaster being used is paramount. Different casting plasters will have hugely different degrees of porosity. A good gauge of plaster porosity is the amount of plaster to water that is required in the mixing process. When plaster is mixed with water it forms a suspension of plaster particles throughout the water in the mix. When the plaster sets and the water evaporates it will leave these particles in suspension with air pockets between the particles. We can see therefore that the less plaster there is in a mix the greater the space between plaster particles once the water has evaporated, producing a more porous set plaster and vice versa.

A general rule of thumb, then, is that the less plaster to water in a mix the more porous the set plaster will be. It would be a mistake, however, to just use less plaster in a mix to produce a more porous set plaster. Different plasters require different additions of water to attain their full strength; reducing the amount of plaster in a mix may affect its set strength.

Generally speaking, Beta plasters require less plaster to water to create a mix than Alpha plasters. Moulds created with less porous plasters will not cast cleanly and will take longer to dry before reuse. There is a dilemma here, however, in that very porous plasters may lose detail with use, due to their inherently less durable nature. Unless stated as specifically porous or for use for slip casting it may be necessary to test plasters for their suitability for slip casting.

Mouldmaking

In relation to creating an efficient slip casting mould we have discussed the importance of plaster porosity; another consideration in mouldmaking is the thickness of the mould walls. When the liquid slip is poured into a mould the plaster needs to absorb the water from the slip quickly and evenly. A thick mould of approximately 50mm will greatly aid this process.

The other advantage of thick moulds is for a quick turnaround of castings. A mould that is saturated with water will not slip cast cleanly and castings will tend to stick to the mould surface. In this case the mould will need to be dried thoroughly before recasting.

Depending on porosity and thickness it may be possible to make several castings in succession before it is necessary to dry the mould.

Pouring moulds in blocks is preferable to achieve the thickness required quickly. However, this may not be possible with moulds in multiple pieces taken from complex originals, in which case moulds can be laminated. If creating moulds by laminating plaster, an even thickness of layers is important and a total thickness of at least 50mm should be achieved.

PROJECT 1

Specification

A two-piece plaster poured block mould from a pumpkin.

Time Required

This project can be completed in three hours not including setting times.

Materials

- ■ British Gypsum® fine casting plaster;
- ■ grey clay;
- ■ vegetable oil; and
- ■ petroleum jelly or wax paste release agent.

Tools

- ■ Linoleum (plastic floor covering);
- ■ a modelling board;
- ■ a clay harp;
- ■ wooden clay tools;
- ■ a rubber kidney;
- ■ a clay knife;
- ■ lengths of bicycle inner tube;
- ■ a spring clamp;
- ■ small plastic or wooden wedges;
- ■ a plaster mixing bowl;
- ■ a surform;
- ■ a hacksaw blade;
- ■ wooden blocks; and
- ■ a permanent marker.

Method

SET-UP AND PREPARATION

As with any project, careful preparation before the start of the job is crucial. Knowing the material quantities and tools needed, undertaking repairs to the original and setting-up the working area will all help to complete the job accurately and efficiently. (Tip: make sure you have enough materials to complete the job before you start. Running out of material halfway through the job is at least a waste of time and, at worst, a loss of previously executed work.)

1. Decide on the location of the division line and mark it with a permanent marker. When making clay slip moulds a small amount of undercutting is acceptable because of the shrinkage of the clay in the mould. If this plaster mould was being made to cast any other material it would need to be made in five pieces to ensure mould pieces pass any undercutting (see Chapter 5). Because the clay slip shrinks in the mould, the cast can pass a small amount of undercutting.
2. Because this will be a sealed mould in two pieces a pouring hole will need to be created in one mould piece to introduce the casting slip. This should be in an area of least significance to the eventual casting as there will be a hole into the casting at this point that will need separate filling or remedial work. In this case the hole will be at the bottom of the casting.
3. Apply release agent to any areas of the pumpkin that might need it – in this case the stalk and a few areas on the skin that seemed dry and porous.

CREATING THE CLAY BED

To define the division of the first mould piece a clay bed is made.

1. Set the pumpkin on the modelling board and secure it with a few pieces of clay.
2. Gradually build up the clay bed with small pieces of clay to 10mm below the division line.
3. Roughly level and smooth the top surface of this preliminary clay bed.
4. Cut a 10mm slab of clay with the clay harp.
5. Lay the slab on the preliminary clay bed to create the top clean surface of the bed. Lay it as closely as possible to the marked division line.
6. With a wooden clay tool make a tight connection between the top surface of the clay bed and the pumpkin. This should be as perpendicular to the surface of the pumpkin as possible to avoid a feathered edge to the mould piece (see Chapter 2 in *Mouldmaking and Casting*).
7. Smooth the clay bed surface with a rubber kidney lubricated with vegetable oil. The vegetable oil will allow the kidney to smooth the surface without picking up the clay.
8. Ensure the outside edge of the whole of the clay bed is cut at right angles to the modelling board as far as possible.
9. Create a series of registration indents in the clay bed at 80–100mm intervals. These will create nipple-and-cup registration points between the two mould pieces.

SETTING UP THE MOULD WALL

A mould wall to contain the poured plaster to create the first mould piece needs to be created. This can be made in a variety of materials as long as it will hold the liquid plaster long enough to set. In this case linoleum makes a good reusable mould wall.

1. Cut and prepare enough linoleum to wrap around the outside of the clay bed one and a half times. The height should be at least 50mm higher than the highest point of the pumpkin.
2. Wrap the lino around the clay bed and temporarily secure it with a spring clamp. Ensure that it wraps around onto itself for at least half as much of the diameter again, to ensure a good seal.
3. Secure with tight-fitting heavy-duty mould bands cut from a bicycle inner tube. Make the bands smaller than the wrapped lino so they need to stretch tightly around it to secure it.
4. Pinch a 'sausage' of clay around the bottom of the lino wall and the modelling board to seal it.

THE FIRST MOULD PIECE

1. Mix a batch of plaster to its specifications.
2. Ideally mix enough to pour the piece in one operation but if you have not mixed enough plaster another batch can be poured immediately onto the first.
3. Pour from one point within the lino wall not directly onto the pumpkin and allow the level to rise, pushing out any air entrapment as it does.
4. Pour to a level 50mm higher than the highest point of the exposed first half of the pumpkin. This will ensure adequate thickness of the mould piece.
5. Introduce your fingertips into the top surface of the poured plaster and move them up and down methodically. This will bring up any trapped air. The outside surface of the lino wall can be lightly tapped to achieve this as well.
6. Allow the plaster to set thoroughly.

THE SECOND MOULD PIECE

1. Remove the lino wall.
2. Invert the first mould piece and clay bed, keeping them together as you do. Do not remove the first mould piece from the pumpkin as you will have to replace it before continuing with the second

mould piece and it will not reregister accurately if removed and then replaced.
3. Remove all of the clay bed. The second half of the pumpkin will now be exposed, sitting in the first mould piece.
4. Sponge off any clay marks left on the now exposed flange of the first mould piece.
5. Sponge off any clay marks left on the now exposed surface of the second pumpkin half.
6. Apply release agent to the exposed flange of the first mould piece.
7. To create the pouring hole into the mould roll out a solid clay cone of diameters 20mm at the base and 15mm at the top, with a height of 50mm. Place this securely at your predetermined spot on the pumpkin surface.
8. Reapply the lino mould wall and secure it as before. Ensure that it is still high enough to cover the pumpkin by at least 50mm.
9. Pour plaster to create the second mould piece as for the first piece.
10. Allow it to set thoroughly.

OPENING AND TRIMMING

Once the mould is complete it can be opened and trimmed.

1. Remove the lino mould wall.
2. Lightly hammer a series of small wooden or plastic wedges into the seam line between the two mould pieces. These should be driven only a little way into the seam until you can just see it parting. Place the wedges in sequence approximately 50mm apart.
3. Drive the wedges in deeper until the mould pieces separate.
4. If the pumpkin remains in one mould piece gently lever it out, taking care not to damage the mould.
5. Trim all sharp edges of the mould to a small chamfer with a surform.
6. Chamfer the edges of the pouring hole at the top and bottom with a clay knife. This is important to avoid any plaster chipping off into the mould when pouring in the slip. Even small particles of plaster introduced into a clay body can cause damage to castings when fired in the kiln.
7. With the mould pieces reassembled, using a hacksaw blade create a line in the plaster across a point where they meet. This will provide a visual reference for where to join the mould pieces.

8. Wash and dry both mould pieces thoroughly.
9. Reassemble the mould and ensure it is thoroughly dry before use. Slip moulds in particular need to be thoroughly dry before use to produce effective castings. Mould pieces should be reassembled while drying in case they warp. Place wooden blocks under the mould to allow air to circulate and water to evaporate from it. The amount of time it takes for a mould to dry completely will depend on mould thickness, the porosity of the plaster used and atmospheric drying conditions. Do not speed up drying by increasing ambient temperatures unduly, as this may affect the dry strength of the mould; a little above room temperature is fine. When the mould feels warm to the touch it is dry and ready to use.

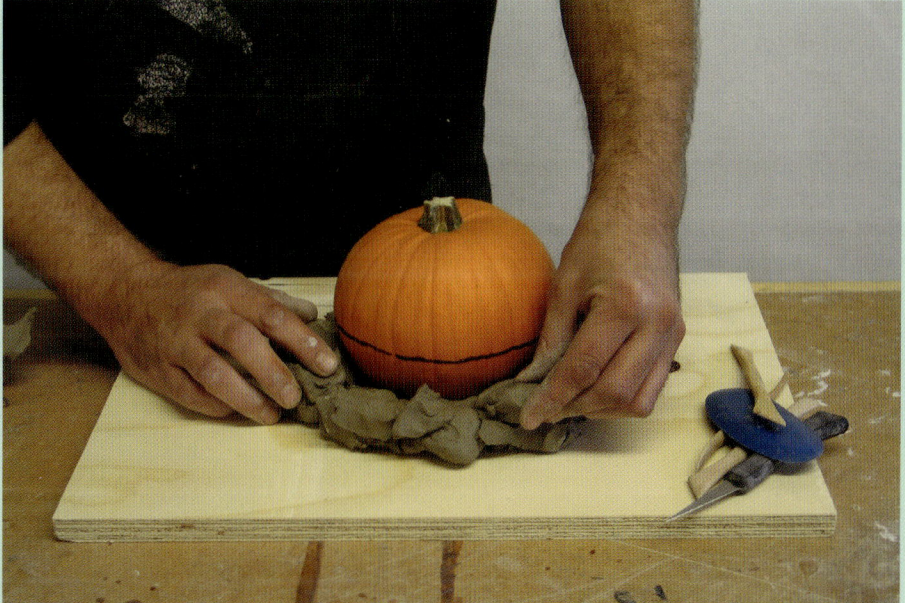

The original is secured in place on a modelling board.

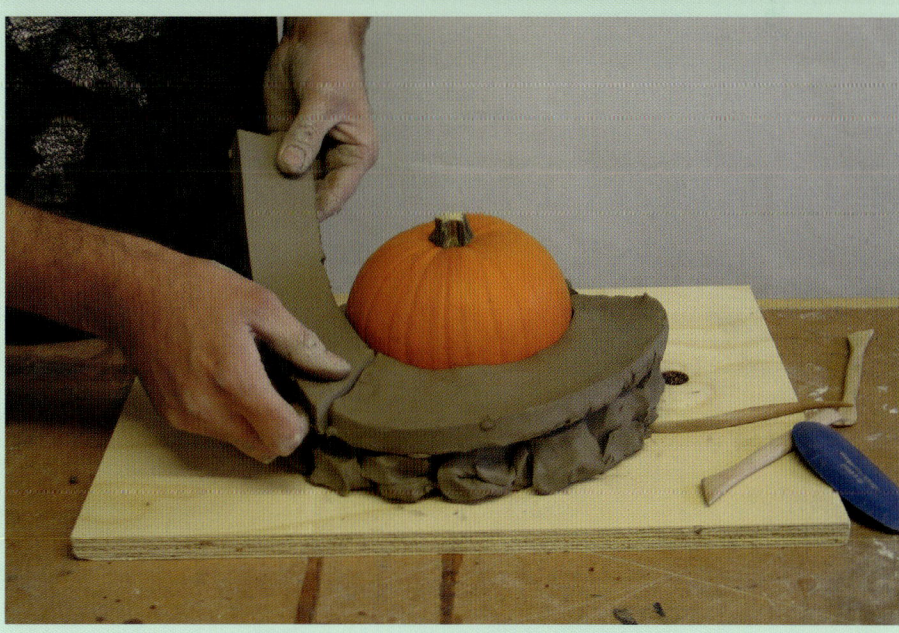

A clay bed and surface slab are created.

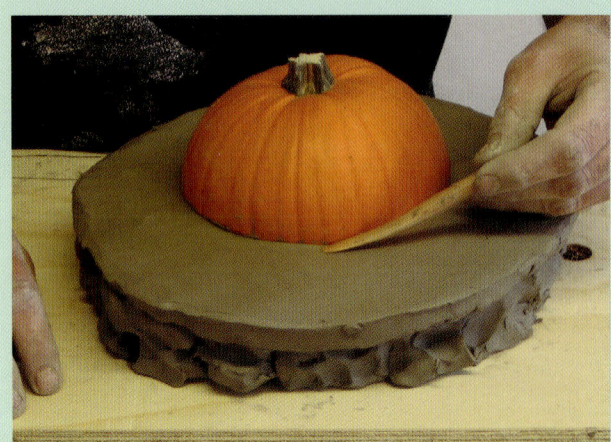

A clean perpendicular join between the clay bed and original is created.

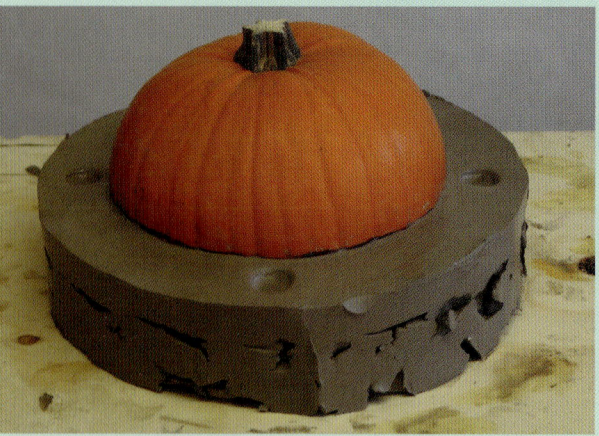

Registration indents are applied to the clay bed surface and the sides cut perpendicular to the modelling board.

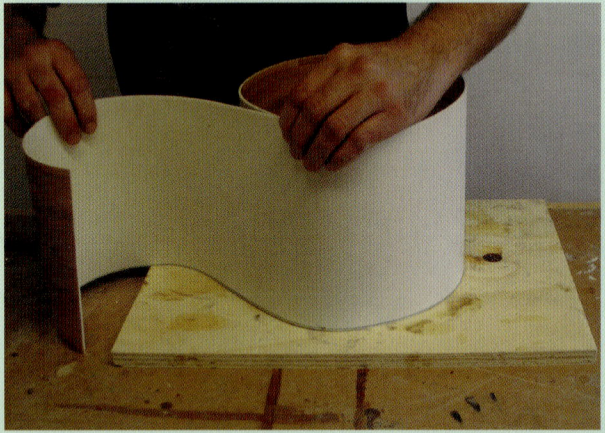

Create a linoleum mould wall around the clay bed.

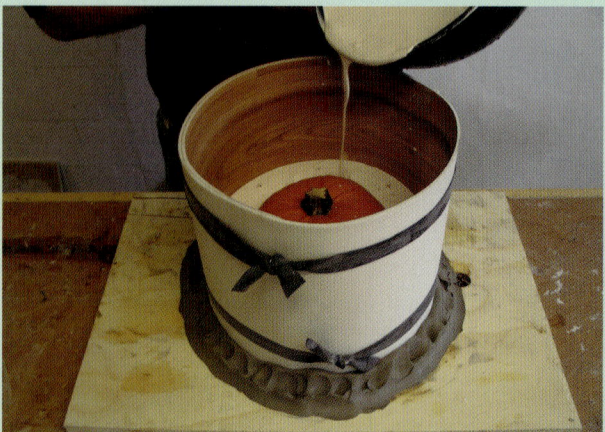

Plaster is poured within the secured mould wall.

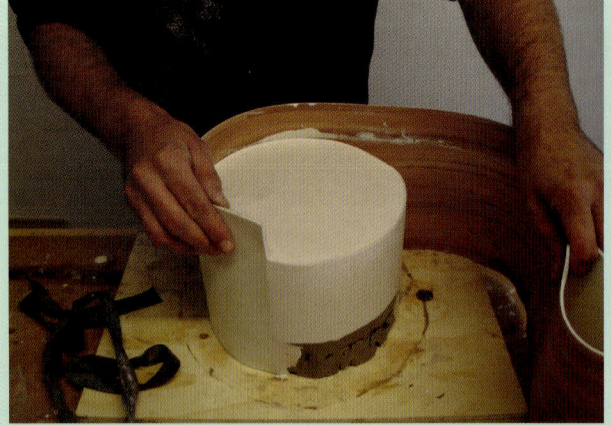

Once the plaster has set the mould wall can be removed.

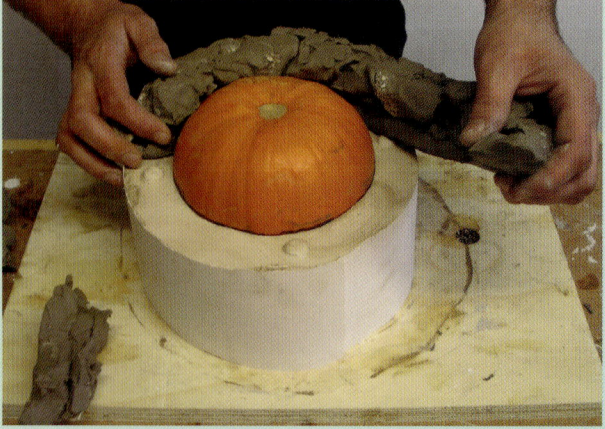

The mould is inverted and the clay bed removed ready to create the second half of the mould.

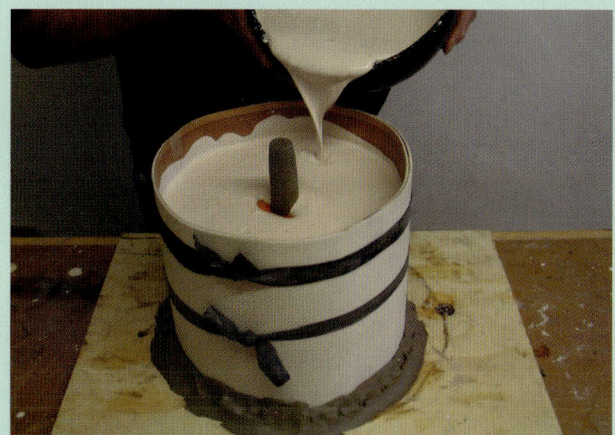

Once the mould walls are reset, the second half of the mould can be poured.

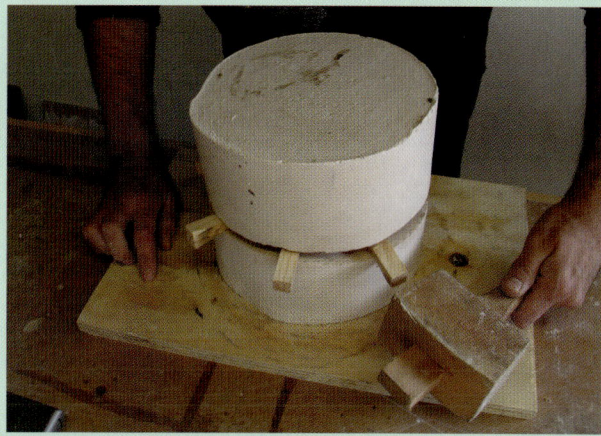

Wooden wedges are sequentially driven in to separate the mould halves.

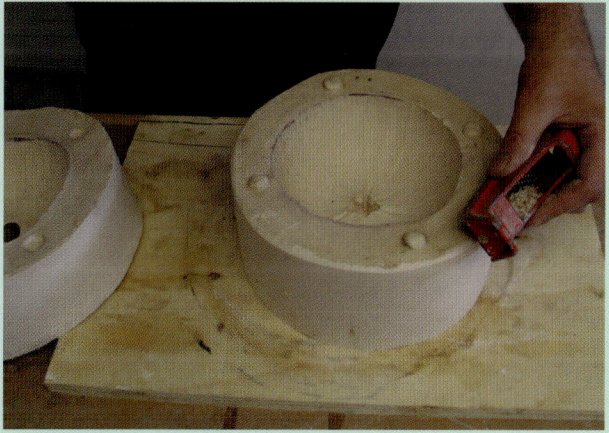

The mould edges are trimmed with a surform.

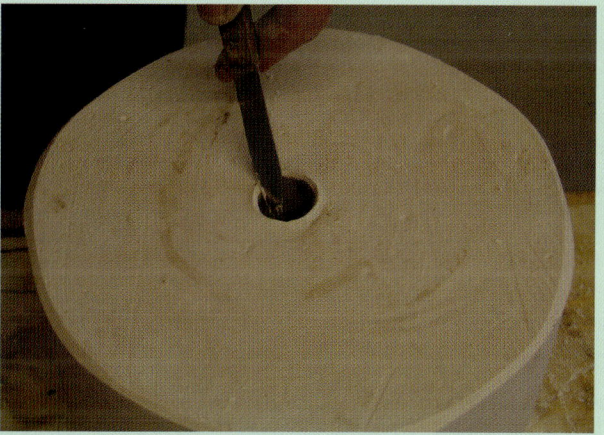

The pouring hole is trimmed with a clay knife.

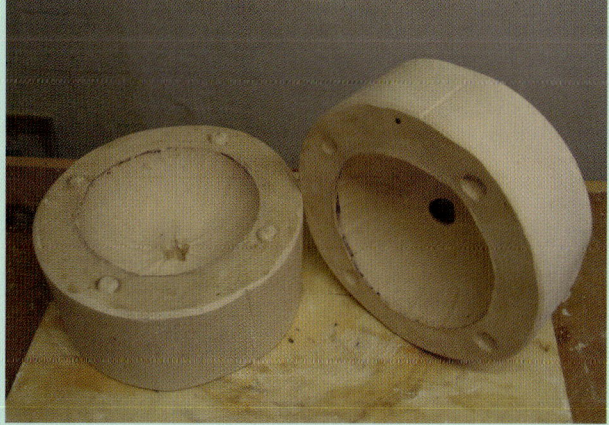

The finished mould.

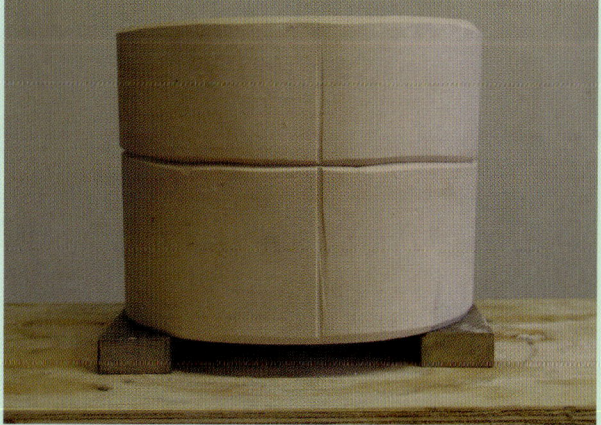

The mould is reassembled and supported on sticks to dry thoroughly before use.

Casting

Clay slip casting is a relatively easy process which involves pouring the liquid clay into a dry plaster mould and allowing it to build up a thickness of plastic clay on the surface of the mould. For a successful casting there are a few choices to be considered and conditions to which one should adhere.

Clay Slip

There are a large number of clays suitable for slip casting, with a wide variety of colours and textures. An understanding of the technical requirements and the effect of these is important in deciding on which materials to use for casting.

It may be obvious to some, but it is important to understand that clay slip castings need to be dried and fired to high temperatures in a kiln in order for them to have any practical strength. Slip castings can be extremely fragile in their 'green' (unfired) state and consideration should be given to ease of access and transport to the kiln. The action of firing clay of any sort will change dramatically its chemical, physical and visual appearance and an understanding of the capabilities of the casting slip being used is crucial.

Firing can be a two-stage process if glazing the piece is required. Glazes need to be matched to the clay body in order that firing temperatures are compatible to both.

Generally speaking the slip casting is fired to a low (bisque) temperature from green and then glazed and refired to a higher (glaze) temperature. Both these firings will have a dramatic effect on the visual appearance of the casting and research and testing should be carried out to determine the desirability, requirements and practicality for the particular piece.

Shrinkage of castings should also be considered. Clay will shrink between 5 and 8 per cent in size when dried and will then shrink a further 5 to 10 per cent when fired.

Another consideration may be the thickness of castings. The process of casting slip involves pouring the liquid clay slip into a mould and allowing it to 'cast' on the surface of the mould. Once the slip has been deposited on the surface of the mould the excess liquid slip is drained out of the mould; leaving the plastic clay behind. The thickness of the casting is determined by how long the casting slip is left in the mould, the longer it is left the thicker the mould will be. The thickness required of different clay slips will vary; some clays will need

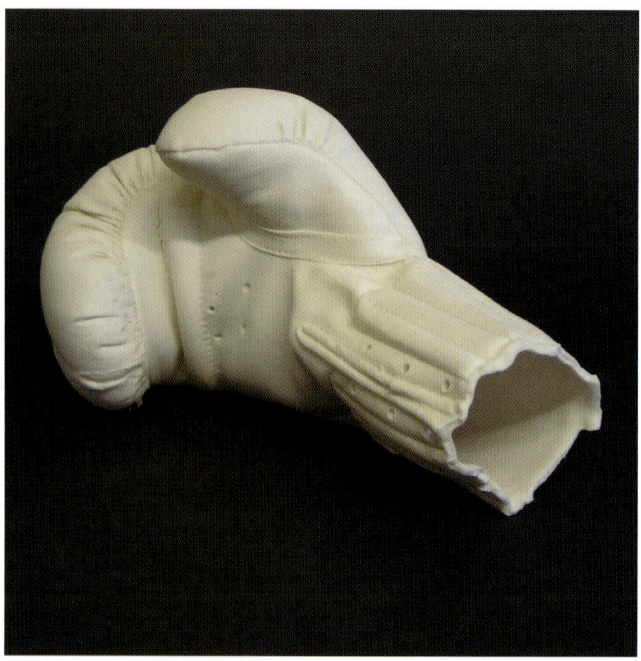

Porcelain slip cast (by Magdalena van Straaten).

to be thicker or thinner than others to attain the correct dry strength.

Once the casting material specifications and finish have been determined casting can proceed.

Porcelain slip casts (by Magdalena van Straaten).

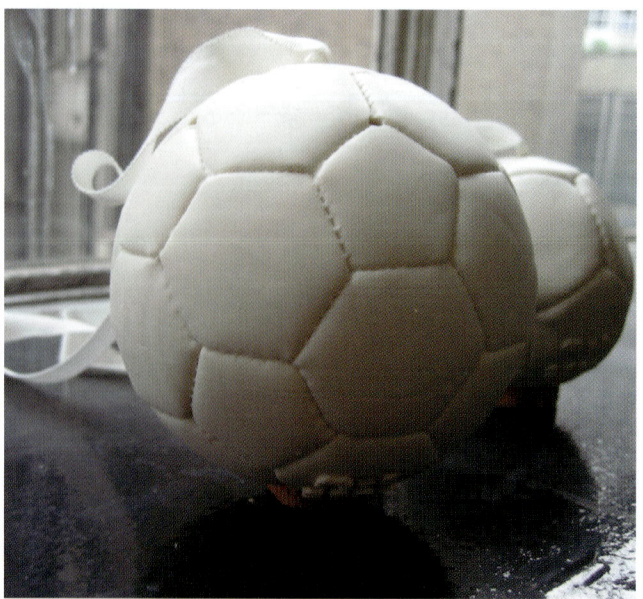

PROJECT 2

Specification

A slip cast of a pumpkin from the two-piece block mould created in Project 1.

Time Required

Approximately one hour (not including firing time).

Materials

■ Porcelain clay casting slip.

Tools

■ A plastic builder's bucket;
■ wooden sticks to place across the top of the bucket × 2;
■ a 120-mesh sieve;
■ a large plastic jug;
■ a clay knife;
■ a small natural sponge; and
■ a wooden drying rack or sticks.

Method

CASTING

1. Ensure the moulds are clean and dry. A dry and slightly warmed mould will cast much more efficiently.
2. Casting slips should be stirred thoroughly and then sieved through a 120-mesh sieve before use. Slips will tend to flocculate when stored even for short lengths of time; stirring and sieving will deflocculate them.
3. Securely fasten the mould together.
4. Set it on wooden sticks placed across the top of a builder's bucket.
5. Dispense enough casting slip into a large plastic jug.
6. Pour the slip evenly in one fluid operation into the pouring hole until it fills the mould. Open-top moulds should be filled to the rim.
7. Maintain the top-filled level while casting. This is important as the cast will cast at different thicknesses if the top level is allowed to drop too much. This can result in bottom-heavy castings.

8. Leave the mould filled until the desired thickness has been achieved. The thickness can be determined by tipping the mould slightly to reveal the edge of the cast.
9. When the desired thickness has been achieved tip out the excess casting slip into the jug or bucket. Initially it may be necessary to clear a pouring hole with a clay knife to allow the slip to pour out. Once a little slip has been poured out it will be possible to trim the plastic clay of the cast back to the outside edge of the pouring hole and then pour out the rest of the slip out more readily. Note: be careful when tipping out excess slip from a mould not to allow any plaster to chip off and drop into casting slip that is to be reused.
10. When all the slip has been poured out invert the mould, pouring hole side down, on the sticks on the bucket to drain out any last little bits of slip.
11. When the cast starts to lose its glossy surface the clay around the pouring hole or mould opening may be trimmed with a clay knife.
12. Allow the cast to firm up until at least 'leather hard' before demoulding.

DEMOULDING

1. Demoulding can occur when the cast is leather hard. However, it may be beneficial to leave demoulding for longer to allow the casting to start shrinking. Remember, clay will shrink by around 5 to 8 per cent while drying, which can be beneficial on moulds that are slightly undercut. In open one-piece moulds it is definitely beneficial to allow the casting to shrink a little before remoulding.
2. Remove the mould parts carefully, supporting the casting as the pieces are removed. Support castings from one-piece moulds as they are tipped out.

TRIMMING, JOINING, CUTTING AND FETTLING

Initial trimming, joining and cutting can be carried out while the clay is leather hard. A secondary fine finish can be achieved when the casting is dry.

1. While the clay is leather hard it can be trimmed with a clay knife. This is the first level of finishing and should not be taken too far. This can involve trimming any excess flashing (clay that has seeped between the mould pieces) or any clay that is excess to the cast surface.

2. A slightly damp small natural sponge can be used to take back any imperfections on the surface of the cast a little further.

3. Cast pieces can be joined to others at this leather-hard stage by using a little casting slip between the join and pressing gently together until secure. A little cross hatching of the surfaces to be joined with a clay or craft knife will help adhesion.

4. The casting can also be cut at this stage using a clay or craft knife. Once the initial trim has taken place the casting should be allowed to dry (see next section).

5. Once completely dry a second level of finishing, fettling, can be achieved by carefully rubbing down any imperfections with very fine wire wool. Be careful when rubbing the surface of dry castings with wire wool as even fine wool will take material away very quickly. Dry castings will be very fragile and care should be taken handling them. (Note: fettling will create clay dust that is carcinogenic. Dust control measures should always be observed and personal protective equipment, including a dust mask, used.)

The mould is secured and placed on sticks over a bucket.

DRYING

Owing to the shrinkage of the clay as it dries castings must be thoroughly dry before firing. Unless the drying process is controlled, the level of shrinkage can put great strains on castings, producing warping and cracking.

1. Ambient temperature will obviously affect drying times. If too high, however, castings will dry too quickly and warp and/or crack. Room temperature is adequate for thin castings, slightly warmer is better for thicker castings.

2. Air should be allowed to circulate around the castings. Placing castings on a wooden drying rack or on sticks will assist airflow and the evenness of drying. Do not use fans or a blow heater to assist this process.

3. Rotating large castings, if possible, while drying will help them to dry evenly.

4. When castings are warm to the touch they are dry and ready for fettling and then firing.

5. Follow the specifications of the casting slip used for the firing schedules.

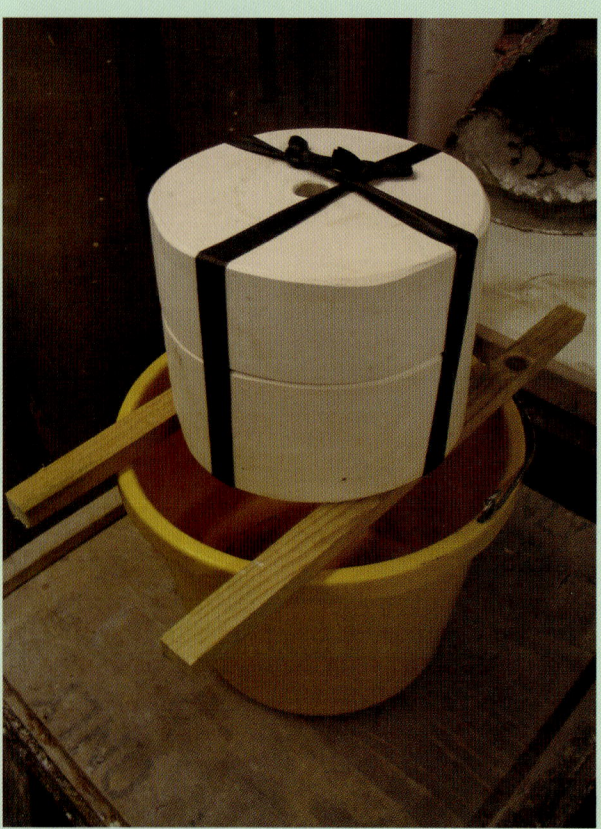

Ready for casting.

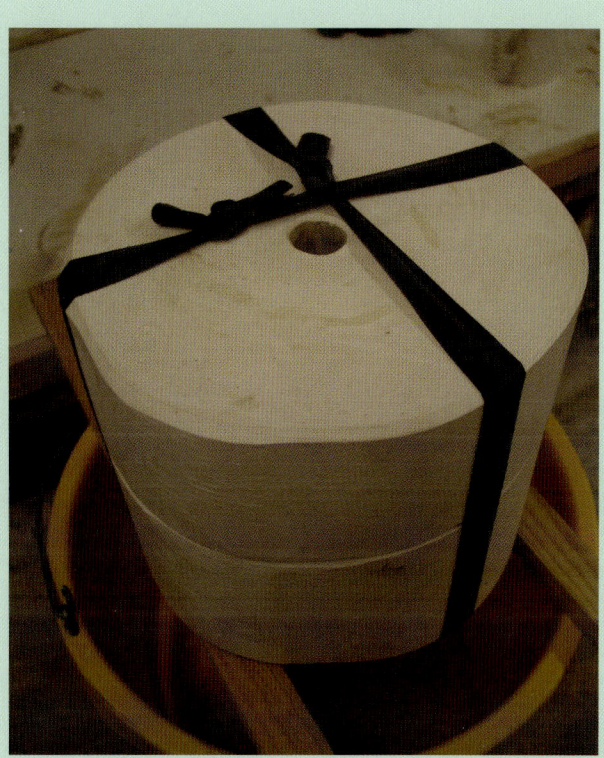

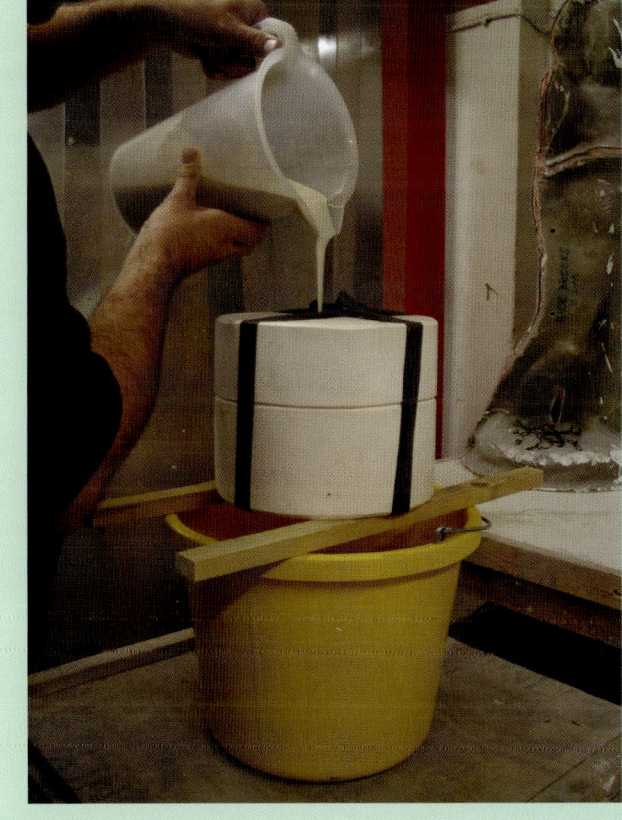

Clay slip is poured into the mould.

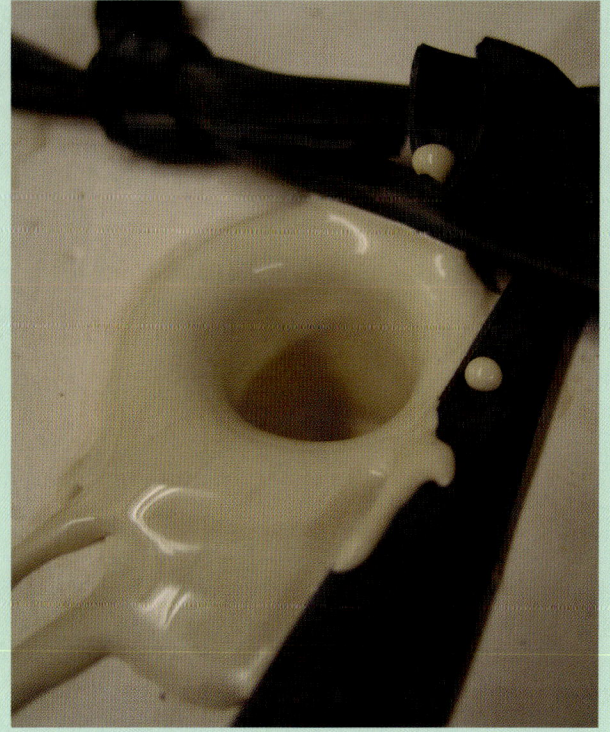

As the water is absorbed from the clay slip the level drops.

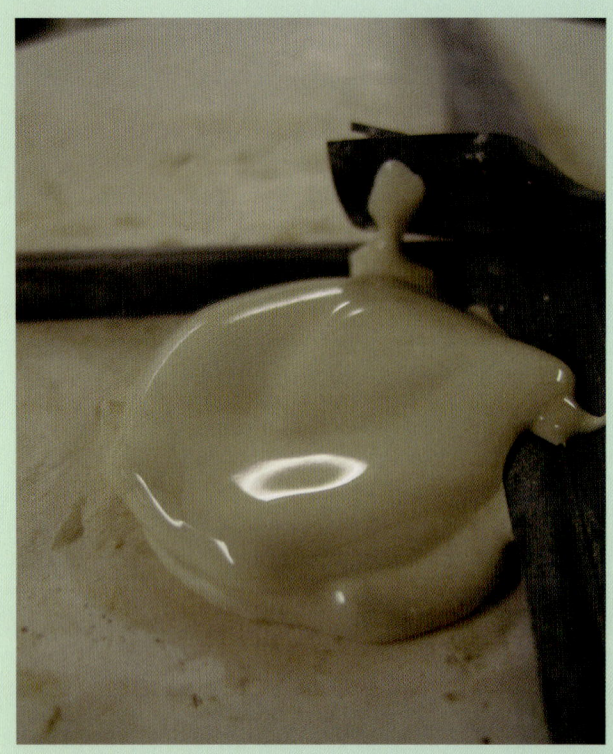

The pouring hole is trimmed before evacuating excess slip from the mould.

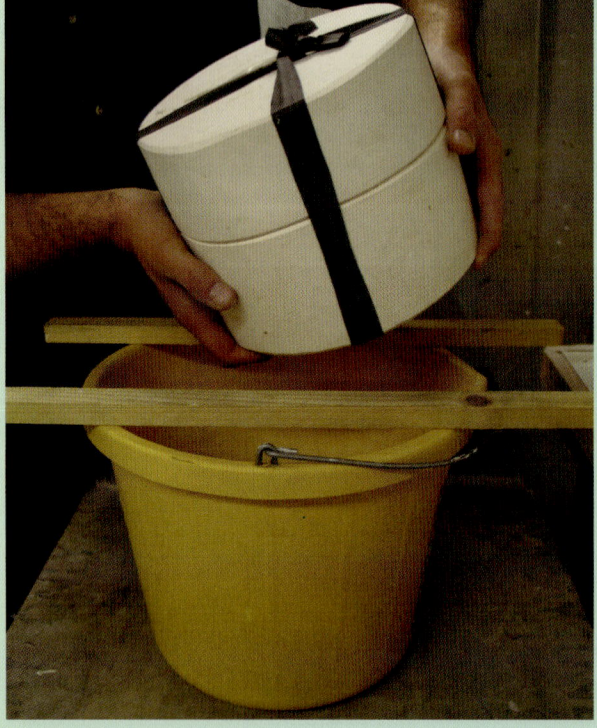

The slip level is topped up.

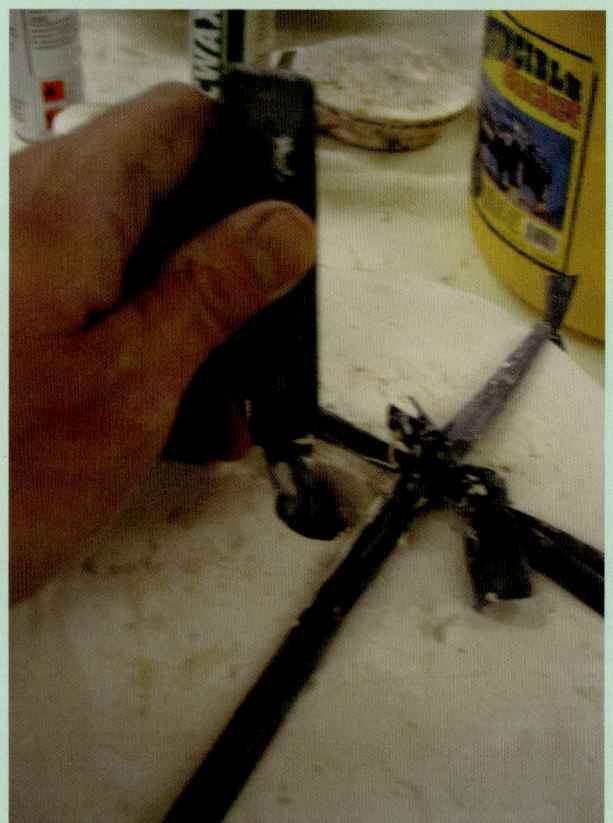

Excess slip is poured out of the mould.

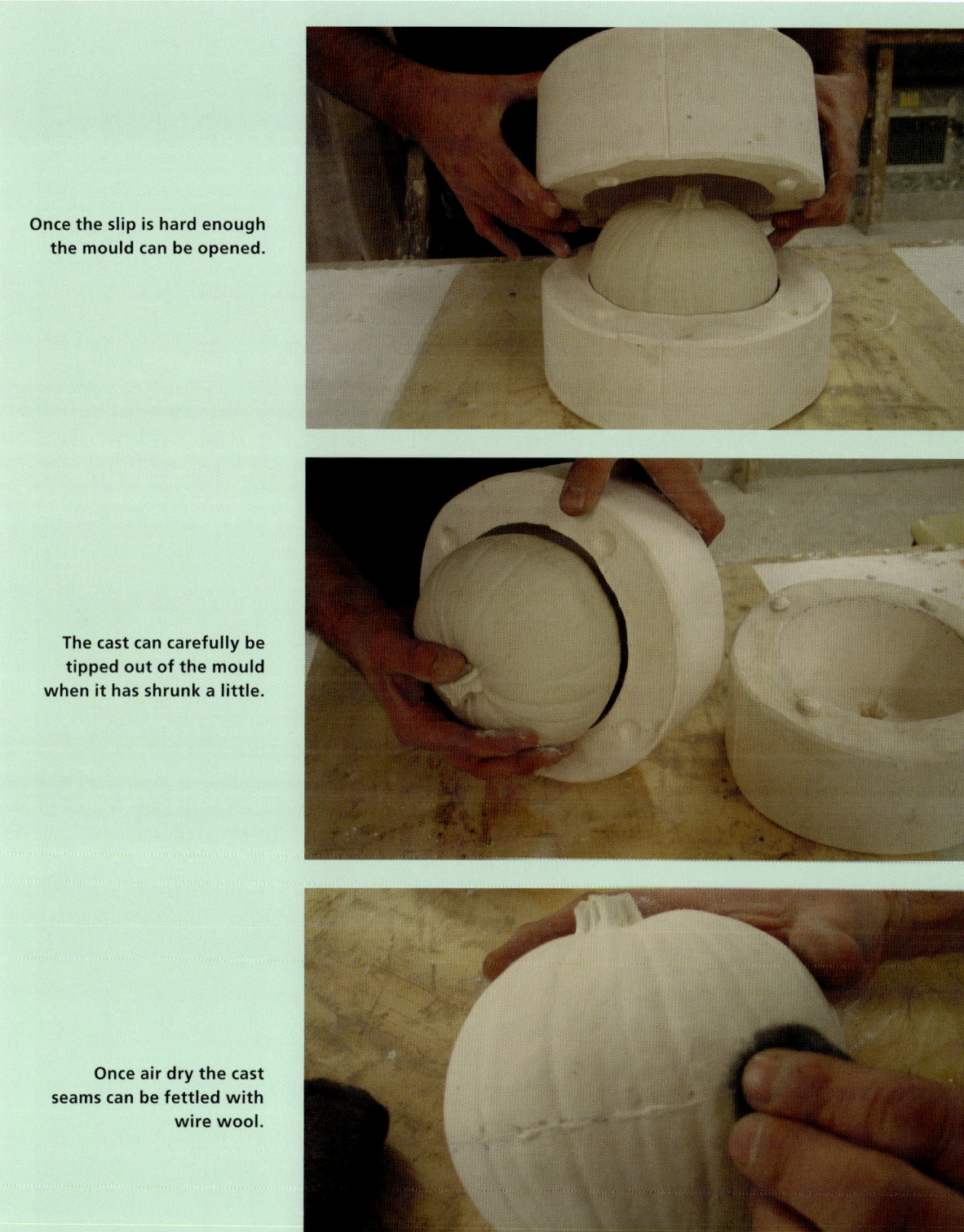

Once the slip is hard enough the mould can be opened.

The cast can carefully be tipped out of the mould when it has shrunk a little.

Once air dry the cast seams can be fettled with wire wool.

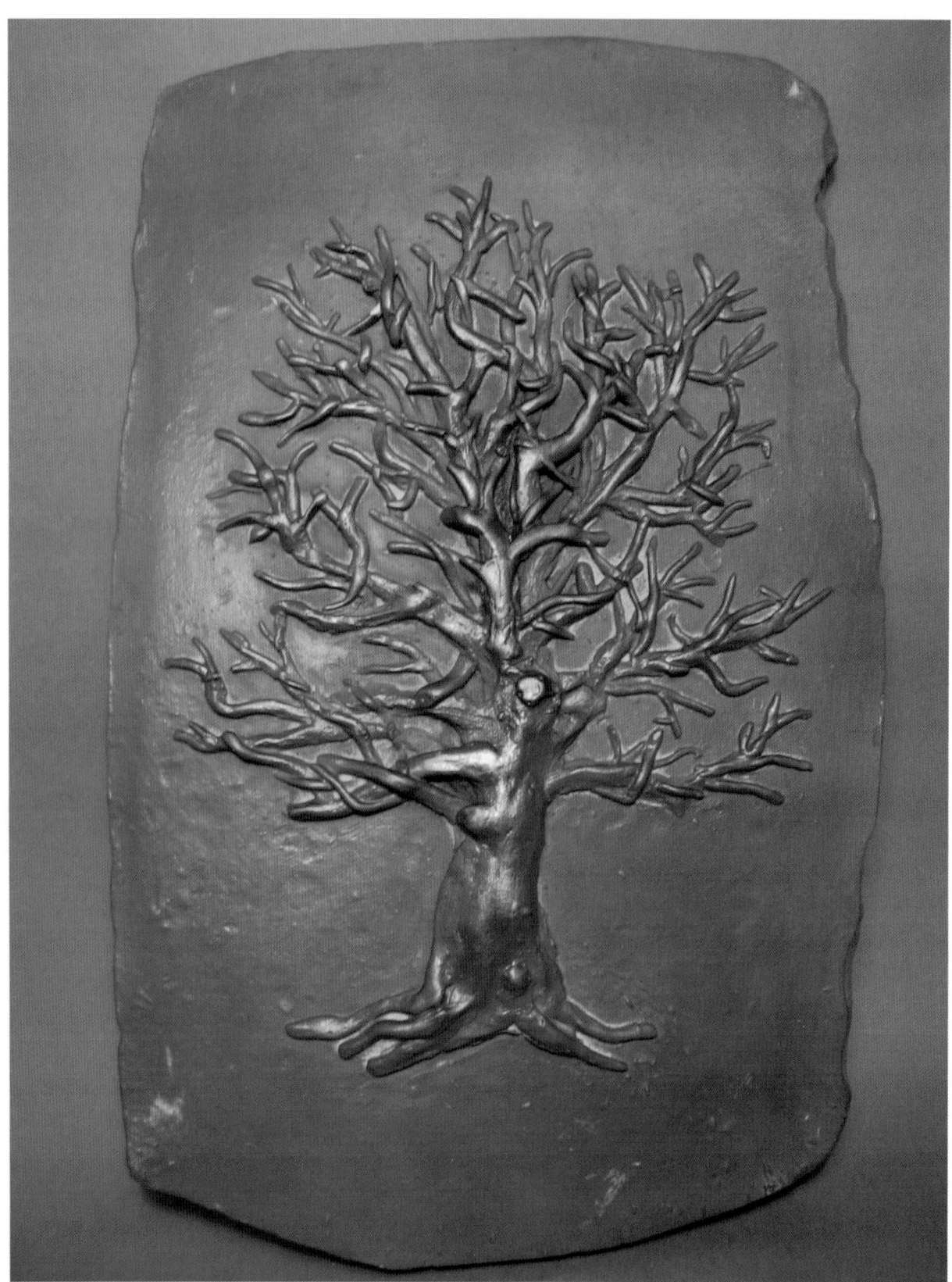

Bronze filled Jesmonite AC100 Cast (H: 330mm).

CHAPTER SEVEN

JESMONITE™

Jesmonite™ is an acrylic polymer and calcium sulphate composite mouldmaking and casting resin system with many advantages over traditional resin systems. Invented in 1984 and developed primarily as a construction material to rival traditional glass reinforced plastic resin systems, its main advantage is minimal toxicological concerns. Being principally water based, there are none of the ventilation and clean-up requirements associated with polyester and polyurethane resins systems. This is clearly advantageous to the user, whether a studio artist or a commercial mould-maker.

There is a range of Jesmonite systems, from very hard composites to softer 'carvable' composites, including systems capable of producing pigmented, metal and stone surfaced castings. The system principally comprises a two-part mix of an acrylic polymer liquid and calcium sulphate powder which when combined produces a set resin that can be cast as a solid or laminated in hollow section. It is an excellent mouldmaking medium, with the advantages of high durability combined with light weight (*see* Chapter 5). The two principal applications of Jesmonite systems are casting and laminating.

Laminating

Jesmonite can be used for hollow casting, mouldmaking and case-making for flexible moulds. This is a two-stage process whereby, first, a 'gel coat' first layer is applied by brush. This can contain pigment, metal or stone fillers for decorative applications in castings or can be used 'neat' for mould-making applications. Second, the gel coat is backed up with a combination of laminating materials.

Casting

Jesmonite is also used for solid filled castings. A composite mix is poured into a mould, which can be pigmented, metal-filled or stone-filled for decorative castings.

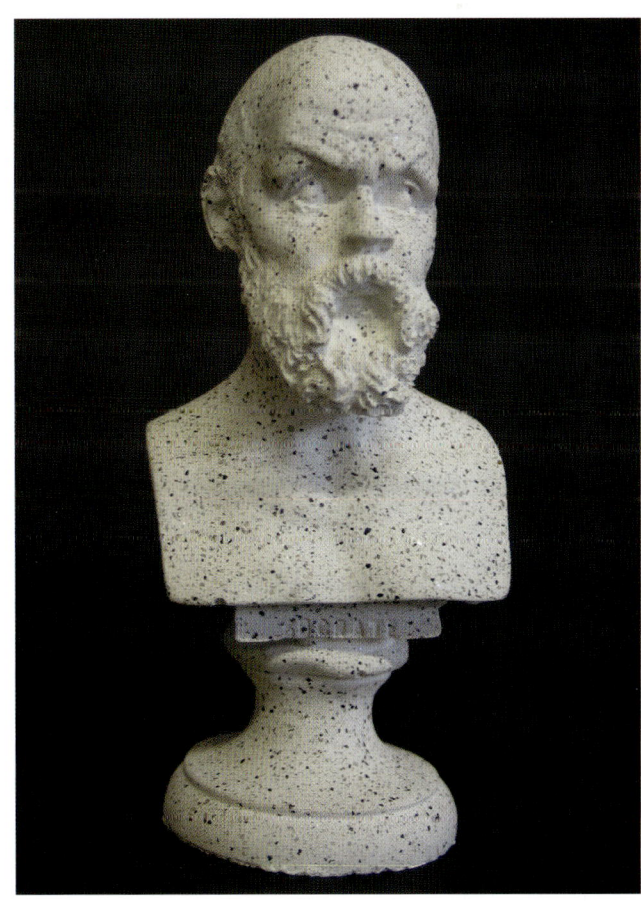

A Jesmonite AC730 granite cast (H: 120mm) (courtesy of Canonbury Arts Ltd).

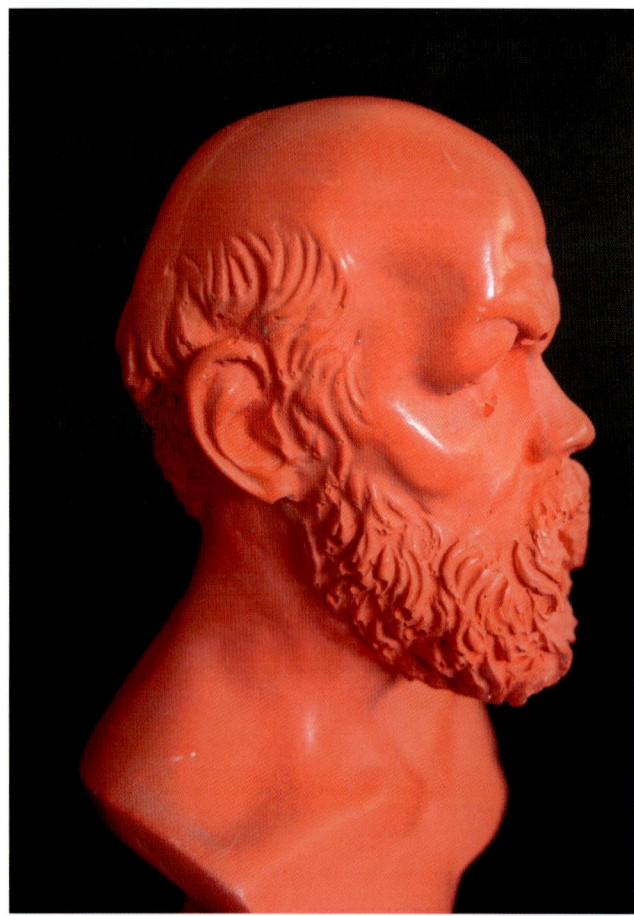

A Jesmonite AC100 pigmented cast (H: 120mm)
(courtesy of Canonbury Arts Ltd).

Materials

Composites

AC100 A standard composite suitable for casting, laminating, pigmenting, and metal and stone finishing.

AC200 A soft composite suitable for carving. Useful applications include the coating of rough-carved foam for further finer carving, or the production of carvable blocks to produce patterns for remoulding (see the Special Notes at the end of the chapter on this material).

AC400 A very hard composite for use where high-impact strengths and external durability are required. It is suitable for casting, laminating, and metal and stone finishing.

AC730 An acrylic polymer 'cement' composite that is externally durable and capable of water submersion. Useful applications include externally sited castings and water features. Suitable for casting, laminating and excellent stone finishes (see the Special Notes at the end of the chapter on this material).

The shelf life for composites is 6 months under dry frost-free conditions.

Sundry Materials

Quadaxial mat A soft mat woven in four directions. Used for laminating hollow castings to provide integral structural strength. (A range of other mats and fabrics is available for jobs of differing specification.)

Chopped strand Glass fibre strands (6–13mm depending on the strength requirements) are used in the laminating process as a sandwiched filler between layers of quadaxial mat.

Thixotropic additive This is used to create 'thixotropic' mixes of the composite that can be applied to a vertical mould surface without running off. Thixotropic addition is only necessary for neat or pigmented gel coats. The addition of metal and stone fillers to the composite mix will create a mix that is thixotropic in its own right.

Retarder This is used in addition to composites to slow setting times and extend the 'pot life' (working time).

Pigments Used in addition to composites to provide integral colour.

Metal and stone fillers Used in addition to composites to produce metal-surfaced and stone-surfaced castings.

Metal Fillers

Metal fillers are fine-mesh metal powders added to composites to produce castings with metallic finishes. Unlike 'metallic' paint finishes these are powders of the actual metal and once cut back with abrasives and polished they will appear as the metals they are. For instance, an iron-filled casting will start to rust if exposed to moisture. Available metal fillers include:

- bronze;
- brass;
- copper; or
- stainless steel flake.

Storage should be at moderate temperatures in dry conditions.

Stone Fillers

Stone fillers are powdered stone materials added to composites to produce stone finishes. They are usually more granular than metal fillers. Available stone fillers include:

- white marble;
- yellow sandstone;
- portland stone; and
- silver-grey granite.

Storage should be at moderate temperatures in dry conditions.

Metal and stone fillers can be used as a 'gel coat' and painted onto the surface of a mould to a thickness of 2 or 3mm, allowed to set and then backfilled with composite or laminated with quadaxial mat and chopped strand.

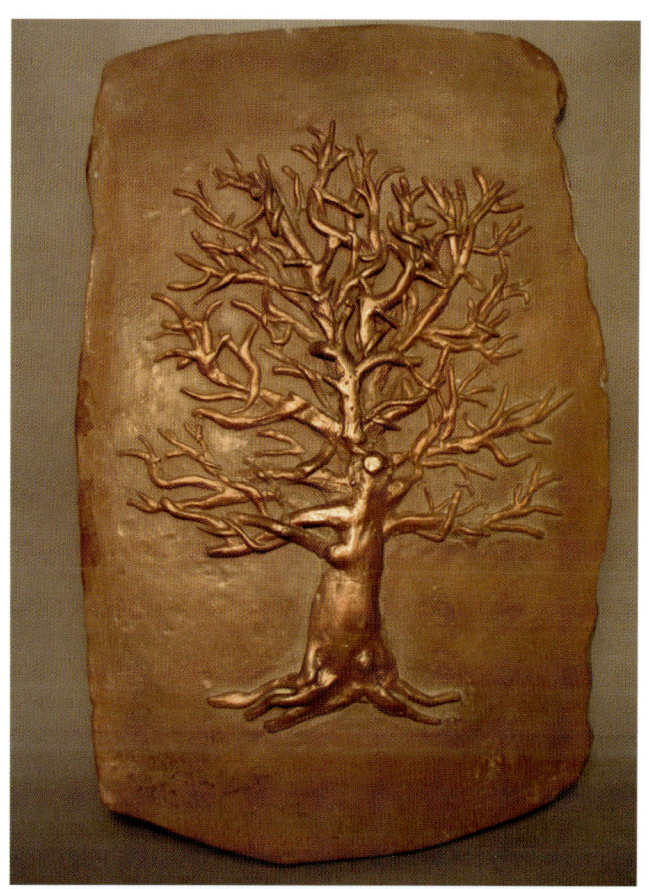

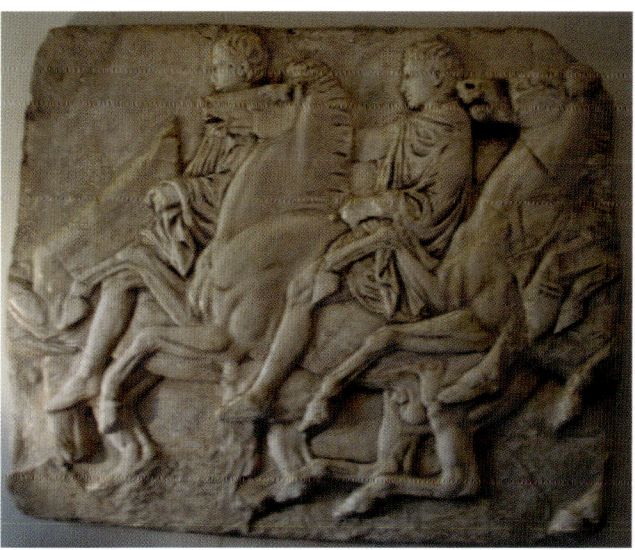

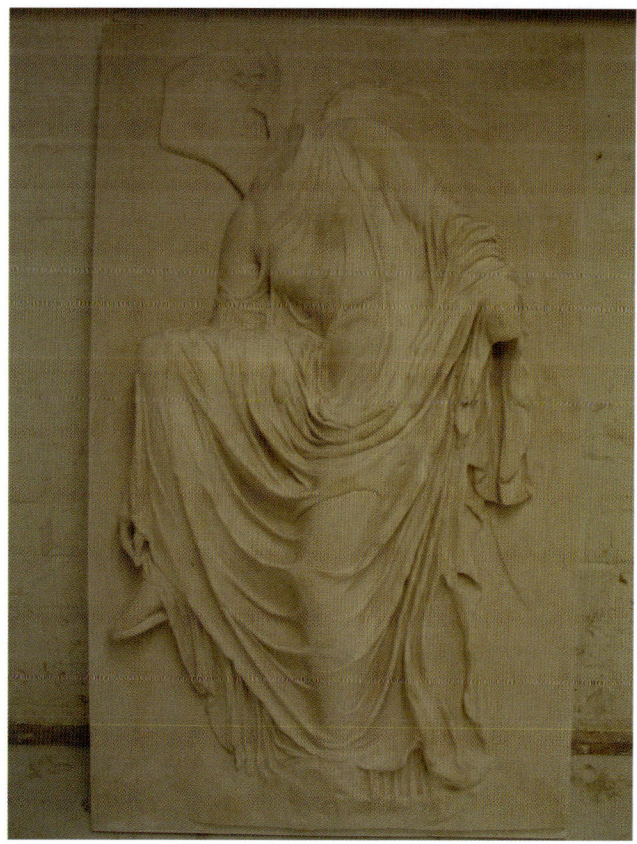

TOP RIGHT: **A Jesmonite AC100 copper cast (H: 330mm).**
RIGHT: **A Jesmonite AC100 unpigmented cast (H: 900mm).**
ABOVE: **An antiqued Jesmonite cast (H: 1030mm, W: 1250mm).**

Tools and Equipment

Dispensing and Mixing

- **Waxed paper cups or white plastic containers**   For dispensing and mixing batches of composite. Plastic containers can be allowed to dry after use and the set composite cracked out to be reused.
- **A variable-speed cordless drill fitted with a high shear blade**   For mixing batches.
- **Disposable wooden spatulas**   For combining composite parts and mixing pigments and fillers into small batches.
- **Scales**   Accurate digital scales should be used to calculate weights and measures of composite parts safely.

Laminating

- **Brushes**   Brushes of various sizes are needed to paint gel coats onto the mould surface. Decorating brushes of a good quality are suitable.
- **Disposable wooden spatulas**   For mixing and applying batches of chopped strand.
- **A plastic paint kettle or builder's bucket**   For cleaning brushes and equipment.

Trimming and Finishing

- **Rasps and files**   These can be used for the initial seam trimming of cured composite casts.
- **A hacksaw**   Used for initial trimming.
- **Tin snips and heavy duty shears**   Used for initial trimming.
- **Powered jigsaws and multi-tools**   These can be very useful to take some of the hard work out of trimming. (Note: observe strict dust control measures.)
- **A power drill**   Holes can be drilled safely mechanically or by hand into set composites.
- **Powered abrasive tools**   For cutting back cast seams and exposing metal or stone surfaces. Beware of cutting back filled casts mechanically as they can take too much away too quickly. (Note: observe strict dust control measures.)
- **Wet-and-dry abrasive paper**   For removing sharp edges after initial trimming and cutting back metal-filled casts prior to polishing.
- **Wire wool**   This comes in different grades and is used for cutting back metal-filled castings.
- **Needle files**   For very fine and difficult-to-access trimming and cutting back.
- **Wire brushes**   For clearing tools clogged with material.
- **Polishing equipment**   For polishing castings after cutting them back with abrasives. This can be done mechanically or by hand.

Safety and Good Studio Practice

- Dust control measures should be applied when working with Jesmonite powders.
- Work surfaces can be protected with a heavy-gauge polythene that can be disposed of or replaced when necessary.
- All tools and equipment can be washed in water.
- Bucket-wash tools and containers to prevent waste material from entering the drainage systems. Allow waste material to settle, then drain off the surface water and put waste sludge in the bin.
- Overalls are a good idea as set composite can be extremely difficult to remove from clothing.
- Disposable gloves or barrier creams are recommended when using Jesmonite.
- Safety data sheets for all materials should be requested from the retailer if not supplied with the products. All health and safety labelling on materials should be understood and adhered to.

Principal Working Information

Mix Ratios

Composite mixes

Composite	Powder to liquid by weight
AC100	2:1*
AC200	2:1
AC400	2:1
AC730	5:1

* This can be increased to 2.5 or 3 parts powder for quicker setting times or for a more thixotropic mix.

Thixotropic additive   Used to produce a paste-like consistency to mixes at a quantity of 1–4g/Kg of total mix (powder and liquid mixed together). In practice thixotropic can be added a drop at a time until the desired consistency is achieved. Thixotropic additives are required when using composite systems neat (with no added fillers) or when making pigmented gel coats.

Retarders   To extend working and slow setting times. Added at a quantity of 2–6g/Kg of total mix.

Metal fillers   Added at a quantity equal to the weight of the total mix. (Note: stainless steel should be added at a ratio of 6 per cent of the weight of total mix.)

Stone fillers   Added at a quantity equal to the weight of the total mix.

Pigments   These should constitute 0.7–1.8 per cent of the total mix weight. They should be added sparingly, a little at a time until the required colour is achieved.

Chopped strand   This should be added at a quantity of 1–2 per cent of the total mix weight.

Note: Only pigments, metal fillers and stone fillers specific to Jesmonite composites should be used.

Mixing

- Powder and liquid should be dispensed and weighed in separate containers.
- Powder is then gradually added to the liquid while mixing continuously.
- A variable-speed cordless drill with a high shear blade fitted should be used to mix batches. Clean the blade in the washing bucket immediately after use.
- Decorative gel coats – pigments, metal and stone fillers – should be added to composite batches after they have been mixed and then thoroughly combined until the mixture is free of lumps.
- Metal-filled and stone-filled gel coats should be kept mixed during application to prevent settlement of the heavy fillers.
- Thixotropic additive should be added (to neat or pigmented gel coats) after the composite batch has been mixed until the desired consistency has been achieved. This can be a fine line: too runny and the

mix will not adhere to the mould walls; too thick and the mix will not pick up fine mould detail.
- Chopped glass fibre strands as used during the laminating process should be added after the composite batch has been mixed. In practice slowly add chopped strand to a mix until it has the consistency of a paste.

Pot Life, Initial Set and Demould Times

Composite	Pot life/Initial set	Demould
AC100	15–20min	45min–2 hours
AC200	15–20min	Dependent on drying and use
AC400	15–20min	1–2 hours
AC730	25–30min	2–3 hours

These times are guidelines only and in practice times will depend on working conditions.

Casting

- The mix should be poured steadily into a mould from one point, to allow entrapped air to be evacuated as it fills.
- Agitation of the mould will help to bring any entrapped air to the surface of the cast once poured.
- Application of a brushed-on or slushed coat, followed by a pour, can also minimize air entrapment.

Release Agents

- Silicone moulds need no release agent.
- GRP, plaster and other rigid or porous moulds should be prepared with release agent. Release agent systems suitable for plaster casting are appropriate.

Laminating

For lamination details see the Project in the following section.

PROJECT

Specification

A granite-filled laminated two-piece casting from a silicone rubber mould of *Kouros of Anaphe* (see also the project section in Chapter 2).

Time Required

Allowing for setting times this project was carried out over two and a half days.

Materials

- Jesmonite AC100 powder (supplied by Notcutt Ltd);
- Jesmonite AC100 liquid;
- coarse granite filler;
- quadaxial mat; and
- chopped strand glass fibre.

Tools

- Mixing beakers;
- brushes;
- a drill and shear blade;
- scissors;
- digital scales; and
- a bucket for washing tools and beakers.

Method

SET-UP AND PREPARATION

As with any project, careful preparation before the start of the job is crucial. Knowing the material quantities and tools needed, undertaking repairs to the original and setting-up the working area will all help to complete the job accurately and efficiently. (Tip: make sure you have enough materials to complete the job before you start. Running out of material halfway through the job is at least a waste of time and, at worst, a loss of previously executed work.)

1. Ensure all work surfaces are clean, clear and well lit. This may sound obvious, but preparation of this sort prior to casting will help greatly in production. It easy to miss parts of the mould surface when in a badly lit work space!
2. Clean and dry the mould surfaces.

3. Support the mould pieces on a work surface. Make sure the mould pieces are secure and will not move about during casting. Ensure there is adequate access all around the mould pieces, particularly that you can reach all areas of the mould surface.

APPLICATION OF THE GEL COAT

1. Prepare a 600g composite batch at a ratio of 2:1. The mix consists of 400g of Jesmonite AC100 powder and 200g of Jesmonite AC100 liquid. A 600g mix can usually be applied within the pot life of a 2:1 ratio, which is approximately 15–20 minutes.
2. Mix with a drill and shear blade for 45 seconds.
3. Add 600g of granite filler and mix for 45 seconds until smooth and lump free.
4. Apply with a soft brush over the entire mould surface to a depth of 2–3mm.
5. On multi-piece moulds work just up to a couple of millimetres below the mould edges.
6. Wipe any excess or splashes off the mould flanges.
7. Allow to set for an hour after application.
8. Moulds with lots of fine detail and or difficult-to-access undercutting can benefit from a second gel coat application.

LAMINATING

The gel coat layer on its own will not be strong enough and needs to be laminated to achieve the full strength of the Jesmonite system. The first stage of the laminating process is a layer of quadaxial mat.

The first layer of quadaxial mat

1. Cut and prepare enough pieces of quadaxial mat to cover the surface of the applied gel coat twice.
2. The size and shape of the pieces should be tailored to the contours of the gel-coated surface. Large open areas can be laminated with large pieces of mat; small and difficult-to-access areas may need to be covered in smaller sections of mat.
3. Set out the cut mat in sequence on the work surface.
4. Prepare a mix of composite (with no filler). The maximum amount of mix that can be used within the pot life of AC100 is about 600g.
5. With a brush apply the mix to the area of the gel coat to be covered with mat first.
6. Lay mat onto the wet mix and push down gently with a brush.

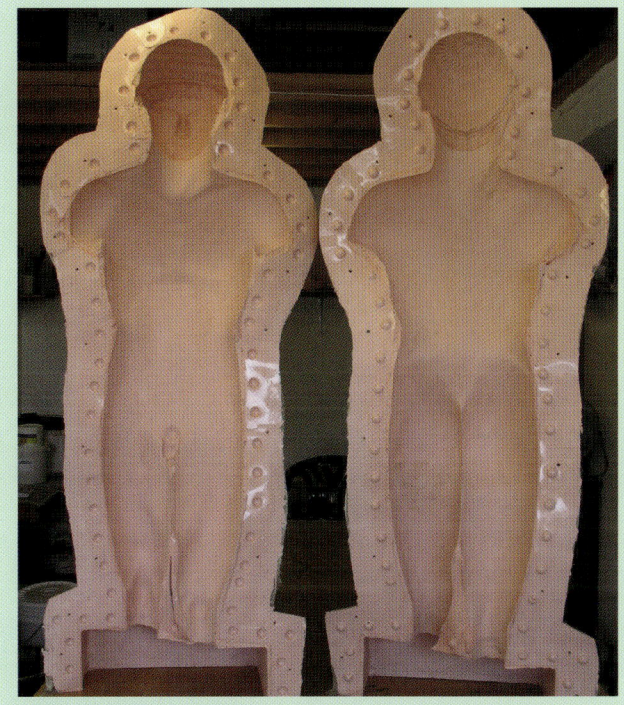

The silicone rubber mould to be cast.

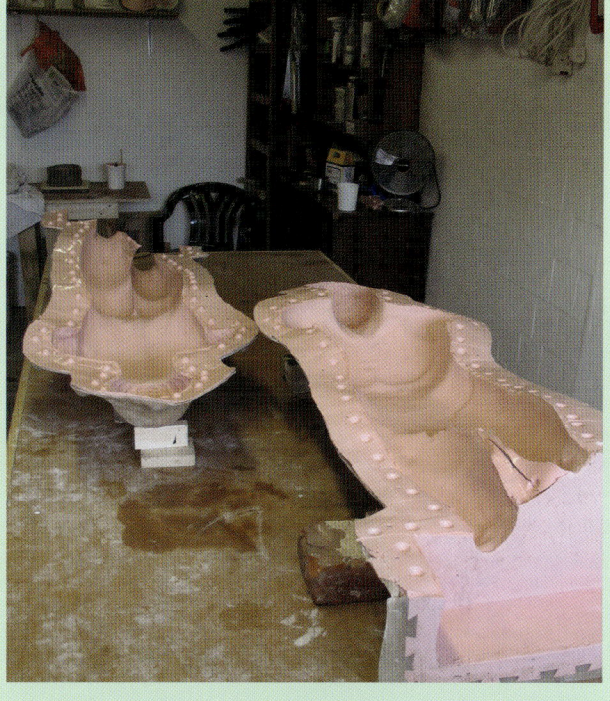

The mould pieces are secured on the bench surface ready for casting.

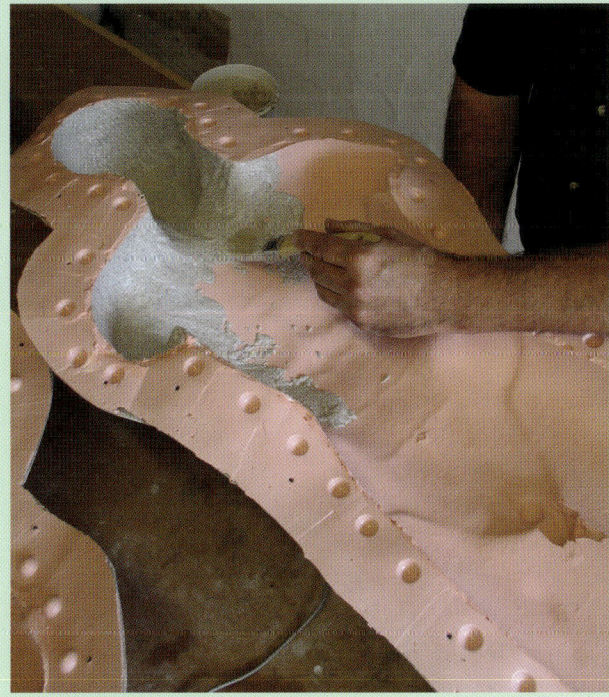

A granite-filled Jesmonite gel coat is applied to the mould surface.

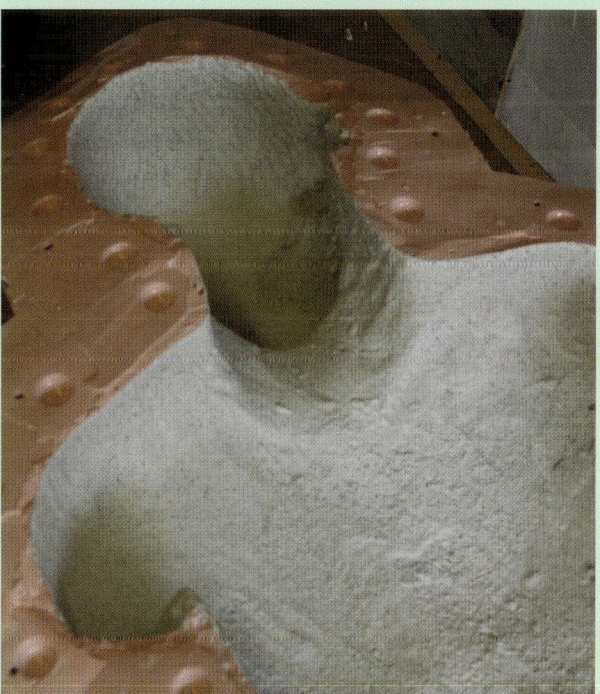

The gel coat is allowed to harden before laminating.

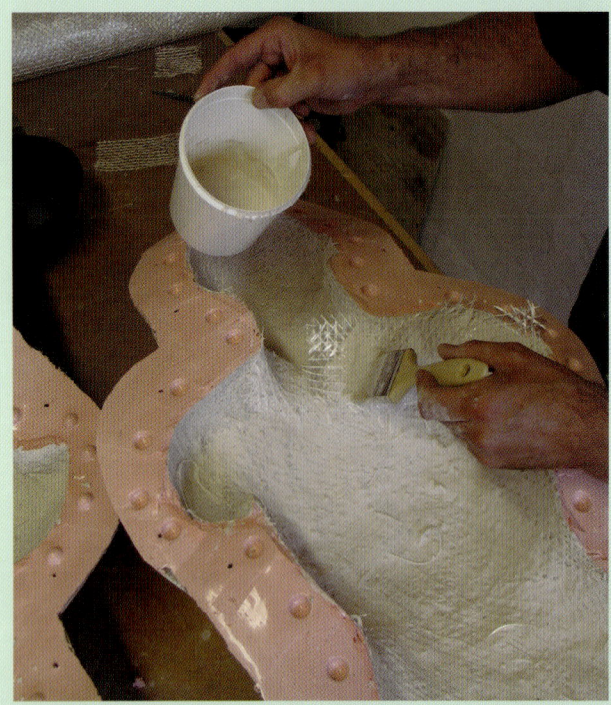

A layer of quadaxial mat saturated with Jesmonite is applied to the gel coat.

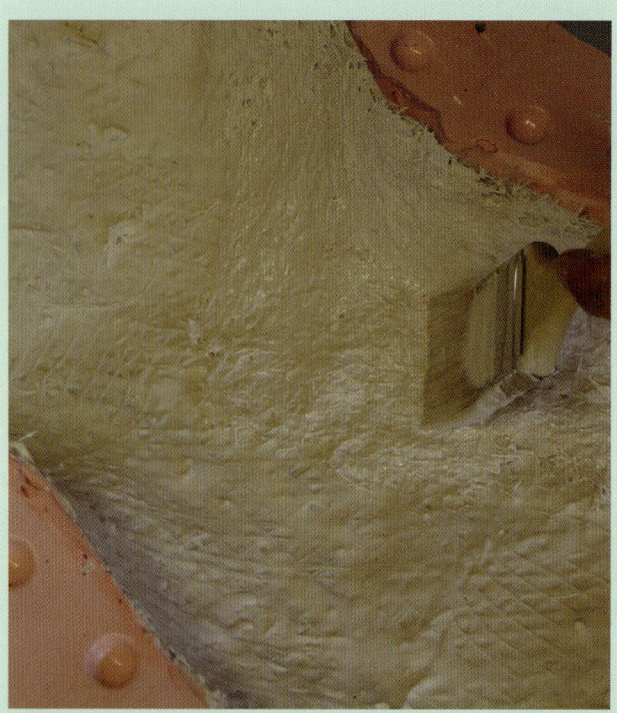

A layer of chopped strand and Jesmonite is applied.

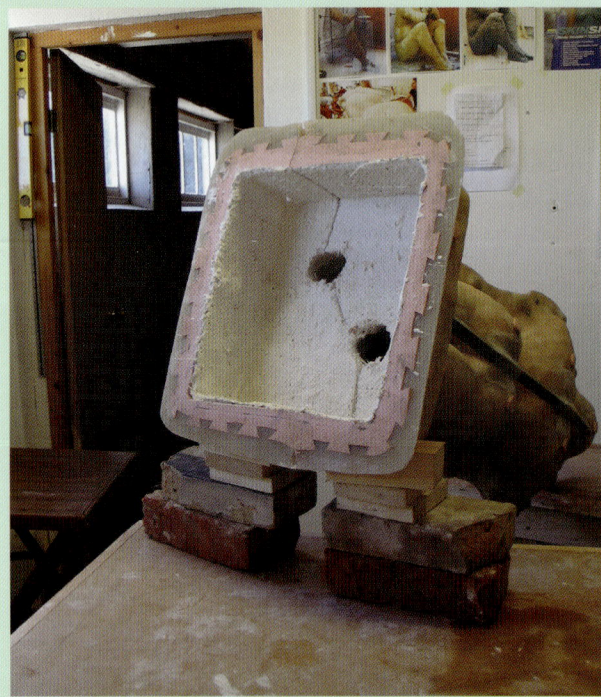

With lamination completed on both halves, the mould is assembled, laid on its side and tilted.

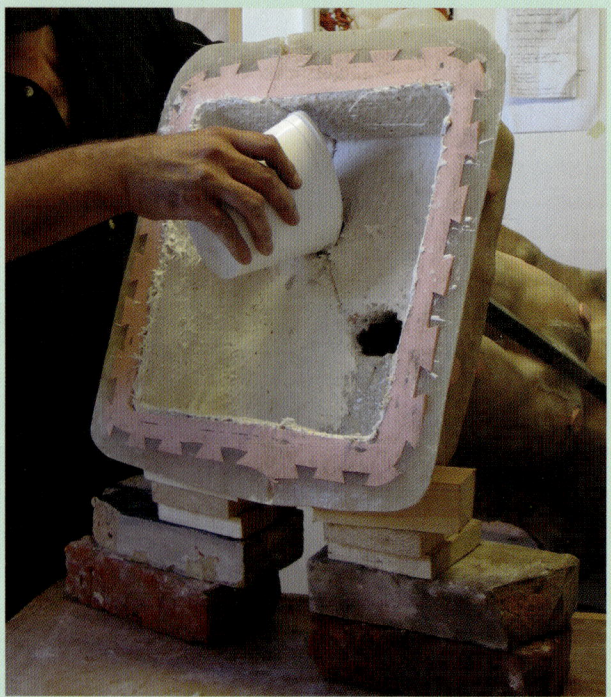

A granite-filled mix is poured into the joined mould.

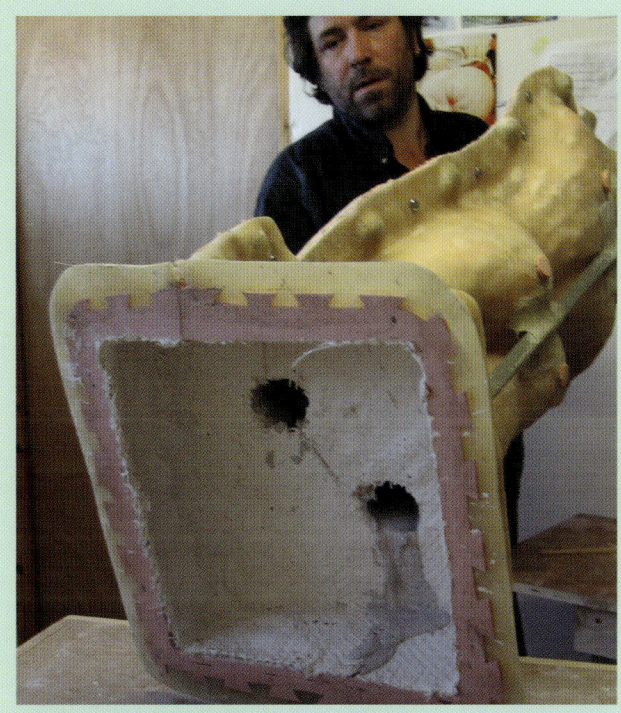

The mould is tilted back and forth to cover the seam internally.

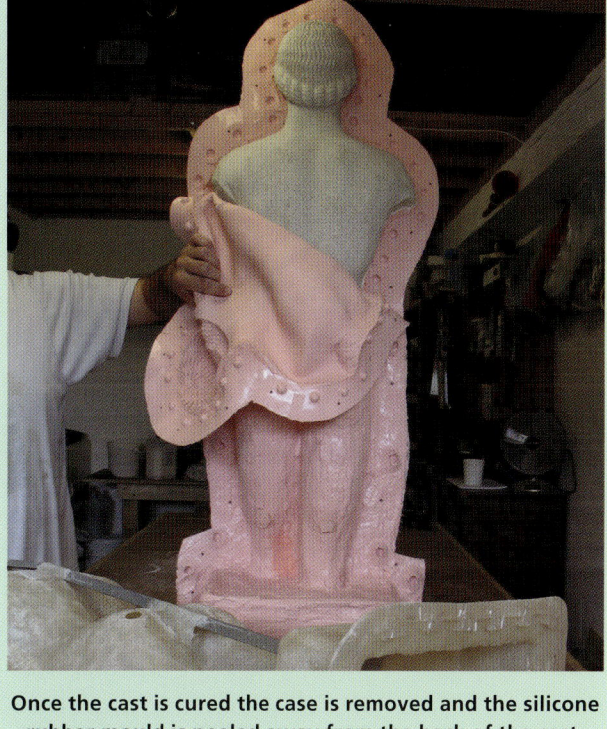

Once the cast is cured the case is removed and the silicone rubber mould is peeled away from the back of the cast.

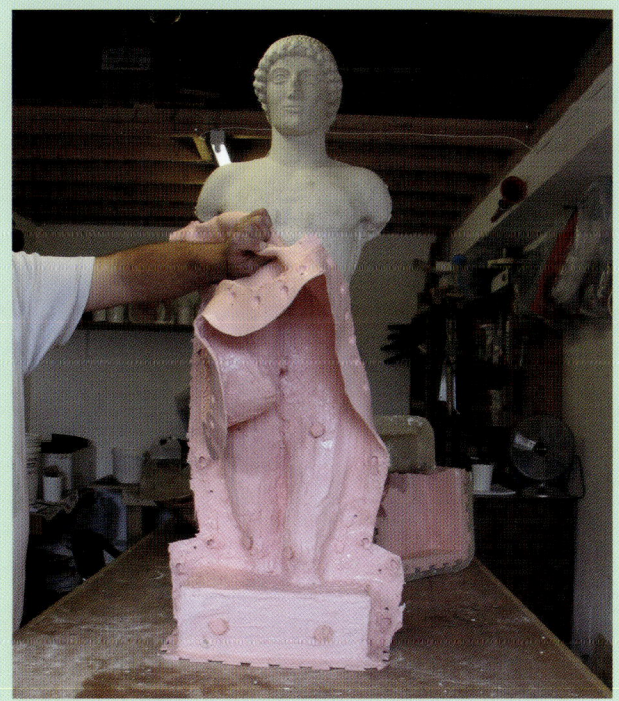

The front half of the silicone mould is removed from the cast.

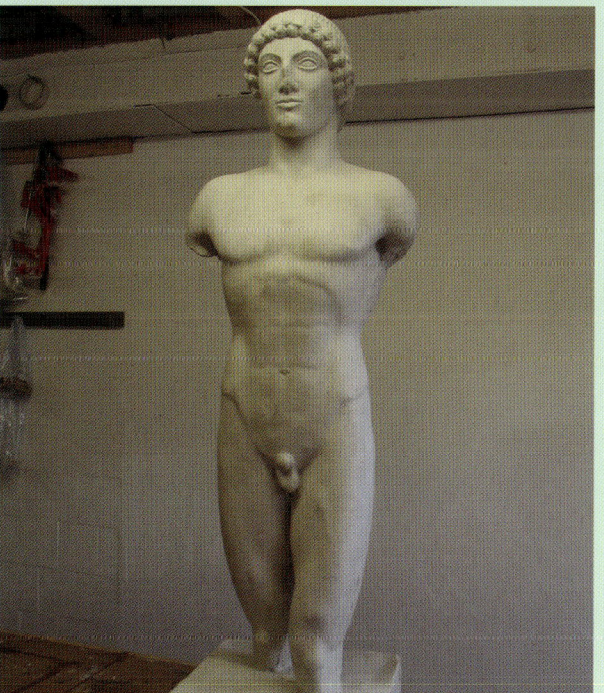

The demoulded cast.

7. Saturate the surface of the mat with more mix. You will find that the mat softens when saturated with mix, enabling it to be laminated closely to the gel coat. Do this by gently stippling the surface of saturated mat, pushing out any air entrapment as you go. The idea is to get tight lamination of the mat to gel coat without any air bubbles.

8. Methodically work over the entire surface of the gel coat, overlapping mat pieces by approximately 5–10mm.

9. On multi-piece moulds work just up to a couple of millimetres below the mould edges.

10. Wipe any excess or splashes off the mould flanges. This is important because otherwise the mould will not go back together accurately.

The chopped strand layer

This is a mix of composite mix and fibreglass chopped strand that is applied between layers of quadaxial mat to give the laminate more strength.

1. Chopped strand should be added to a pre-mixed batch of composite mix at a rate of 1–2 per cent by weight of the mix. The consistency should be that of a thick spreadable paste. Use a wooden mixing stick to mix in the chopped strand.

2. Apply with a brush and spread out to a depth of 2–4mm.

3. Use a stick to push the mix into difficult-to-access areas.

4. Methodically work over the entire surface of the first layer of quadaxial mat. On multi-piece moulds work just up to a couple of millimetres below the mould edges.

5. Wipe any excess or splashes off the mould flanges. This is important because otherwise the mould will not go back together accurately.

The second layer of quadaxial mat

1. Apply a second layer of quadaxial mat, in the same way as for the first layer, over the layer of chopped strand.

2. Allow to set for at least an hour before joining the cast sections.

The total laminating process will produce a casting 5–6mm thick. At this thickness castings will have a weight of 9–11 kg/m². Increasing the thickness of the chopped strand layer will produce stronger castings.

CURING AND DRYING

As the composite starts to set an exothermic reaction takes place which produces heat between the initial and final set of approximately 30°C. After approximately one hour the chemical reaction is complete and the casting will have achieved 60 per cent of its total strength.

Full strength will be achieved dependent on drying conditions and the thickness of the casting. Thin sections will dry faster than thicker ones and dry atmospheric conditions will increase the speed of the drying process.

JOINING MOULDS CAST IN SECTIONS

Moulds cast in sections will need to be joined to complete the casting process. A point of access into the mould is required to introduce material to join the cast pieces. Sections can be joined internally with several layers of composite mix, but if possible some laminating material should be applied as well.

1. For this project the mould has been cast in two sections into two mould pieces. The pieces containing the cast sections must be joined securely. Access into the mould in the case of this project is provided through the holes where the legs join the base.

2. A 2:1 mix of composite with granite filler addition is made up and poured into the mould down one side, seam side down.

3. The mould is tilted to allow the mix to run down the mould, internally covering the seam line. Tilt back and forth to cover the seam line as many times as possible until the mix starts to set and stops 'running'.

4. Repeat this process with new mixes 2 or 3 times to strengthen up the join.

5. If access allows, laminate the seam following the same steps as for the rest of the cast.

6. Multi-piece moulds of more than two pieces should be joined securely sequentially. If the mould is created as a sealed unit around an original with no base, access into the mould can be provided by a pouring hole created in one of the mould pieces. A pouring hole will only allow the joining of sections with a liquid mix of composite. In order to apply some laminate it is possible to leave one mould piece (with a pouring hole) open, allowing hand access into the mould to apply some laminate. This last section can then be secured and joined with a liquid composite mix (see Chapter 13).

7. Allow the cast to cure fully before demoulding.

Demoulding

The techniques for demoulding (removing the finished cast from the mould) will largely depend on what type of mould is being used.

Plaster one-piece Moulds can be tapped or levered out from the inside of the cast using a chisel. Soaking in hot soapy water can help to ease out difficult casts.

Plaster multi-piece Moulds should be eased apart piece by piece. Small moulds can usually be parted using a strong-bladed knife. Larger moulds may require a thin chisel to initially crack the seam until a wooden or plastic wedge can be driven in. On particularly long seams a series of wedges can be gradually driven in sequentially until the seam is parted.

Plaster waste See Chapter 4 of *Mouldmaking and Casting* for detail on chipping out plaster waste moulds.

Fibreglass As above, although there can be a certain degree of flexibility in a fibreglass mould depending on how thickly it has been made.

Flexible moulds (without a case) Demoulding from flexible moulds without a case involves a combination of flexing and peeling the mould while easing out the cast.

Flexible moulds (with a case) First remove the case (this should be carried out as for plaster one-piece moulds) and then peel the mould away from the cast. It is possible to peel the mould away from the cast with these moulds as they are thinner and more flexible than flexible moulds without a case.

Trimming and Cutting Back

Once the cast has been demoulded any excess cast and seam lines (flashing) can be trimmed back.

1. Initially the extremities of any excess can be broken off carefully by hand or a pair of pliers, but be careful not to break off too much. Then a number of tools can be employed depending on the size of the cast and how much composite is to be removed (for example, chisels, hacksaw blades, surforms, rasps and so on).

2. The initial trim should not be taken right back to the surface of the cast and should only be used to remove bulk excess.

3. Smaller and smaller tools should be used as you get closer to the cast surface (*see* Chapter 14).

4. Fine files including needle files can be useful to get into difficult-to-access areas of the cast (note that a fine brass or wire brush is useful to clear clogged files).

5. Once excess flashing has been taken back to the surface final cutting back and/or polishing of the entire cast surface can be tackled.

Surface Finishing and Polishing

Casts that have coloured gel coats will usually come out of moulds with a matt surface finish; metal-filled or stone-filled gel coats will be matt and the base material not fully visible. To obtain the full effect from metal and stone and achieve gloss colours, castings will need to be cut back and/or polished.

Metal-Filled Castings

Freshly demoulded casts will have a fine acrylic film on the surface that needs to be removed to expose the metallic finish. This is achieved by abrasion with wire wool of progressive grades, working from coarse to fine. The cast should be air-dried and hard.

1. Start rubbing with coarse grades of wire wool, working sequentially through to the finer grades.

2. Work methodically over the entire surface of the casting.

3. Replace wool as it clogs to ensure it maintains its abrasive action.

4. Once exposed, metal surfaces can be polished to a high shine or paginated using cold pagination processes.

Note: Stainless steel filled castings should not be abraded. Once demoulded and allowed to air dry a wax polish can be applied to enhance the surface finish.

Polishing

Polishing can be done either mechanically or by hand using specifically designed polishing compounds. Polishing compounds come as either a hard waxy block or as a cream and are applied to the cast surface with lint-free cloth or a mechanically spun polishing mop.

Cloth polishing mops for block compounds and sponge mops for cream compounds can be mounted, using the correct arbour, to a standard electric drill with variable speed control or in a dedicated polishing machine. Polishing machines are bench mounted so this will restrict the size of the cast that can be polished. Electric drills can be used freehand or can be bench mounted securely using a clamping system specific to the machine you are using. Care should be taken when polishing using electric drills as they have no guards and whichever system of polishing is being used goggles should always be worn.

Polishing compounds are a very fine level of abrasive and come in grades of coarseness, like the abrasive papers, which should be used in sequence from coarse to fine methodically over the entire surface of the cast. Compounds usually come in two or three grades and castings should be washed between grades of polish. Cold-cast metal castings (castings with a metal-filled gel coat) can be given a final polish using a proprietary metal polish suitable to the base metal used.

If after polishing through the grades of compound the levels of brightness required have not been achieved it may be necessary to return to the abrasive process to cut back more material and then to repolish.

Stone-Filled Castings

Four different levels of finish can be achieved on stone-surfaced castings.

Smooth acrylic finish The cast should be air dry and waxed with a solvent-thinned wax furniture polish. Allowed the polish to soak into the acrylic film, which enhances the surface finish of the stone.

Exposed stone finish Freshly demoulded cast surfaces should be wetted with water, which is then allowed to soak into and soften the acrylic film. Scrub the surface with a nylon washing-up pad to expose the stone finish. Longer wetting and scrubbing will reveal coarser stone surfaces as required.

Acetone can be used to speed up this process (but wear rubber washing-up gloves for this).

Exposed stone finish (smooth ground) Casts should be air dried and hard before abrading the surface with consequential grades (180–240 grit) of wet-and-dry paper, used wet. Rinse the paper as it clogs and replace when worn. Exposed areas can be ground mechanically using adequate dust extraction methods or can be wet ground with air-powered tools.

Exposed stone finish (coarse textured) Sand-blasting systems can provide a range of coarse textures to castings. Castings should be thoroughly air dried and hard before sand blasting.

Sealer

Jesmonite sealer can be applied to all cast surfaces for a number of reasons.

■ If castings are to be sited externally, apply two coats by brush or spray.

■ For internally sited castings Jesmonite sealer can prevent finger marking and give a clear matt finish.

■ Adding pigments and water to sealer produces colour washes.

Special Notes on Jesmonite AC200 and AC730

Jesmonite composites AC200 and AC730 share many of the principal mixing and practical applications of the other Jesmonite composites but there are a few exceptions and additions as follows.

AC200

■ AC200 is used to produce cast blocks of compound that can be carved. These could be remoulded to cast in other materials. To avoid air entrapment thixotropic addition AC200 should be brushed onto the mould surface and then it should be backfilled with standard mix once set. Carving can be carried out immediately after demoulding.

- Jesmonite sealer can be used to seal AC200 before remoulding.
- AC200 can be used as a coating compound for foam or polystyrene. After roughly carving foam or polystyrene to shape coat with thixotropic addition AC200 to allow further fine carving to the surface. A final coat of AC100 will provide a durable surface for the finished cast.
- AC200 is also suitable as an adhesive for polystyrene, styrofoam and polyurethane foam products.
- AC200 is not suitable for laminating or hollow casting.

AC730

- Thixotropic additions are not necessary when using AC730 because of the higher powder mix ratios.
- Adjustments to a mix ratio of 4.5:1 (powder to liquid) will provide a thinner mix but will marginally affect strength.
- Retarder can be added at 3–6g per kilogram of mix weight to extend the pot life by up to 45 minutes.
- If using stone fillers in the mix ensure they are specific to AC730.

- 13mm coarse chopped fibreglass strand should be used in the laminating process.
- The minimum laminated thickness of castings should be 8mm, weighing 15–16kg/m^2.
- Castings should not exceed temperatures of 35°C while curing to allow for the correct crystal growth to form. Large castings will produce excessive exothermic heat and should be wrapped in damp sacking when curing.
- Once demoulded, castings should be wrapped in wet sacking and polythene to achieve full strength.
- Castings develop 80 per cent of their total strength in 24 hours at a temperature of 16–18°C.
- Castings should be kept at temperatures not exceeding 40°C after the initial cure.
- Textured finishes can be achieved very effectively with 2 or 3 applications of proprietary brick cleaner.
- Metal-surfaced castings can be obtained using Flex Metal Gel Coats® in conjunction with AC730; these are available in Bronze, Copper, Brass and Silver Bronze.
- GRP, plaster and other rigid or porous moulds should not be used with Flex Metal systems.

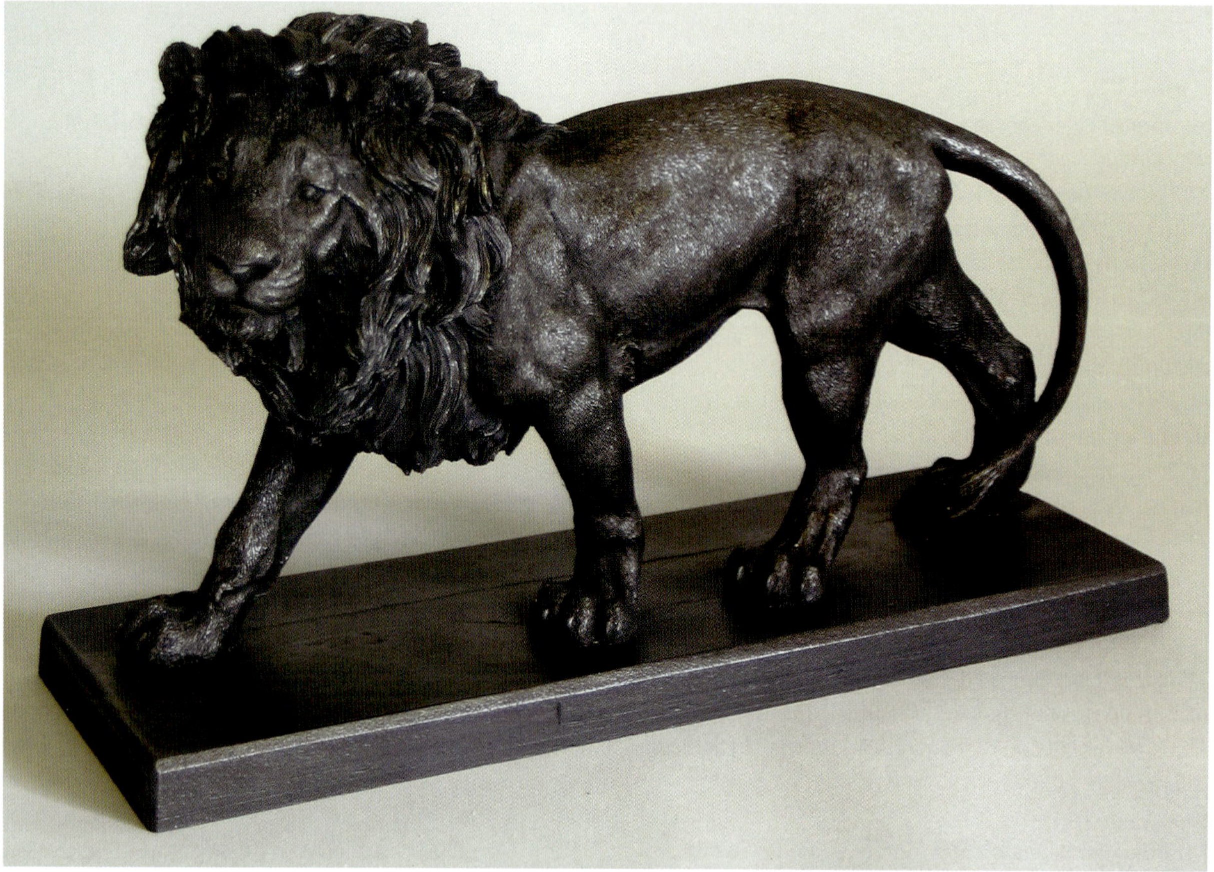

Above: Black-pigmented and applied graphite paste polyurethane resin cast (L:320mm; W: 110mm; H: 200mm).
Below: Polyurethane expanded foam cast (L: 320mm; W: 110mm; H: 200mm).

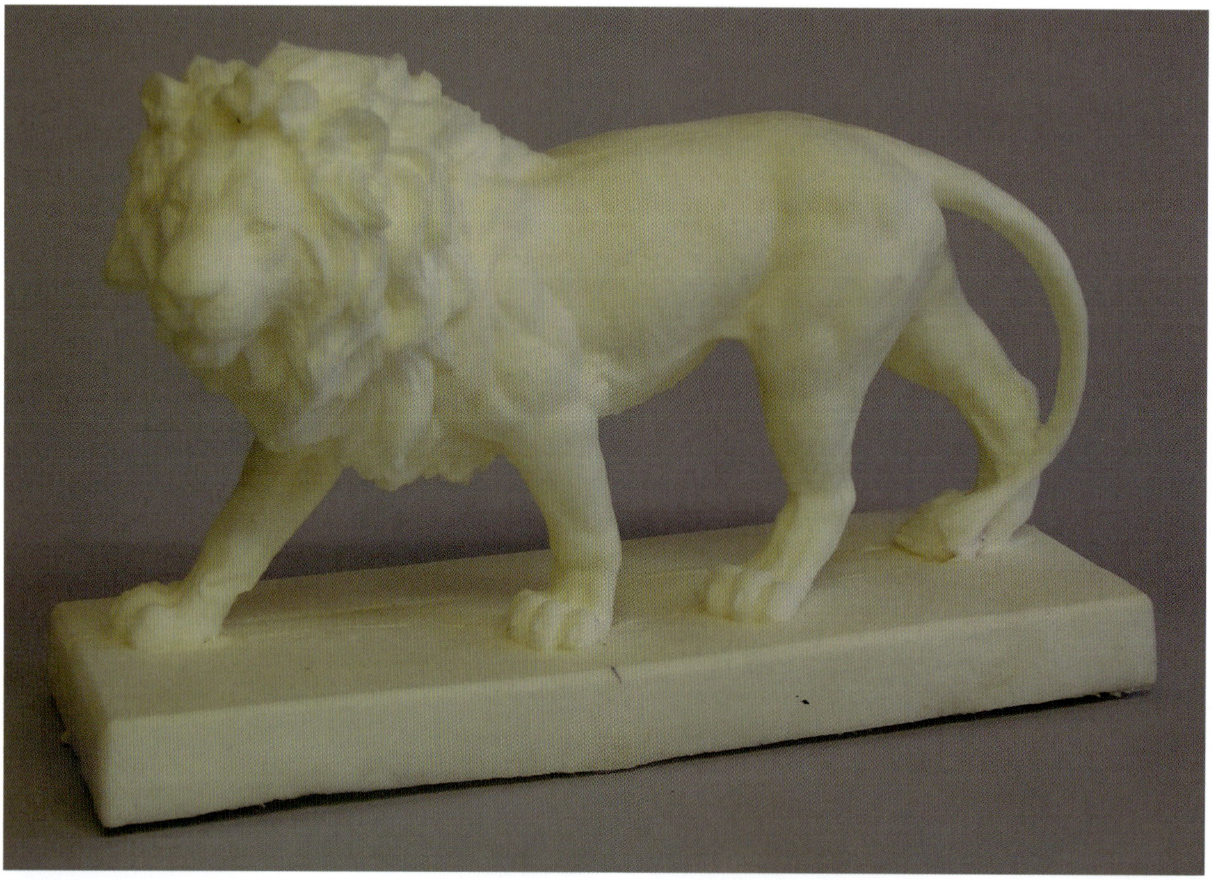

CHAPTER EIGHT

POLYURETHANE RESINS AND EXPANDING FOAM

Polyurethane Resins

Polyurethane resins are fast-curing casting resins from the Methylene bis(phenylisocyanate) chemical family. They are usually supplied as a two-part pack with a very easy-to-mix ratio of 1:1. These resins have a very low viscosity, which makes them ideal for small and bubble-free castings without the use of degassing equipment.

With setting times of between two and five minutes and demoulding times of between ten and thirty minutes very quick turn-around can be achieved for multiple-cast runs. Polyurethane resins can be coloured using dedicated polyurethane resin pigments. Powdered metal and stone additions can be used to achieve metallic and stone-finished castings.

Due to very high Shore hardness, the advantages of polyurethane resins over polyester resins in tensile strength without brittleness are significant. They enable the creation of slushed thin-section hollow castings of great strength (*see* Chapter 12).

Materials

Fast cast   As the name suggests these resins have a very fast setting time of approximately two minutes and demould times of ten to thirty minutes (but do check individual manufacturer's specifications). These are good for very fast multiple-cast production and have very low viscosity for bubble-free castings.

Slow cast   Although still fast these resins have a slightly longer pouring/setting time of approximately five minutes and demould times of twenty minutes to an hour. Slower setting times can be advantageous for pigmented or filled gel coat castings.

Clear   These are used for both clear and coloured translucent castings. They are also good for pigmented or metal/stone-filled castings.

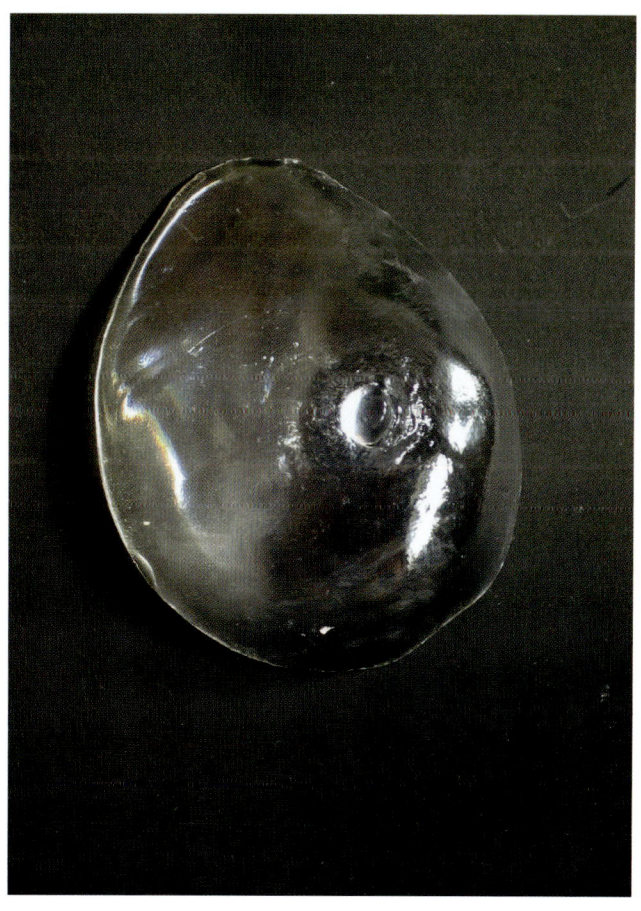

A polyurethane resin life cast.

Fillers

Fillers can collectively, in general terms, be described as very fine mesh powders that are mixed into the resin. They can be broken down into three main groups.

Inert fillers (aluminium trihydrate) These are very fine inert mineral powders that are mixed in equal parts with the resin. Mixing the resin with a filler reduces the amount of resin needed to fill a cast solid, which is useful for two reasons: first, to lower exotherm (the heat generation during setting), and second, to reduce casting costs. Calcium carbonate can be added to resin to produce a very white casting. Storage should be at moderate temperatures in dry conditions.

Metal fillers These are fine mesh metal powders added to resins to produce castings with metallic finishes. Unlike metallic paint finishes these are powders derived from the metal itself and once cut back with abrasives and polished will appear as the metals they are (for instance, an iron-filled casting will start to rust if exposed to moisture). Storage should be at moderate temperatures in dry conditions.

Stone fillers These are powdered stone materials added to the resin to produce stone finishes. They are usually more granular than metal fillers. Storage should be at moderate temperatures in dry conditions.

Metal and stone fillers can be used as a gel coat and painted, to a thickness of 2–3mm, onto the surface of a mould, allowed to set and then backed up with resin or resin/inert filler mix to cut down on the cost of metal and stone fillers.

Tools and Equipment

Dispensing and Mixing

Waxed paper cups or white plastic containers For dispensing and mixing batches of resin. Plastic containers can be allowed to dry after use and the set resin cracked out for reuse.

Disposable wooden spatulas For combining resin parts and mixing pigments and fillers into batches.

Scales Although polyurethane resins are often 1:1 two-part mixes some types are 1:0.9 and accurate digital scales should be used to calculate weights and measures of resin parts safely according to manufacturer's instructions.

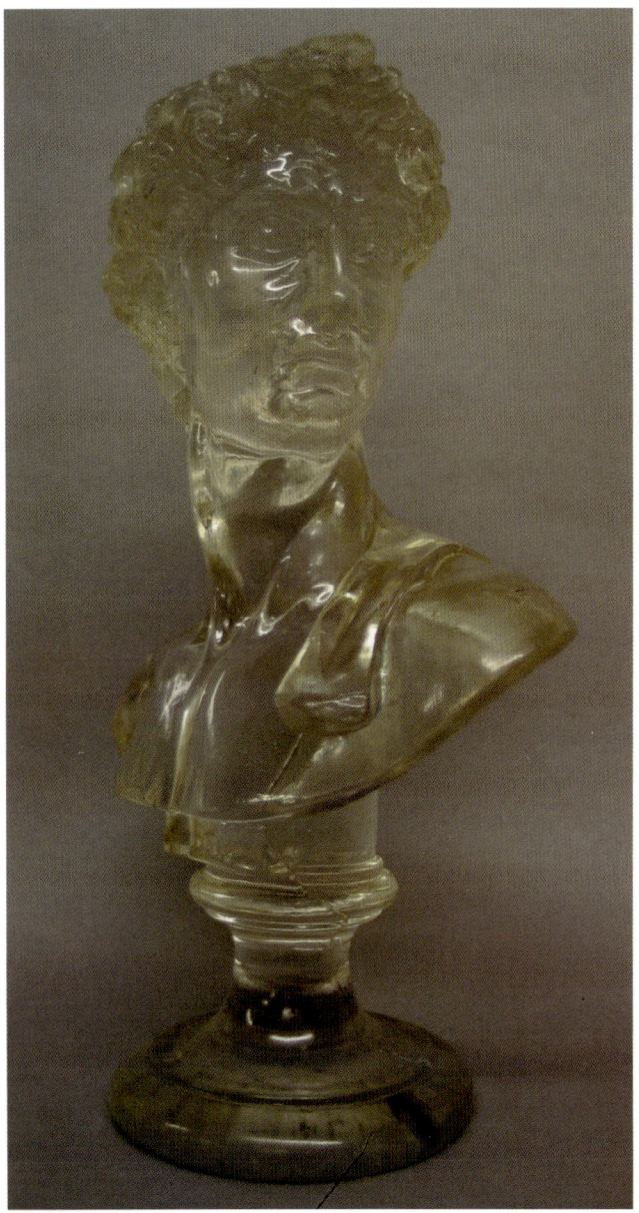

A polyurethane cast (H: 400mm).

Shelf Life

The shelf life of these resins is at least six months at room temperature. Opened containers of resin should be resealed tightly after use, as any atmospheric moisture contamination can cause foaming when next used. A moisture purging dry-gas aerosol can be sprayed into open containers to prolong the shelf life.

Laminating

Brushes   Brushes of various sizes are needed to paint gel coats onto the mould surface. Specially manufactured brushes are available that will withstand the harsh chemicals involved and not lose bristles; however, ordinary decorating brushes of a good quality will last quite a long time.

Disposable wooden spatulas   For mixing batches.

Trimming and Finishing

Rasps and files   These can be used for the initial trimming of cured resin casts.

A hacksaw   Used for initial trimming.

Tin snips and heavy duty shears   Used for initial trimming.

Powered jigsaws and multi-tools   These can be very useful to take some of the hard work out of trimming (ensure strict dust control measures are observed).

A power drill   Holes can be drilled safely mechanically or by hand into set resins.

Powered abrasive tools   For cutting-back flashing on seams and exposing metal/stone-filled surfaces. Beware of cutting backfilled casts mechanically as they can take too much away too quickly (ensure strict dust control measures are observed).

Wet-and-dry abrasive paper   This is used for removing sharp edges after initial trimming and cutting back metal-filled casts prior to polishing.

Needle files   For very fine and difficult-to-access trimming and cutting back.

Wire brushes   For clearing tools clogged with material.

Polishing equipment   For polishing castings after cutting back with abrasives, this can be done mechanically or by hand.

Safety and Good Studio Practice

▨   Polyurethane resins emit isocyanate fumes at working temperatures above 40°C, which can be hazardous.

Keep working temperatures below 40°C and provide adequate ventilation measures.

▨   In addition to good ventilation personal respiratory equipment can be used. It is essential that respiratory equipment is specified as suitable for use with polyurethane resin. Using equipment that is not designed for use with resins is sometimes worse than wearing none at all; always check the manufacturer's specifications.

▨   Work surfaces can be protected with a heavy-gauge polythene that can be disposed of or replaced when necessary.

▨   Overalls are a good idea as resins are extremely difficult to remove from clothing.

▨   Working with resins and their associated products can cause skin reactions, particularly if you have a sensitive skin type. Barrier creams provide a protective barrier between you and these materials and should always be employed even for those without sensitive skin. Disposable plastic or rubber gloves will provide further levels of hand protection. The only efficient and safe way to clean hands is to use specific proprietary hand cleaners.

▨   Disposal of excess resins, empty storage and dispensing containers and any other associated materials should be carried out with regard to an understanding of flammability and environmental consequences. If possible follow the guidelines set out by manufacturers, which should be available through the retailer.

▨   Safety data sheets for all materials should be requested from retailer if not supplied with the products. All health and safety labelling on materials should be understood and adhered to.

Principal Casting Techniques

Mixing

Polyurethane resins are supplied as two-part systems. Ensure the ratios of parts are correct and exact by weighing on digital scales. Ensure both resin parts and moulds are at room temperature; studio temperature should be above 15°C and maintained at that temperature during setting and curing times. Ensure mixing vessels and tools are dry.

Combine both resin parts in a mixing vessel and stir vigorously for one minute, scraping the sides and bottom to ensure thorough mixing.

Additional catalysts can be used to speed up curing times but should be batch tested for the job beforehand. Do not use more than 1 per cent of additions. Pour into the mould immediately.

Pigment and Filler Addition

Use a slower-setting resin for pigmented and filler-addition castings to allow for the additional mixing time. Mix both resin parts before introducing additions. Ensure fillers are dry.

COLOURED GEL COATS

To obtain castings with integral colour, pigments can be added to the resin to create a gel coat layer of the casting. These are not gel coats in the traditional polyester resin sense as polyurethane resin is not thixotropic, but if worked with quickly enough mixes can be applied to a thickness of 2–3mm to create a first layer to the casting. Specific polyurethane resin pigments have been developed that are raw earth pigments suspended in a resin binder. A gel coat resin is used to carry the pigment of the casting.

1. Dispense the amount of resin required to apply a layer approx 2–3mm thick to the mould surface. If laying up large moulds be aware of the amount of resin that can be applied within the working time or pot life of a batch. If it will be necessary to lay up the mould with several batches of gel coat it will be necessary to colour-match each batch. Add the pigment in small amounts until the colour required is obtained; note that only small amounts of pigment are needed to produce very vivid colours. Additions of approximately 2–5 per cent by weight of resin should be adequate, but in practice it is much easier to mix by eye.
2. Once thoroughly mixed the batch can be applied to the mould surface with a brush or can be slushed (see Chapter 12). Be aware that it will set very quickly and that it will need to be kept moving over the surface of

the mould in order to coat it evenly, to a thickness of about 2–3mm. Use batches of a size that can be used within the pot life.

3. It is sometimes a good idea to apply a second gel coat to moulds with a lot of detail. In such cases allow the first gel coat to cure and dry before application of the second.
4. Allow the gel coat to set before backfilling with resin or resin/inert filler mix.

METAL/STONE-FILLED GEL COATS

Metal and stone effect castings can be obtained using very fine mesh (finely ground) metal and stone powders (known as fillers) mixed into the resin. A wide range of fillers is available, including:

■ bronze;
■ copper;
■ iron;
■ brass;
■ marble;
■ slate; or
■ stone.

Fillers are added to the resin to form a brushable gel coat that is applied to the mould surface and then backfilled with a resin or a resin/inert filler mix that fills the mould. When calculating the amount of metal filler a rough rule of thumb is to use equal quantities by volume of resin to filler.

1. Dispense the required amount of resin into a container and then dispense an equal quantity by volume of the filler required. Do not mix the resin and filler at this stage. For a gel coat mix the quantity of resin and filler combined will need to cover the entire surface of the mould to a thickness of approximately 2–3mm, depending on the amount of detail. Moulds containing a combination of raised and deep fine detail may need a second application of gel coat once the first has set.
2. Laying up a large mould will require several batches of gel coat in order to apply it within the pot life (working time). Colour-matching of metal and stone fillers needs to be considered when laying up several batches of gel coat.

3. Mix consistencies will depend on their use. Gel coats should be brushable but thixotropic; that is, they can be painted onto the mould surface to a thickness of 2–3mm but will not run off. The use of equal quantities of resin and filler should be taken as only a rough guide, and where possible more filler should be used without compromising the required consistency. Using less than 50 per cent filler will not produce good metal and stone effects.

4. Once thoroughly mixed the batch can be applied to the mould surface with a brush or can be slushed (*see* Chapter 12). Be aware that it will set very quickly and that it will need to be kept moving over the surface of the mould in order to coat it evenly, to a thickness of about 2–3mm. Use batches of a size that can be used within the pot life.

5. Allow the gel coat to set before backfilling with resin or resin/inert filler mix.

Solid and Backfilled Castings

Polyurethane resins can be poured in one operation for solid castings or for backfilling gel-coated castings. (See Project 1 for an illustrated example of a pigmented solid-filled casting.)

1. Arrange the mould so that it can be levelled in two directions. This is done easily using small balls of clay under each corner or opening the flange of the mould and pushing the mould down into them to obtain a level that can be checked with a spirit level.

2. Estimate the amount of resin needed.

3. Estimate the amount of pigment or filler needed (see previous section). Bear in mind that the mix needs to pour well, so do not overestimate the filler.

4. Mix the resin and pigment or filler together very quickly but thoroughly for one minute.

5. Fill the mould by pouring from one spot and allowing the mix to rise, pushing out any air entrapment as it does. A little agitation of the mould will bring up any air bubbles and allow the mix to seep into the mould detail.

6. Exotherm (heat generation) should be considered when pouring polyurethane resins to form a solid. Different polyurethane resins will have varying maximum and minimum casting size limits so always check the individual specifications of the resin being used. (See Chapter 10 for an understanding of exotherm and resin casting.)

7. Allow to set thoroughly.

CLEAR CASTINGS

1. Follow the stages as described above.

2. An additional pre-coat of clear resin can be applied before the mould is cast to achieve highly polished clear castings. This should be poured as above and the excess poured out of the mould. Allow to set before pouring the main casting.

3. As for step 6 in the previous section, careful consideration should be given to the exothermic heat that will be generated when casting. Always adhere to the size limits and specifications of the resin being used.

4. Polyurethane clear castings will benefit greatly if degassing techniques are employed (*see* Chapter 9).

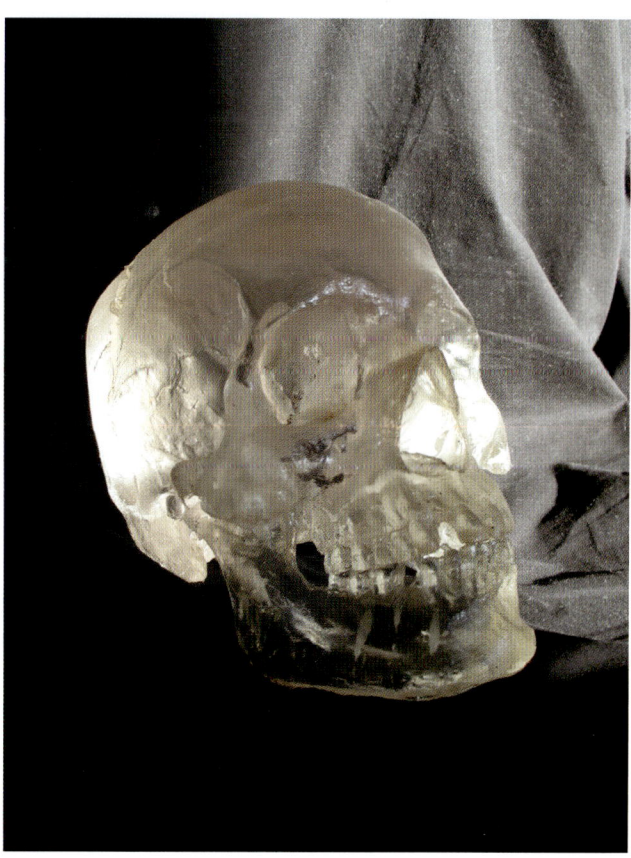

Clear polyester resin (life size).

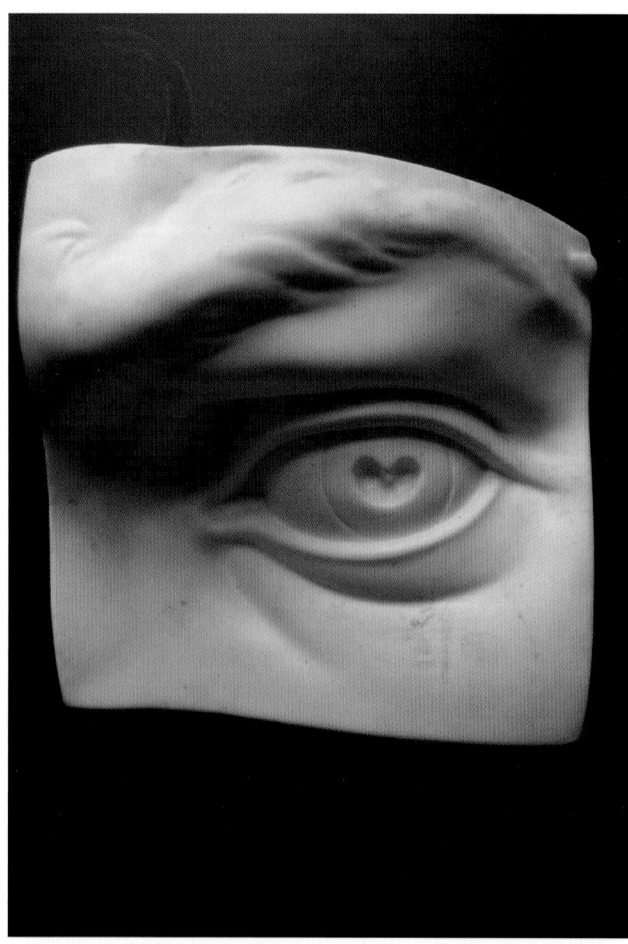

Unpigmented polyurethane resin (H: 120mm, W: 180mm).

HOLLOW CASTINGS

1. Follow the mixing, additions and pouring stages as above.
2. Hollow castings can be achieved by slushing (*see* Chapter 12). Moulds should be filled approximately a third full and then constantly and evenly rotated until the resin sets. This is easiest with a mould 'in-the-round', where the pouring hole of the mould can be bunged and it can be rotated in all directions. However, tilting an open mould carefully to allow the resin to cover up to the edges is also possible.
3. Moulds may need several coats in this way, allowing time for the resin to set between coats, to achieve an adequate thickness of 3–5mm.
4. Allow to set thoroughly.

Demoulding

The techniques for demoulding – removing the finished cast from the mould – will largely depend on what type of mould is being used.

Plaster one-piece   Moulds can be tapped or levered out from the *inside* of the cast using a chisel. Soaking in hot soapy water can help to ease out difficult casts.

Plaster multi-piece   Moulds should be eased apart piece by piece. Small moulds can usually be parted using a strong-bladed knife. Larger moulds may require a thin chisel to initially crack the seam until a wooden or plastic wedge can be driven in. On particularly long seams a series of wedges can be gradually driven in sequentially until parted.

Plaster waste   See Chapter 4 of *Mouldmaking and Casting* for detail on chipping out plaster waste moulds.

Fibreglass   As above, although there can be a certain degree of flexibility in a fibreglass mould depending on how thickly it has been made.

Flexible moulds (without a case)   Demoulding from flexible moulds without a case is a combination of flexing and peeling the mould while easing out the cast.

Flexible moulds (with a case)   First remove the case (this should be carried out as for plaster one-piece moulds) and then peel the mould away from the cast. It is possible to peel the mould away from the cast with these moulds as they are thinner and more flexible than flexible moulds without a case.

Gelflex moulds   Resin casts from gelflex moulds should be allowed to cool down thoroughly after the setting process as the mould may soften slightly due to the high exotherm generated and will need time to reset.

Trimming and Cutting Back

Once the cast has been demoulded any excess cast and seam lines (flashing) can be trimmed back.

1. Initially the extremities of any excess can be broken off carefully by hand or a pair of pliers, but be careful not to break off too much. Then a number of tools can be employed depending on the size of the cast and how much resin is to be removed (chisels, hacksaw blades, surforms, rasps and so on).

2. The initial trim should not be taken right back to the surface of the cast and should only be used to remove bulk excess.

3. Smaller and smaller tools should be used as you work closer to the cast surface.

4. Final cutting back to the surface of the cast should be achieved with increasingly finer grades of abrasive paper. Fine files including needle files can be useful for getting into difficult-to-access area of the cast (a fine brass or wire brush is also useful to clear clogged files).

5. Once excess flashing has been taken back to the surface the final cutting back and/or polishing of the entire cast surface can be tackled.

Surface Finishing and Polishing

Casts that have coloured gel coats and clear casting resins will usually come out of their moulds with a matt surface finish; metal/stone-filled gel coats will be matt and the base material not fully visible. To obtain the full effect of metal and stone, or to achieve gloss colours or glass-clear surfaces, castings will need to be cut back with abrasive papers and then polished.

CUTTING BACK WITH ABRASIVES

Wet-and-dry abrasive papers are used to cut back cast surfaces and these should be used wet to avoid dust (which can be carcinogenic) and prevent the paper from clogging. The papers are graded by the number of particles of grit per square inch of paper and a variety of grades should be used in sequence from coarse to fine. Depending on the job 100–600 grit paper (100 being coarsest and 600 finest) should be used in succession, with the very fine grades usually being reserved for clear casting resins.

■ Standard sheets of abrasive paper should be cut up into pieces that are suitable for the size of the job and laid out in sequence.

■ Initially use the coarsest grade just to take off the worst of any seam lines and to give the whole surface 'bite'. With metal and stone surfaces this will just remove the surface layer of resin and expose the base material. Where there are smooth areas or areas that have little detail coarse papers should be used sparingly and it may be preferable to start with a finer paper.

■ As the paper becomes clogged either rinse it under a running tap or in large bowl of water.

■ Once the whole surface has been cut back with one grit size wash the cast, change your rinsing water and move on to the next grit size. In this way the whole surface of the cast is cut back progressively using finer and finer paper, with scratches created by the coarser grades being removed by the finer grades.

■ You will notice that metal fillers will become more and more visible as the abrasive exposes them.

■ Clear resins will remain cloudy even after the finest grade and will not become clear until polished unless they are pre-coated.

■ It is difficult to gauge whether casts have been thoroughly abraded enough until after polishing, but a thorough and methodical abrading will produce better polished results. If polished results are not good it will usually mean returning to the abrasives before polishing again.

■ Once exposed, metal surfaces can be polished to a high shine or paginated using cold pagination processes (see 'Finishing' section).

POLISHING

Polishing can be done either mechanically or by hand using specifically designed polishing compounds. Polishing compounds come as either a hard waxy block or a cream and are applied to the cast surface with lint-free cloth or a mechanically spun polishing mop.

Cloth polishing mops for block compounds and sponge mops for cream compounds can be mounted, using the correct arbour, to a standard electric drill with variable speed control or can be mounted in a dedicated polishing machine. Polishing machines are bench-mounted so this will restrict the size of the cast that can be polished mechanically. Electric drills can be used freehand or bench-mounted securely using a clamping system specific to the machine you are using. Care should be taken when using electric drills for polishing as they have no guards; goggles should always be worn whichever system of polishing is being used.

Polishing compounds are a very fine level of abrasive and come in grades of coarseness like the abrasive papers. They should be used in sequence from coarse to fine methodically over the entire surface of the cast. Compounds usually come in two or three grades and castings should be washed between grades of polish. Cold-cast metal castings can be given a final polish using a proprietary metal polish suitable to the base metal used.

If after polishing through the grades of compound the levels of gloss, brightness or clarity required have not been achieved it may be necessary to return to the abrasive papers to cut back more and then to repolish.

TIPS

- When cutting back and polishing cold-cast metal casts with a lot of difficult-to-access detail different grades of wire wool or very fine wire brushes can be used. These should be used dry so care should be taken not generate too much dust and a dedicated dust mask should be worn.
- Wire wool should not be used on white or light-coloured castings as they may discolour.
- When cutting back any casting with abrasives the object is to remove the surface layer of resin to expose the colour or base materials. On castings with very fine detail this process may remove some detail; there is no way round this so the balance of how far to cut back without losing too much should be considered carefully.
- Castings with areas of high and low detail will produce areas that are brighter on the high points. This can look very effective if a 'foundry sculpture' effect is required.
- Once cut back and polished cold-cast metal castings will begin to oxidize over time and can be brought back to brightness with a proprietary metal polish.
- Cold-cast bronzes (and other metals) can be displayed as such, as long as they are labelled 'cold cast' to distinguish them from 'foundry cast'.
- Toothpaste is an ultra-fine abrasive polish and can be a good final polishing compound.

FINISHING

Cold-cast bronze, copper and brass castings can be 'paginated' following the same methods as for full bronzes although pagination times may need to be reduced due to the smaller amounts of metal contained within the resin (for pagination techniques research other publications).

- Casts can be wax-polished to retain brightness.
- Metal shellacs can be used to create permanent seals.
- Domestic metal polishes can be used to rejuvenate brightness on oxidized castings.
- Iron-filled castings can be submerged in water to produce a 'rusted bloom' on the surface.
- Unpigmented castings will yellow if exposed to direct sunlight and should be painted or sealed if they are intended for exterior use.
- Castings can be painted with oil-based paints and should be degreased thoroughly beforehand.
- Castings can be drilled, sanded and machined.

Faults and Repairs

- Small holes or cracks can be filled from the surface with additional mixes. A mix of resin and the appropriate metal powder combined at a ratio of one part resin to at least two parts powder produces a thick paste that is useful for filling and making repairs. Overfill, cut back any excess and finish in the usual way.
- Broken-off cast pieces can be glued back with resin mix containing a little metal powder or colour.
- Wax gilt crayons can be used to touch up minor blemishes.
- Breaks can be also be repaired with epoxy resin adhesives.

PROJECT 1

Specification

A polyurethane resin pigmented black lion on a base, from a silicone rubber 'core' mould. Size: 320mm (L), 110mm (W) and 200mm (H).

Time Required

Allowing for setting times this project can be carried out in approximately two hours.

Materials

- Easyflo 60 polyurethane resin (supplied by Notcutt Ltd); and
- black polyurethane resin pigment.

Tools

See 'Tools and Equipment' section for polyurethane resins.

Method

This project was carried out using the multi-piece cored silicone rubber lion mould produced by the project in Chapter 1. To create the cast follow the steps from the earlier section in this chapter from 'Solid and Backfilled Castings' onwards.

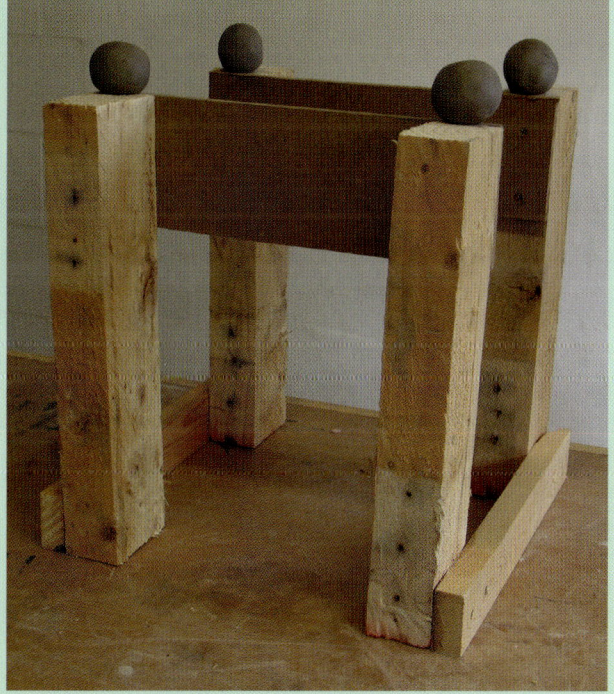

Balls of clay are placed on the four corners of the mould support.

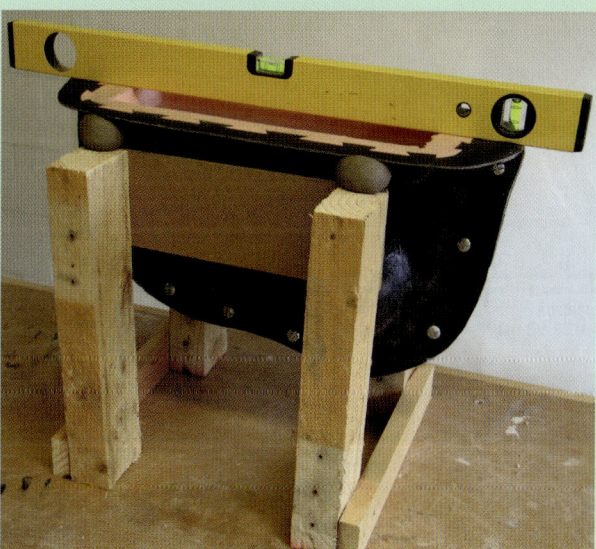

The mould levels are set in two directions by pushing the mould down into the clay balls.

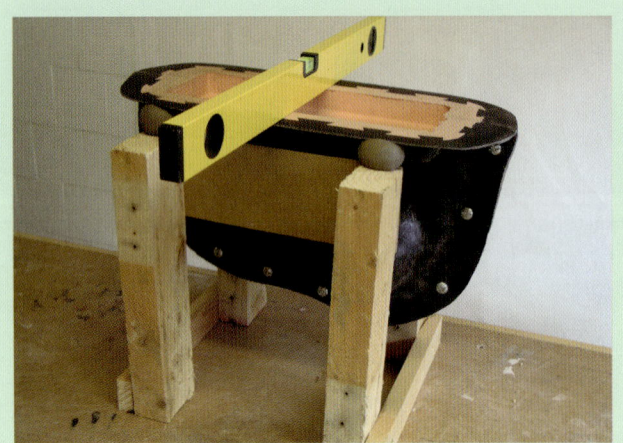

The mould is levelled.

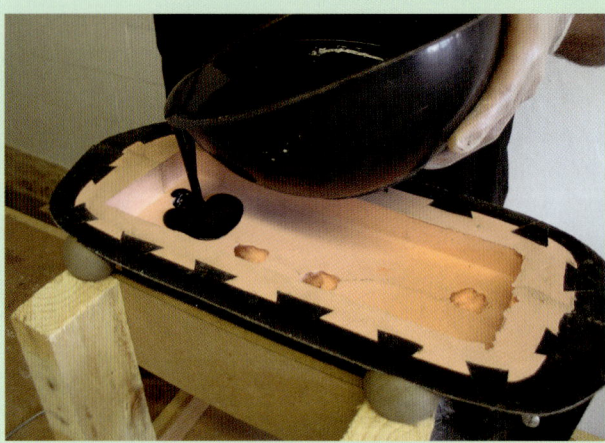

Pigmented polyurethane resin is poured into the mould from one point.

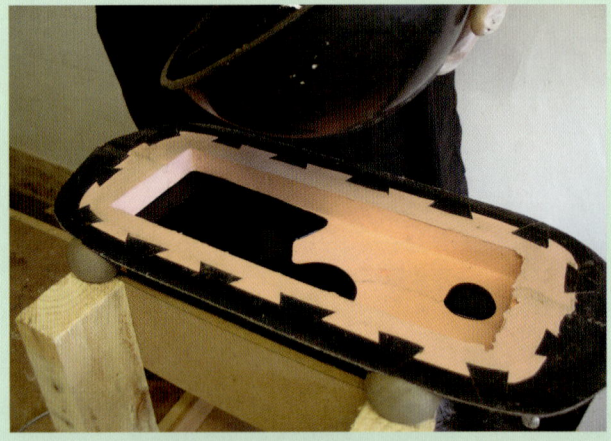

The resin is allowed to rise in the mould, pushing out any air entrapment as it does.

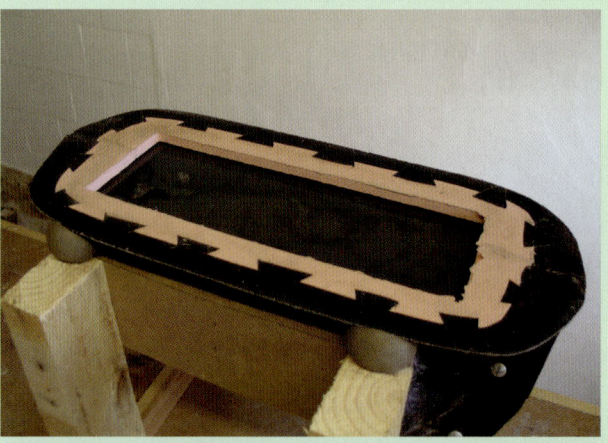

Once the mould is filled the resin should be allowed to set fully and harden.

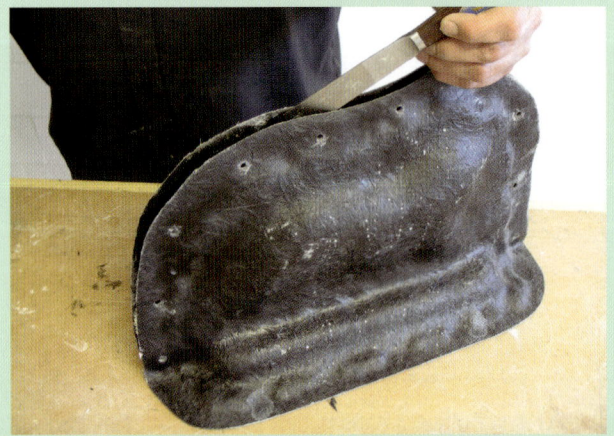

The case seam is helped open with a knife.

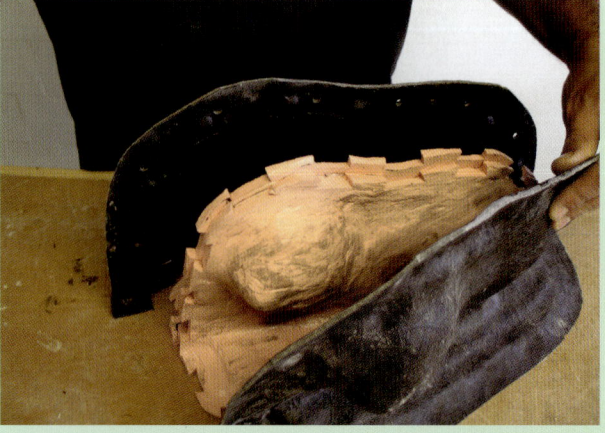

The case pieces are removed from the silicone mould.

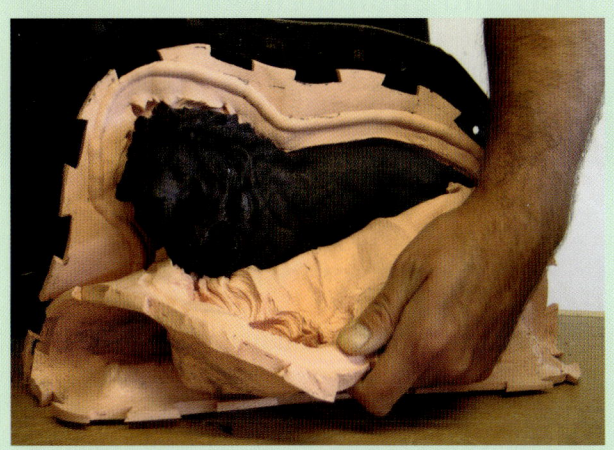

The two silicone side pieces are pulled away from
the cast.

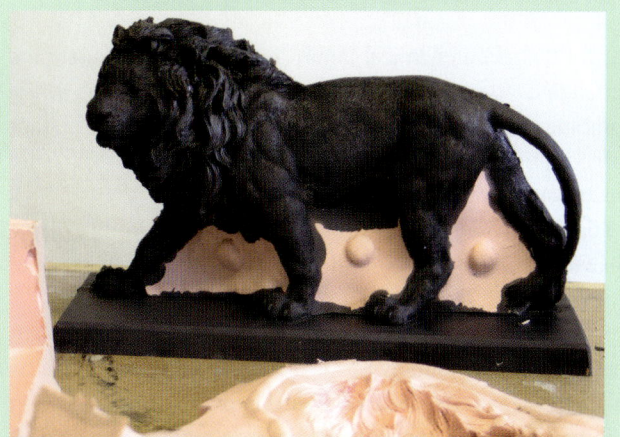

The cast with silicone mould core in situ.

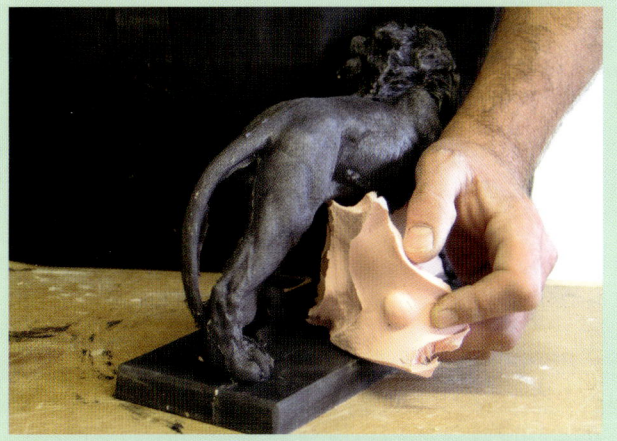

The core is removed last.

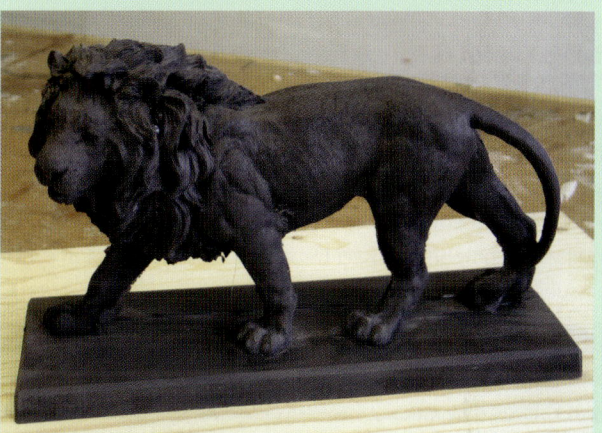

The demoulded pigmented polyurethane cast.

Polyurethane Expanding Foam

Part of the same chemical family as the resins, polyurethane expanding foams are two-part liquid systems that when combined expand and then set to form a solid. The resultant solid can be of infinitely varying flexibility, from a firm to very flexible set foam.

Foams have advantages for all sort of uses, from variable flexible castings to semi-rigid backfillings for any number of cast materials.

Flexible castings can be advantageous to the initial mould-making process. Moulds for flexible casts can sometimes be made in fewer parts, with the flexibility of the casting allowing it to bend and contract past minor undercuts.

Materials

Flexible foam Variable density foams are available in a range of flexibilities. The 'open' (bubbled) textured surface varies depending on the density. Flexible foam is good for the backfilling of hollow castings to reduce the cost of the original material. It can also be used for casting if surface detail is not an issue.

Self-skinning flexible foam As above but this has a smooth skin that develops while setting. This is preferable when casting fine detail.

Pigments Specific polyurethane foam pigments can be added at the mixing stage to produce integrally coloured castings.

Shelf Life

The shelf life for polyurethane foams is at least six months at room temperature. Opened containers of resin should be tightly resealed after use, as any atmospheric moisture contamination can cause foaming when next used. A moisture purging dry-gas aerosol can be sprayed into open containers to prolong shelf life.

Some liquids can become crystalline, develop sediment and become cloudy if stored below room temperature and this will reduce the physical properties of the foam. To restore it, loosen the lid and warm to 48–71°C until clear.

Tools and Equipment

Dispensing and Mixing

- **Polyethylene plastic containers** These can be used for mixing and can often be reused when the excess is set and removed after use.
- **Flat-bladed spatulas or a palette knife** Used to mix small batches.
- **A cordless drill and mixing blade** These allow for mechanical mixing, useful for larger amounts.

Trimming and Finishing

RIGID FOAMS

Rasps and files These can be used for initial trimming.

A hacksaw This can also be used for initial trimming.

Tin snips and heavy duty shears These can also be used for initial trimming.

Powered jigsaws and multi-tools These can be very useful to take some of the hard work out of trimming (ensure strict dust control measures are observed).

A power drill Holes can be drilled safely mechanically or by hand.

Powered abrasive tools Beware of cutting back mechanically as powered tools tend to take too much away too quickly (ensure strict dust control measures are observed).

Wet-and-dry abrasive paper This is used in a selection of grades for fine-surface trimming.

Needle files These are used for very fine and difficult-to-access trimming and cutting back.

FLEXIBLE FOAMS

A Stanley knife or craft knife Used for initial trimming.

A scalpel or razor blade Used for secondary or fine-surface trimming.

Note: Foam dust can ignite readily and care should be taken with waste dust from abrasive action.

Safety and Good Studio Practice

Safety and good studio practice should be followed in the same way as for polyurethane resins (*see* previous section).

Principal Casting Techniques

Project 2 at the end of this chapter provides an illustrated example of flexible foam casting. See also Chapter 11 for an example of backfilling.

Compaction and Volume Calculation

To calculate the required density of foam for the job and the resultant volume of liquid foam to use, a compaction calculation should be performed. The 'set' foam density will determine the weight and detail pick-up of the casting. The density of material is calibrated in weight per cubic area. 'Free rise' density describes the density of foam allowed to set not contained within a mould and this will be a lower density than the 'moulded density'. Moulded density is therefore the figure to consider when determining casting densities.

The more liquid the mix of foam you put into a mould (referred to as 'packing'), the denser the resultant set foam will be. As the liquid mix starts to set bubbles are formed as it expands. The less room there is inside the mould for it to expand, the less bubbles can form and the denser the casting will be and vice versa.

Note that packing the mould with too little foam will hinder self-skinning properties and therefore detail pick-up. Packing the foam to a minimum of 2–3lb per cubic foot above free rise density will result in good detail pick-up.

Mould Preparation

Moulds should be clean and dry and preferably heated to 23–9°C for best results. For open moulds a lid should be made with a pouring hole and vent holes to allow air to escape while the foam is rising. Blocks should be prepared to block these holes securely once the foam has started to rise and the required packing is achieved. Moulds, lids and blocks should be prepared with release agents.

Mixing

The amounts of the liquids to combine to create the foam are usually in ratios of two parts, i.e. 2:1 or 1:1. Always check the manufacturer's instructions for the specific material you are using. The amount of liquid foam to be used should be found by weighing and not calculated by volume.

Dispense both parts of the liquid foam into one container to avoid a loss of material from pouring from one container into another to combine (which can result in under-curing and tackiness). Mix small batches with a flat-bladed palette knife, scraping material from the sides and bottom of the container to combine thoroughly. Larger batches should be mixed with a cordless drill and mixing blade.

The amount of time to mix batches is known as 'cream time' and this can be 15–45 seconds (always check the manufacturer's individual material specifications).

Pouring

Mixes should be poured as soon as they are mixed, in one continuous steady operation to avoid air entrapment. Do not scrape the sides and bottom of mix containers to avoid introducing unmixed liquid foam parts (which can result in under-cured or soft areas of the casting).

Curing

The amount of time the foam takes to fully expand is known as 'rise time', and this can be 1–6 minutes. Demould times can be 20–45 minutes. These are minimum times before remoulding and for certainty full cure should be achieved before demoulding.

Full cure times can be 12–24 hours. Some foams can benefit from 'post-curing' at raised temperatures to achieve their full properties. Check the manufacturer's individual material specifications for all these stages and times.

Demoulding

The techniques for demoulding, removing the finished cast from the mould, will largely depend on what type of mould is being used.

■ Moulds used in rigid foam casting should be removed as for resin demoulding but with extra care to avoid damaging the cast surface as some can be quite soft.

■ Flexible foam castings have the advantage of being able to be bent and contorted to release them from their moulds. Be careful not to tear any cast seam lines (flashing) when demoulding.

Trimming and Cutting Back

Once the cast has been demoulded any excess flashing can be trimmed back.

RIGID FOAMS

■ Initially the extremities of any excess can be broken off carefully, by hand or with a pair of pliers, being careful not to break off too much. Then a number of tools can be employed depending on the size of the cast and how much foam is to be removed (chisels, hacksaw blades, surforms, rasps and so on).

■ The initial trim should not be taken right back to the surface of the cast and should only be used to remove bulk excess.

■ Smaller and smaller tools should be used as you work closer to the cast surface.

■ Final cutting back to the surface of the cast should be achieved with increasingly finer grades of abrasive paper. Fine files including needle files can be useful for getting into difficult-to-access area of the cast (a fine brass or wire brush is also useful to clear clogged files).

■ Once excess flashing has been taken back to the surface the final cutting back can be done in the same way as for resins (see the section earlier in this chapter on Surface Finishing and Polishing).

Note: Foam dust can ignite readily and care should be taken with waste dust from abrasive action.

FLEXIBLE FOAMS

■ Flexible foams can really only be trimmed.

■ A Stanley knife, craft knife or nail scissors can be used for the initial trimming.

■ A scalpel or razor blade should be used for secondary or fine-surface trimming.

■ For the final trim the foam can be stretched a little, with tweezers if necessary, cut and then allowed to spring back to achieve a close-to-the-surface cut.

Finishing

■ Foam castings can yellow and become chalky with exposure to sunlight and should be painted and sealed before exterior use.

■ Castings can be painted once fully cured. The compatibility of primer and paints should be tested before commitment.

Faults and Repairs

■ Tears or breaks in polyurethane foam castings can be repaired using water-based flexible adhesives such as liquid latex glues. Proprietary polyurethane mastics are also available for this purpose.

■ Holes are more problematic to repair. Additions of more foam will adhere to casting surfaces but will need to be trimmed and sculpted back to the cast surface once expanded and set.

PROJECT 2

Specification

A polyurethane flexible foam lion on a base, from a silicone rubber 'core' mould. Size: 320mm (L), 110mm (W) and 200mm (H).

Time Required

As for polyurethane resin (see Project 1).

Materials

■ Polyfoam F5 polyurethane casting foam (supplied by Notcutt Ltd).

Tools

See 'Tools and Equipment' section for polyurethane expanding foam.

Method

This project was carried out using the multi-piece cored silicone rubber lion mould produced by the project in Chapter 1. To create the flexible foam cast follow the steps from the section 'Principal Casting Techniques' for polyurethane expanding foam. (*See also* Chapter 11 for another example.)

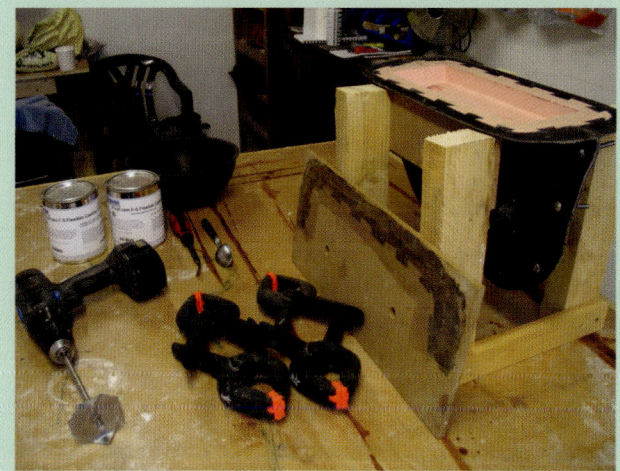

The mould, materials and equipment set up for polyurethane foam casting.

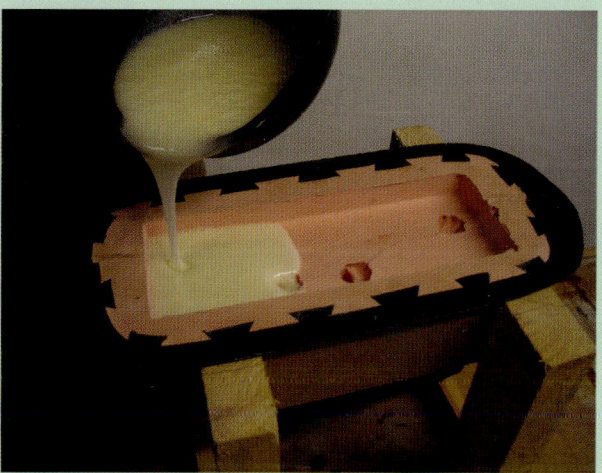

The foam is mixed and poured into the mould quickly.

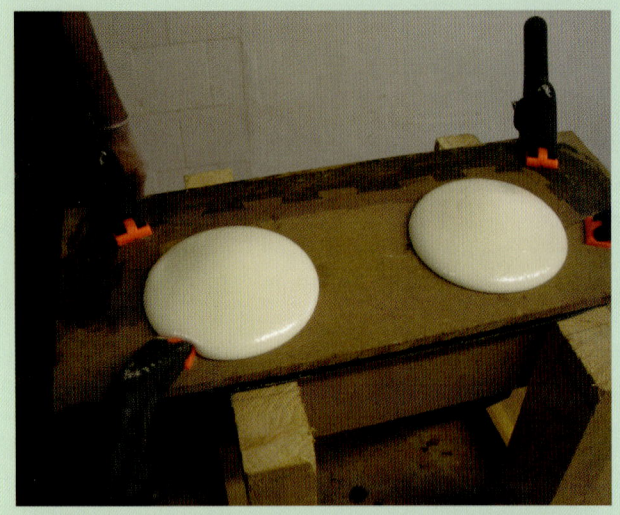

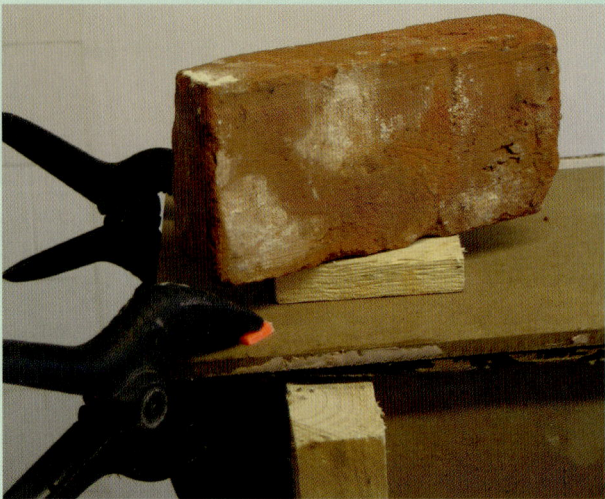

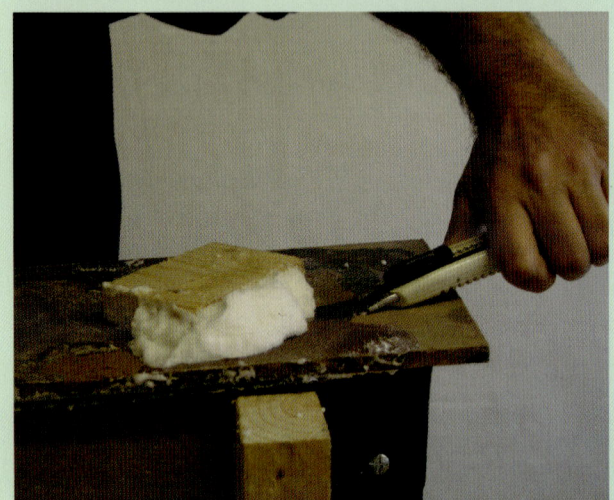

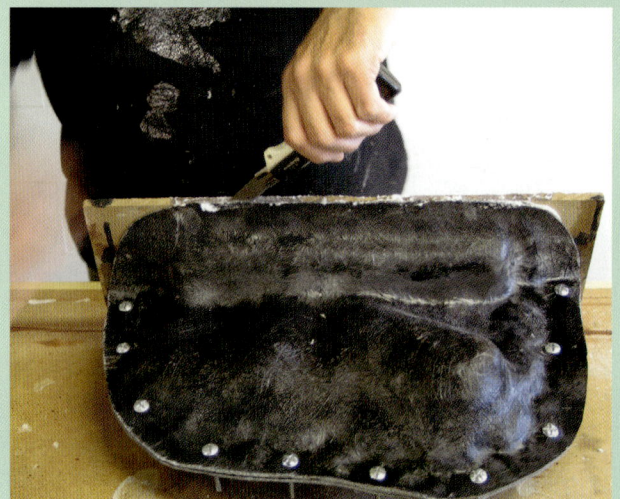

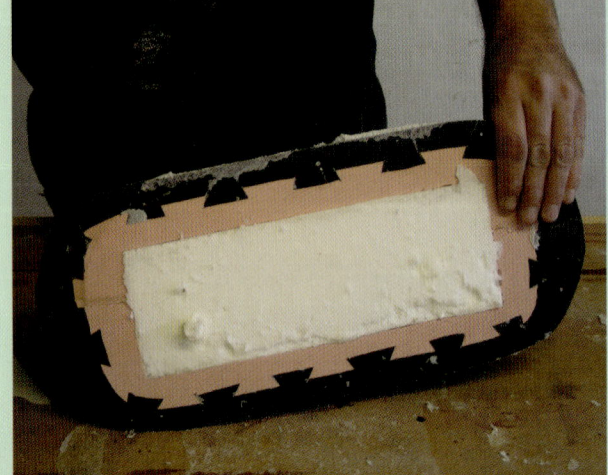

TOP LEFT: **A top board is secured to the mould opening and foam is allowed to rise from the vent holes.**

TOP RIGHT: **If a tighter foam compaction is required the vent holes can be blocked and weighted to prevent the foam from rising further.**

MIDDLE LEFT: **Once the foam has set blocks can be cut away from the top board.**

MIDDLE RIGHT: **The top board may need to be cut away from the mould opening.**

LEFT: **The top board has been removed from the mould.**

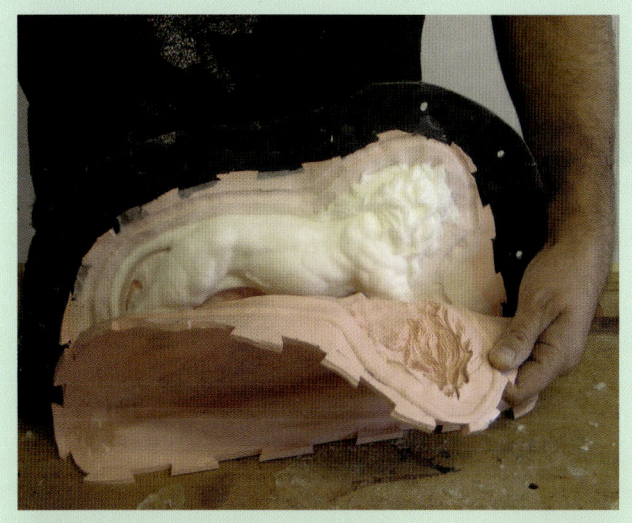

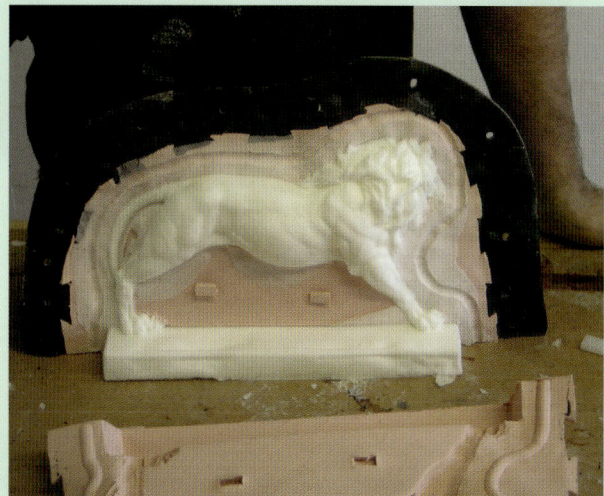

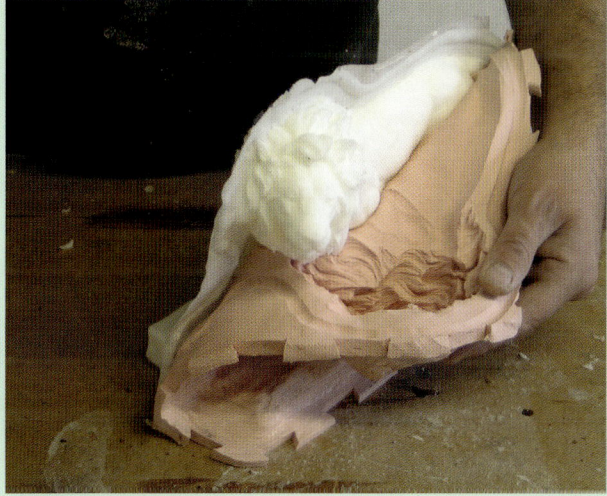

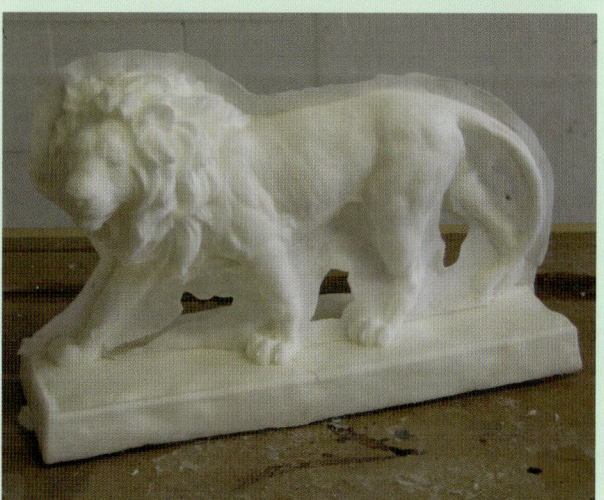

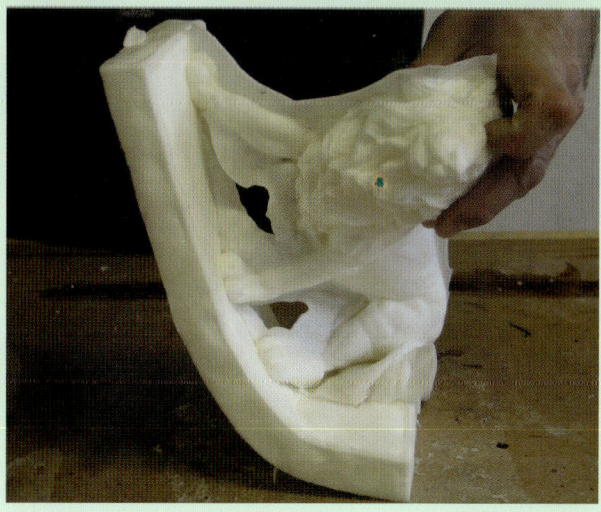

TOP LEFT, TOP RIGHT, MIDDLE LEFT: The mould case is removed and the silicone mould pieces are removed in sequence.

MIDDLE RIGHT: The demoulded cast.

RIGHT: Showing the flexibility of the polyurethane foam cast.

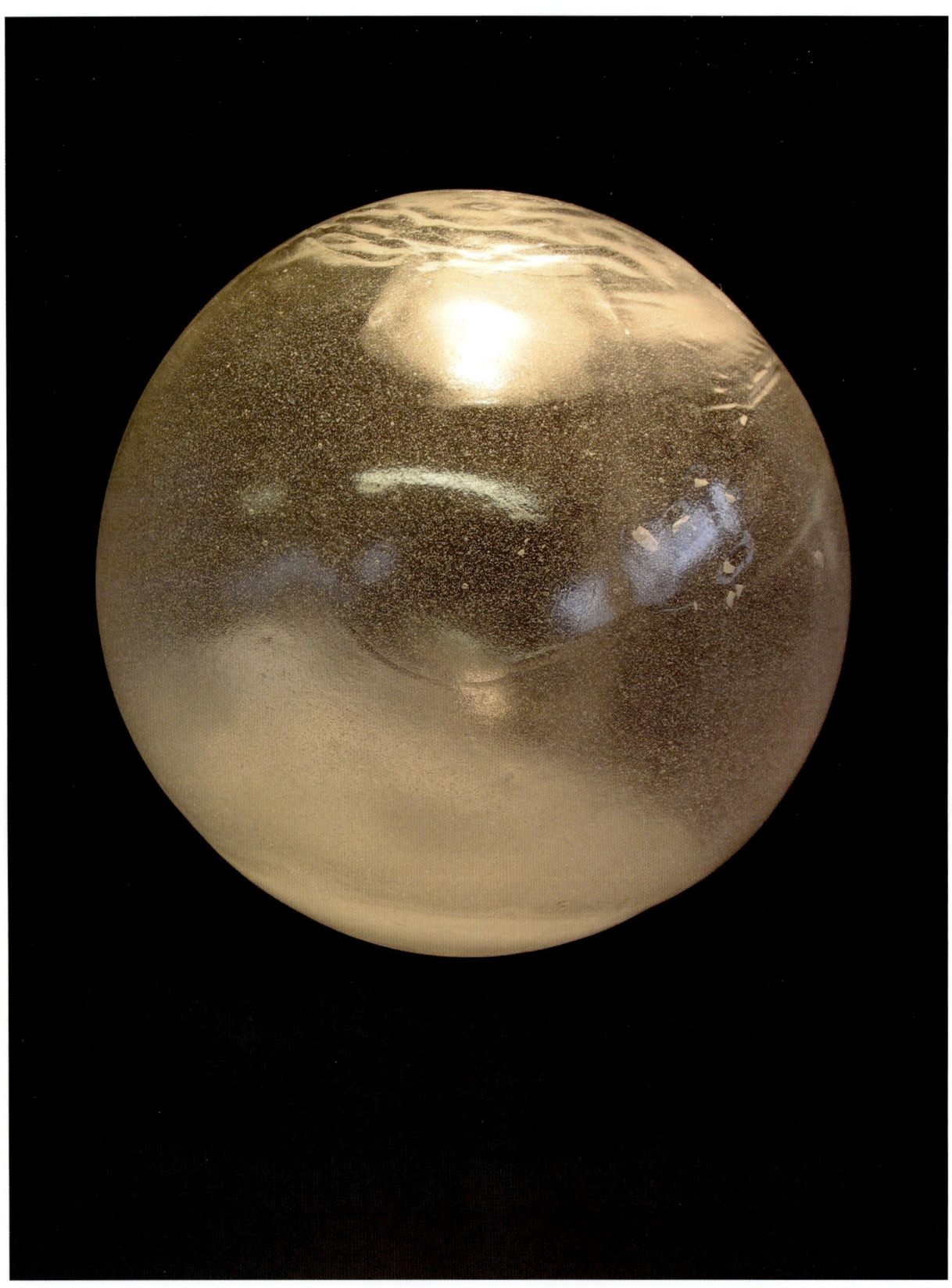

Bioresin sphere cast (700mm circumference).

CHAPTER NINE

BIORESIN®

Developed as a non-toxic alternative to polyresin and epoxy resin systems, Bioresin® is a relatively new material available to the domestic mouldmaking and casting market.

The wide range of toxicological hazards present in polyresin and epoxy resin systems can render them extremely hazardous to work with, particularly in a small studio or workshop environment, where adequate protective systems may not always be available.

Although recognized as hazardous for some time, extensive research in the last ten years has shown that poly and epoxy resin systems contain a number of toxic components that can produce a wide range of toxicological effects, such as allergies, contact dermatitis (including skin lesions/ulceration/sensitization), blood and nerve damage, sensitization of the respiratory system and narcosis. Although it has been widely accepted that working with these potential hazards is a 'containable risk' with appropriate health and safety procedures in place, clearly a non-toxic resin system is a very attractive alternative option. Additionally, issues such as the negative environmental impact and sustainability of petrol-based resin systems cannot be ignored, particularly in the current climate of ecological awareness.

The Bioresin systems are formulated from plant-based derivatives such as sunflower seed oil, soya and several other proprietary natural additives. This means they do not require toxic labelling and are safe to use in the studio/workshop environment with minimal health and safety concerns.

Material Specifications

A wide range of Bioresin systems are available with working and production possibilities similar to other resin systems. These include:

- variable Shore hardness (for an explanation of the Shore scale of hardness see Chapter 11);
- variable pot life, setting and demould timings;
- transparency and variable degrees of translucency;
- pigmentation addition;
- metal/stone-filled systems;
- laminating;
- embedding;
- flexibility; and
- being food-safe.

Note: Bioresins come in many varieties within the numbered system. Unless stated specifically, figures are for maximum and minimum times within the whole system. Maximum and minimum time figures are for the 'individually' numbered 'system', but should be checked against 'individually' numbered 'resin' within the system being used.

1775–1777 This is a range of resins suitable for multiple use. Their properties include:

- transparency;
- suitability for very small to large castings;
- suitability for slush casting;
- a pot life time of 2min–5hr;
- a demould time of 8min–14hr;
- an ultimate hardening time of 1hr–8 days;
- a Shore hardness (*see* Chapter 11) from 72–78D;
- a compressive strength of 110 N/mm^2;
- a mix ratio of 1:1.5;
- a vacuum degas time of 1–5min;
- heat resistance to 110–140°C;
- suitability for polishing (certain systems only); and
- UV stability.
- 1777 is a clear flexible system.

1780   These comprise a variety of multiple-use resins with a higher Shore hardness range and longer pot life and demould times. Their properties include:

- transparency and semi-translucency;
- suitability for very small to very large castings (more than 50 litres);
- suitability for slush casting;
- a pot life time of 2min–8hr;
- a demould time of 8min–3 days;
- an ultimate hardening time of 1hr–14 days;
- a Shore hardness of 78–88D;
- a compressive strength of 110–140 N/mm^2;
- a mix ratio of 1:1.5;
- a vacuum degas time of 1–5min;
- heat resistance to 110–140°C;
- suitability for polishing (certain systems only);
- UV stability; and
- low shrinkage.

1784–1786   This is a range of optically transparent resins that are particularly suitable for embedding, very hard and suitable for polishing. Properties include:

- optical transparency;
- suitability for very small to large (over 200mm) castings;
- a pot life of 40min (1784/1785) or 5min–8hr (1786);
- a demould time of 2–4hr (1784/1785) or 15min–24hr (1786);
- an ultimate hardening time of 6–8hr (1784/1785) or 2hr–3 days (1786);
- a Shore hardness of 80–87D;
- a compressive strength of 110–180 N/mm^2;
- a mix ratio of 1:2 (1784/1786) or 1:2.5 (1785);
- a vacuum degas time of 2–5min;
- heat resistance to 110–170°C;
- suitability for polishing (all systems);
- UV stability; and
- low shrinkage.

611, 616, 625   This range of very hard and durable resins is suitable for metal/stone filling and laminating. Properties include:

- translucency or being opal in appearance;
- suitability for laminating and filling;

- a pot life of 4–35min;
- a demould time of 8min–3hr;
- an ultimate hardening time of 1–8hr;
- a Shore hardness of 83–87D;
- a tensile strength of 124 N/mm^2
- a mix ratio of 1:1.5/1.8;
- a vacuum degas time of 2min;
- heat resistance to 170–190°C;
- suitability for polishing (all systems); and
- shrinkage of 1–2 per cent.

SHELF LIFE (ALL SYSTEMS)

Shelf life is 12 months in sealed original containers in dry conditions at temperatures of 15–30°C.

Fillers

Fillers can collectively be described as very fine mesh powders that are mixed into the resin. They can be broken down into three main groups.

- **Inert fillers (microballoons)**   These are very fine inert mineral powders that are mixed in equal parts with the resin. Mixing the resin with a filler reduces the amount of resin needed to fill a cast solid, which is useful for two reasons: one, to reduce exotherm (the heat generated during setting) and, two, to decrease casting costs. Calcium carbonate can be added to resin to produce a very white casting. Storage should be at moderate temperatures in dry conditions.
- **Metal fillers**   These are fine-mesh metal powders added to resins to produce castings with metallic finishes. Unlike metallic paint finishes the powders used are powders of the actual metal and once cut back with abrasives and polished they will appear as the metal itself – for instance, an iron-filled casting will start to rust if exposed to moisture. Storage should be at moderate temperatures in dry conditions.
- **Stone fillers**   These are powdered stone materials added to the resin to produce stone finishes. They are usually more granular than metal fillers. Storage should be at moderate temperatures in dry conditions.

Metal and stone fillers can be used as a gel coat and then painted or slushed (*see* Chapter 12) to a thickness of 2 or 3mm onto the surface of a mould, allowed to set and then backed up with resin or resin/inert filler mix to cut down on the cost of metal and stone fillers. To paint on gel coats systems with a slow setting (long pot life) should be used.

Tools and Equipment

Dispensing and Mixing

- **Waxed paper cups or white plastic containers** For dispensing and mixing batches of resin. Plastic containers can be allowed to dry after use and the set resin cracked out for re-use.
- **Disposable wooden spatulas** For combining resin parts and mixing pigments and fillers into batches.
- **Scales** Accurate digital scales should be used to calculate weights and measures of system parts safely. Bioresins are a two-part system of resin and hardener that need to be combined at different ratios by weight.
- **A degasser** Bioresins need to be degassed in a pressurized vacuum chamber, to remove air entrapment before mould application. Degassing times vary slightly for different Bioresin systems. Reducing degassing times will produce castings with trapped air bubbles. This can be quite attractive if controlled, but can affect the set strength.

Laminating

- **Brushes** Brushes of various sizes are needed to paint gel coats onto a mould surface. Specially manufactured brushes are available that will withstand the materials involved and not lose bristles; however, ordinary decorating brushes of a good quality will last quite a long time.
- **Disposable wooden spatulas** For mixing batches.
- **A plastic paint kettle** For cleaning brushes and equipment in white spirit.

Trimming and Finishing

Trimming and finishing can really only be achieved effectively on the harder Bioresin systems.

- **Rasps and files** These can be used for initial trimming of cured resin casts.
- **A hacksaw** Used for initial trimming.
- **Tin snips and heavy-duty shears** Used for initial trimming.
- **Powered jigsaws and multi-tools** These can be very useful to take some of the hard work out of trimming. (Note: observe strict dust control measures.)
- **A power drill** Holes can be drilled safely mechanically or by hand into set resins.
- **Powered abrasive tools** For cutting back flashing on seams and exposing metal/stone-filled surfaces. Beware of cutting back filled casts mechanically as they can take too much away too quickly. (Note: observe strict dust control measures.)
- **Wet-and-dry abrasive paper** For removing sharp edges after initial trimming and cutting back metal-filled casts prior to polishing.
- **Needle files** For very fine and difficult-to-access trimming and cutting back.
- **Wire brushes** For clearing tools clogged with material.
- **Polishing equipment** For polishing castings after cutting back with abrasives. This can be done mechanically or by hand.

Safety and Good Studio Practice

- Although they are non-toxic, Bioresin systems do emit fumes so your working area should be well ventilated.
- Work surfaces can be protected with a heavy-gauge polythene that can be disposed of or replaced when necessary.
- Overalls are a good idea as resins are extremely difficult to remove from clothing.
- Working with any resins and their associated products can cause skin reactions, particularly if you have a sensitive skin type. Barrier creams provide a protective barrier between your skin and these materials and

should always be employed, even for those without 'sensitive' skin. Disposable plastic or rubber gloves will provide further levels of hand protection. Specific proprietary hand cleaners are the only efficient and safe way to clean hands.

■ White spirit should be used to clean brushes and tools prior to washing with detergent.

■ Disposal of excess resins, empty storage and dispensing containers, solvents and any other associated materials should be carried out with regard to an understanding of flammability and environmental consequences. If possible follow the guidelines set out by manufacturers, which should be available through the retailer.

■ Safety data sheets for all materials should be requested from retailer if not supplied with the products. All health and safety labelling on materials should be understood and adhered to.

Principal Casting Techniques

Mix Ratios and Mixing

Bioresin systems are supplied as a two-part system of resin and hardener. Ensure the ratio of the parts is correct by weighing on digital scales. It is also important that both resin parts and the moulds are at room temperature. Your studio should be maintained at room temperature during setting and curing times. Mixing vessels and tools should be clean and dry.

When making up your resin combine both resin parts in a mixing vessel and stir vigorously for one minute, scraping the sides and bottom to ensure thorough mixing. Bioresin systems have a wide combination of mix ratios to allow for different requirements for pot life, setting and demould times (*see* the earlier section 'Material Specifications').

Exotherm

Bioresin will produce an exothermic (heat-generating) reaction when setting. Although the inherent problems associated with this are reduced considerably when using Bioresin as opposed to polyresin systems, an understanding of the effects of exotherm on resin castings should be understood

(*see* Chapter 10). Consideration of the effects of exotherm should be given according to the nature of the casting; large-scale castings need to be allowed to set and cure very slowly, whereas small castings can be set and cured faster. Mix ratios and system specifications should to be considered according to the particular job at hand.

Degassing

Bioresin systems need to be degassed immediately after mixing using degassing equipment to eliminate air entrapment. The mixed batch should be introduced into the vacuum chamber and then vacuumed under pressure until bubbles start to appear and pop on the surface of the mix. When the bubbles start to subside the mix will be ready to use.

Degassing times vary between one and five minutes; adhere to the specifications of the specific system being used to ensure bubble-free castings. Immediately after degassing the mix can be poured or painted into the mould.

Pigment and Filler Addition

If you wish to use pigment or filler addition use a slower-setting system, specified for pigmented and filler addition castings, to allow for the additional mixing time. Mix both resin parts before introducing additions and ensure fillers are dry. Degas as described above.

COLOURED GEL COATS

To obtain castings with integral colour, pigments can be added to the resin to create a gel coat layer of the casting. These are not gel coats in the traditional polyester resin sense, as Bioresin is not thixotropic, but if worked with quickly enough the mix can be applied to a thickness of 2–3mm while setting to create a first layer to the casting. Specific Bioresin pigments have been developed that are raw earth pigments suspended in a resin binder. A gel coat resin is used to carry the pigment of the casting.

1. Dispense the amount of resin required to apply a layer approximately 2–3mm thick to the mould surface. If laying up large moulds be aware of the amount of resin that can be applied within the working time or pot life of a batch. If it will be necessary to lay up

the mould with several batches of gel coat, it will be necessary to colour-match each batch. Add the pigment in small amounts until the required colour is obtained; be aware that only small amounts of pigment are needed to produce very vivid colours. Additions of approximately 2–5 per cent by weight of resin should be adequate, but in practice it is much easier to mix 'by eye'.

2. Once mixed thoroughly the batch can be applied to the mould surface with a brush or can be slushed (*see* Chapter 12). Be aware that it will set very quickly and it will need to be kept moving over the surface of the mould in order to coat it evenly, about 2–3mm thick. Use batches of a size that can be used within the pot life.

3. It is sometimes a good idea to apply a second gel coat to moulds with a lot of detail, in this case allow the first gel coat to cure and dry before applying the second layer.

4. Allow the gel coat to set before backfilling with neat resin, or resin/inert filler mix, or laminating.

METAL/STONE-FILLED GEL COATS

Metal and stone effect castings can be obtained using very fine mesh (finely ground) metal and stone powders, known as fillers, mixed into the resin. A wide range of fillers is available, including:

- bronze;
- copper;
- iron;
- brass;
- marble;
- slate; or
- stone.

Fillers are added to the resin to form a brushable gel coat that is applied to the mould surface and then backfilled with neat resin or a resin/inert filler mix. When calculating the amount of metal filler required a rough rule of thumb is equal quantities by volume of resin to filler.

1. Dispense the require amount of resin into a container and then dispense an equal quantity by volume of the filler required. Do not mix the resin and filler at this stage. For a gel coat mixture the quantity of resin and filler combined will need to cover the entire surface of the mould to a thickness of approximately 2–3mm, depending on the amount of detail. Moulds containing a combination of raised and deep, fine detail may need a second application of gel coat once the first has set.

2. Laying up a large mould will require several batches of gel coat in order to apply it within the pot life (working time). Colour matching of the metal and stone fillers needs to be considered when laying up several batches of gel coat.

3. Mix consistencies will depend on their intended use. Brush-applied gel coats should be brushable but thixotropic; that is, they can be painted onto the mould surface to a thickness of 2–3mm but will not run off. Slushed gel coats will need to be thinner in order to run on the mould surface. Equal quantities of resin and filler is only a rough guide, and where possible more filler should be used without compromising the required consistency. Less than 50 per cent filler will not produce good metal and stone effects.

4. Once mixed thoroughly the batch can be applied to the mould surface with a brush or can be slushed (*see* Chapter 12). Be aware that it will set very quickly and it will need to be kept moving over the surface of the mould in order to coat it evenly, to a thickness of around 2–3mm. Use batches of a size that can be used within the pot life.

5. Allow the gel coat to set before backfilling with neat resin, resin/inert filler mix or laminating.

Solid and Backfilled Castings

Bioresin systems can be pigmented or filled and poured in one solid casting or can be applied as a gel-coated layer and backfilled.

1. Set the mould levels in two directions. This is done easily using small balls of clay under each corner or opening flange of the mould and pushing the mould down into them to obtain a level (see illustration sequence for Project 1 in Chapter 8).

2. Estimate the amount of resin needed.

3. For solid-filled castings estimate the amount of pigment or filler needed (see previous section). Bear

in mind that the mix needs to be pourable, so do not add too much filler.

4. Create your mix and stir very quickly but thoroughly for one minute and degas before pouring.

5. Fill the mould by pouring from one spot and allowing mix to rise, pushing out any air entrapment as it does. A little agitation of the mould will bring up any air bubbles and allow the mix to seep into the mould detail.

6. Allow to set thoroughly.

CLEAR CASTINGS

1. Follow the stages as described above.

2. Be aware that degassing becomes of particular importance with clear castings as any bubbles will be highly visible in the set casting.

3. Objects can be encapsulated or embedded in Bioresin at the casting stage if desired (*see* Chapter 10).

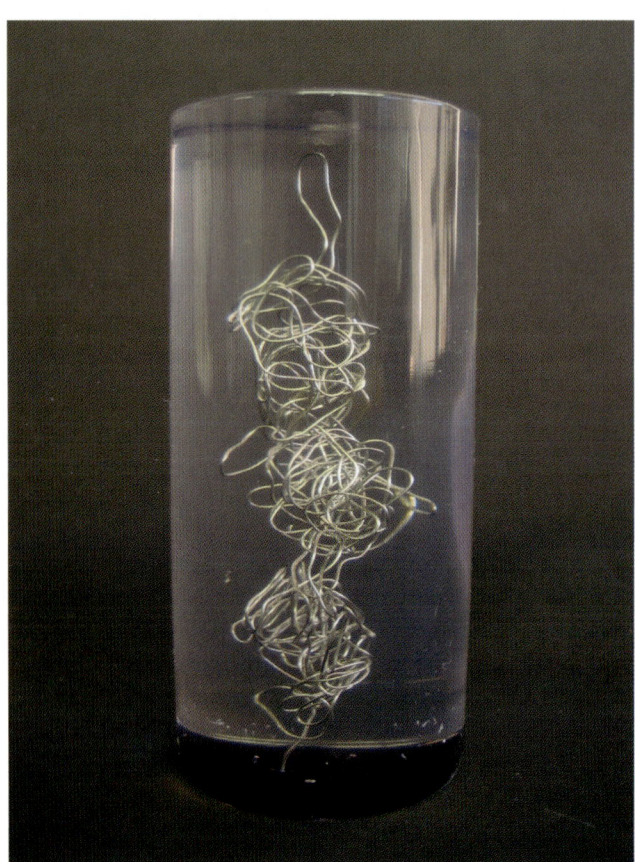

Embedded Bioresin (H: 80mm).

HOLLOW CASTINGS

1. Follow the directions for mixing, additions and pouring as described above.

2. Hollow castings can be achieved by slushing (*see* Chapter 12). Moulds should be filled approximately a third full and then constantly and evenly rotated until the resin sets. This is easiest with a mould 'in-the-round', where the pouring hole of the mould can be bunged and it can be rotated in all directions. However, tilting an open mould carefully to allow the resin to cover up to the edges is also possible.

3. Moulds may need several coats in this way, allowing time for the resin to set between coats, to achieve an adequate thickness of 3–5mm.

4. Allow to set thoroughly.

Laminating

It is possible to produce laminated hollow castings using certain Bioresin systems (primarily the 600 range). Fibreglass mat can be used in conjunction with Bioresin and the laminating processes to be employed are the same as for polyester resin systems (see Chapter 11 in *Mouldmaking and Casting* for further information).

Demoulding

The techniques for demoulding, removing the finished cast from the mould, will largely depend on what type of mould is being used.

■ **Plaster one-piece** Moulds can be tapped or levered out from the *inside* of the cast using a chisel. Soaking in hot soapy water can help to ease out difficult casts.

■ **Plaster multi-piece** Moulds should be eased apart piece by piece. Small moulds can usually be parted using a strong-bladed knife. Larger moulds may require a thin chisel to crack the seam initially until a wooden or plastic wedge can be driven in. On particularly long seams a series of wedges can be gradually driven in sequentially until parted.

■ **A plaster waste mould** See Chapter 4 of *Mouldmaking and Casting* for detail on chipping out plaster waste moulds.

- **Fibreglass**   As above, although there can be a certain degree of flexibility in a fibreglass mould depending on how thickly it has been made.
- **Flexible moulds (without a case)**   Demoulding from flexible moulds without a case is a combination of flexing and peeling the mould while easing out the cast.
- **Flexible moulds (with a case)**   First remove the case (this should be carried out as for plaster one-piece moulds) and then peel the mould away from the cast. It is possible to peel the mould away from the cast with these moulds as they are thinner and more flexible than flexible moulds without a case.
- **Gelflex moulds**   Resin casts from gelflex moulds should be allowed to cool down thoroughly after the setting process as the mould may soften slightly due to the high exotherm generated and will need time to reset.

Post-Curing After Demoulding

Many of the Bioresin systems either benefit from or require post-curing to achieve their full hardness and set strength. This can be done in a domestic oven or via an external heat source (careful control of constant temperatures should be observed). See the post-curing time specifications on individual systems.

Trimming and Cutting Back

Once the cast has been demoulded any excess cast and seam lines (flashing) can be trimmed back. Note that only the harder Bioresin systems are suitable for cutting back and polishing. Trimming with a scalpel or craft knife is possible on the softer systems.

1. Initially the extremities of any excess can be broken off carefully by hand or a pair of pliers, but be careful not to break off too much. Then a number of tools can be employed depending on the size of the cast and how much resin is to be removed (chisels, hacksaw blades, surforms, rasps and so on).
2. The initial trim should not be taken right back to the surface of the cast and should only be used to remove bulk excess.

3. Smaller and smaller tools should be used as you work closer to the cast surface.
4. Final cutting back to the surface of the cast should be achieved with increasingly finer grades of abrasive paper. Fine files including needle files can be useful for getting into difficult-to-access area of the cast (a fine brass or wire brush is also useful to clear clogged files).
5. Once excess flashing has been taken back to the surface, final cutting back and/or polishing of the entire cast surface can be tackled.

Surface Finishing and Polishing

Casts that have coloured gel coats and clear casting resins will usually come out of moulds with a matt surface finish; metal/stone-filled gel coats will be matt and the base material not fully visible. To obtain the full effect of metal and stone, or to achieve gloss colours or glass-clear surfaces, castings will need to be cut back with abrasive papers and then polished.

CUTTING BACK WITH ABRASIVES

Wet-and-dry abrasive papers should be used to cut back cast surfaces and these should be used wet to avoid dust (which can be carcinogenic) and prevent paper from clogging. The papers are graded by the number of particles of grit per square inch of paper and a variety of grades should be used in sequence from coarse to fine. Depending on the job 100–600 grit paper (100 being coarsest and 600 finest) should be used in succession, with the very fine grades usually being reserved for clear casting resins.

1. Standard sheets of paper should be cut up into pieces that are suitable for the size of the job and laid out in sequence.
2. Initially use the coarsest grade just to take off the worst of any seam lines and to give the whole surface 'bite'. With metal and stone surfaces this will just remove the surface layer of resin and expose the base material. Where there are smooth areas or areas that have little detail coarse papers should be used sparingly and it may be possible to start with a finer paper.
3. As the paper becomes clogged either rinse it under a running tap or in a large bowl of water.

4. Once the whole surface has been cut back with one grit size wash the cast, change your rinsing water and move on to the next grit size. In this way the whole surface of the cast is cut back progressively using finer and finer paper, with scratches created by the coarser grades being removed by the finer grades. Metal castings can also be cut back with progressive grades of wire wool. You will notice that the metals will become more and more visible as the abrasive exposes them. Clear resins will remain cloudy even after the finest grade and will not become clear until polished.

5. It is difficult to gauge whether casts have been thoroughly abraded enough until after polishing, but thorough and methodical abrading will produce better polished results. If the polished results are not good it will usually mean returning to abrasives before polishing again.

6. Once exposed, metal surfaces can be polished to a high shine or paginated using cold pagination processes.

POLISHING

Polishing can be done either mechanically or by hand using specifically designed polishing compounds. Polishing compounds come as either a hard waxy block or as a cream and are applied to the cast surface with a lint-free cloth or a mechanically spun polishing mop.

Cloth polishing mops for block compounds and sponge mops for cream compounds can be mounted, using the correct arbour, to a standard electric drill with variable speed control, or can be mounted in a dedicated polishing machine. Polishing machines are bench-mounted so this will restrict the size of the cast that can be polished mechanically. Electric drills can be used freehand or bench-mounted securely using a clamping system specific to the machine you are using. Care should be taken when using electric drills for polishing as they have no guards; goggles should always be worn whichever system of polishing is being used.

Polishing compounds are a very fine level of abrasive and come in grades of coarseness like the abrasive papers. They should be used in sequence from coarse to fine methodically over the entire surface of the cast. Compounds usually come in two or three grades and castings should be washed between grades of polish. Cold-cast metal castings can be given a final polish using a proprietary metal polish suitable to the base metal used.

If after polishing through the grades of compound the levels of gloss, brightness or clarity required have not been achieved it may be necessary to return to the abrasive papers to cut back more and then to repolish.

TIPS
■ See the 'Tips' section in Chapter 8.

FINISHING
■ Cold-cast bronze, copper and brass castings can be 'paginated' following the same methods as for full bronzes although pagination times may need to be reduced due to the smaller amounts of metals contained within the resin (for pagination techniques research other publications).
■ Casts can be wax-polished to retain brightness.
■ Metal shellacs can be used to create permanent seals.
■ Domestic metal polishes can be used to rejuvenate brightness on oxidized castings.
■ Iron-filled castings can be submerged in water to produce a 'rusted bloom' on the surface.
■ Castings can be painted with oil-based paints and should be degreased thoroughly beforehand.
■ Castings can be drilled, sanded and machined.

Faults and Repairs

■ Small holes or cracks can be filled from the surface with additional mixes. A mix of resin and the appropriate metal powder combined at a ratio of one part resin to at least two parts powder produces a thick paste that is useful for filling and making repairs. Overfill, cut back any excess and finish in the usual way.
■ Broken-off cast pieces can be glued back with resin mix containing a little metal powder or colour.
■ Wax gilt crayons can be used to touch up minor blemishes.

PROJECT

Specification

A slush-cast transparent Bioresin sphere with reduced degassing time to create some bubble entrapment in the casting. From a five-piece Jesmonite mould. Size: 700mm circumference.

Time Required

This project consists of three slush-cast applications of Bioresin over approximately 90min, allowing for setting times.

Materials

▣ **1775 Bioresin 1775 RSSS** (supplied by Canonbury Arts Ltd). The two resins were combined at a ratio to produce a setting time of approximately 10min.

▣ A combination release agent system for the mould.

Tools

▣ Mixing beakers;
▣ wooden spatulas for mixing;
▣ digital scales; and
▣ a degasser.

Method

This project was carried out using the five-piece Jesmonite mould from a ball produced by the project in Chapter 5. To create the cast follow the steps from the earlier section in this chapter from 'Solid and Backfilled Castings' for a hollow casting. See Chapter 12 for slush casting principles and methods.

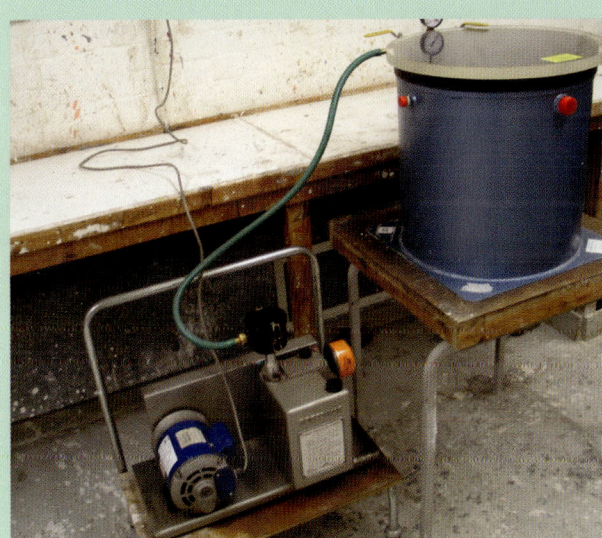

A degasser for removing air from mixes of Bioresin.

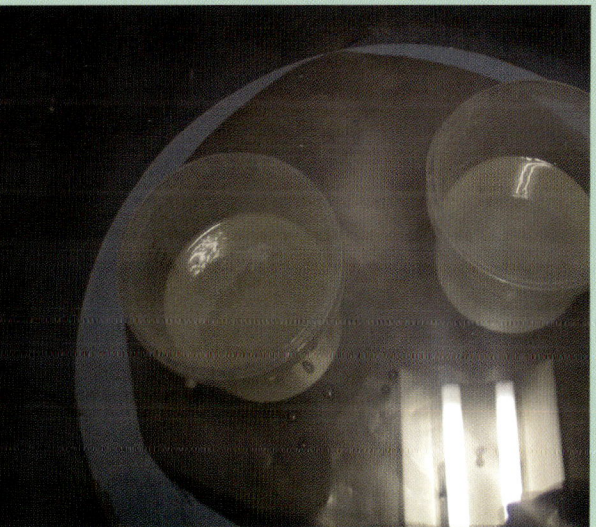

Cups of Bioresin are placed in the degasser and a vacuum is created.

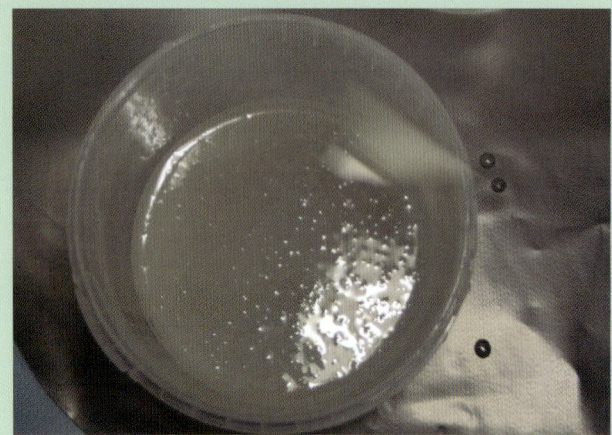

Bubbles appear and burst on the surface of the Bioresin as the vacuum is increased.

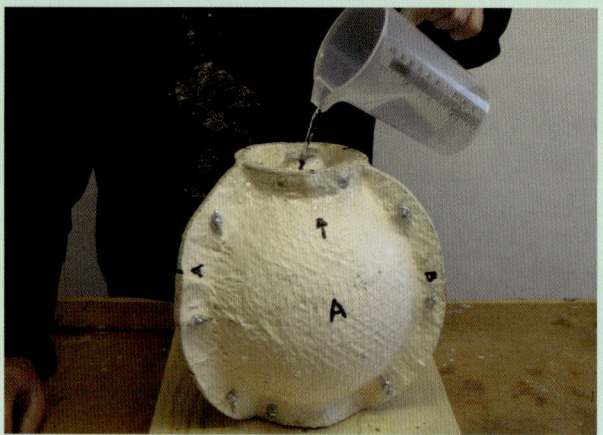

The degassed Bioresin is poured into the mould.

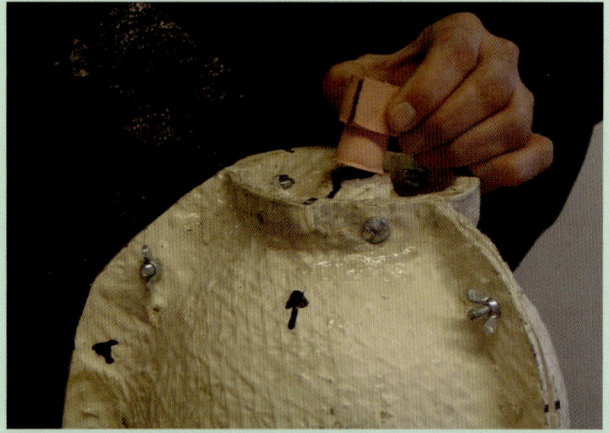

The mould is sealed with a silicone rubber bung.

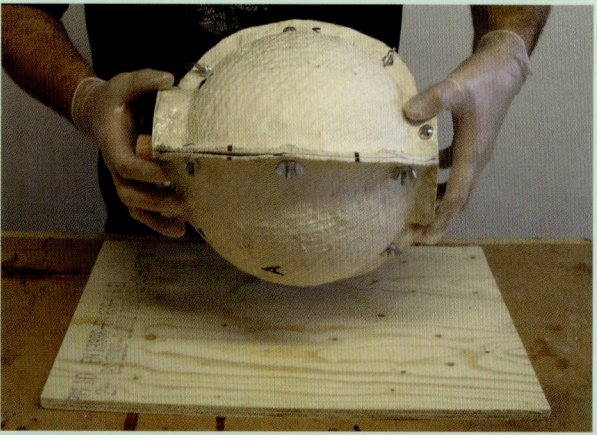

A rotation pattern is employed to slush cast the Bioresin within the mould.

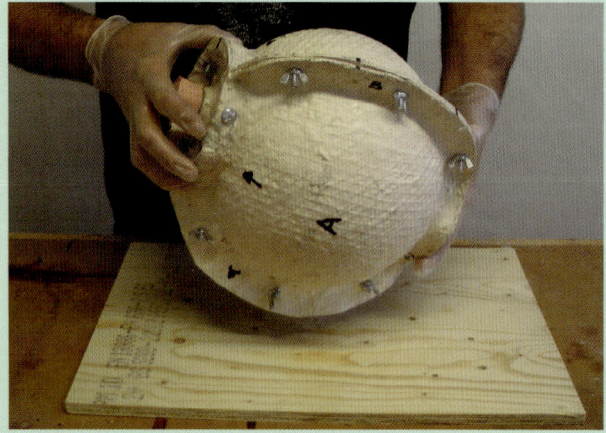

A rotation pattern is employed to slush cast the Bioresin within the mould.

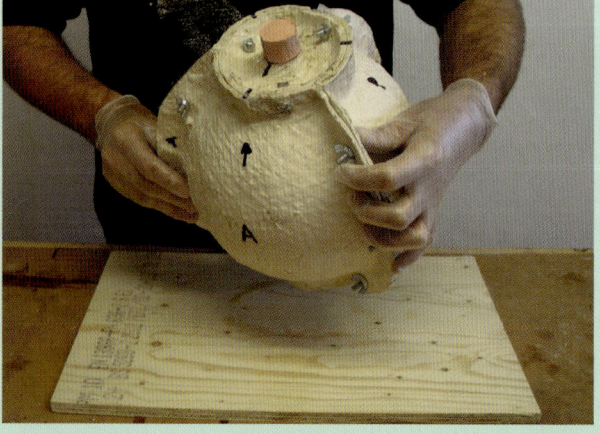

A rotation pattern is employed to slush cast the Bioresin within the mould.

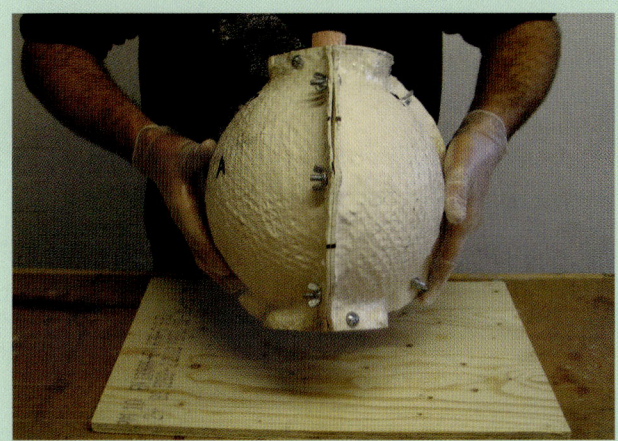

A rotation pattern is employed to slush cast the Bioresin within the mould.

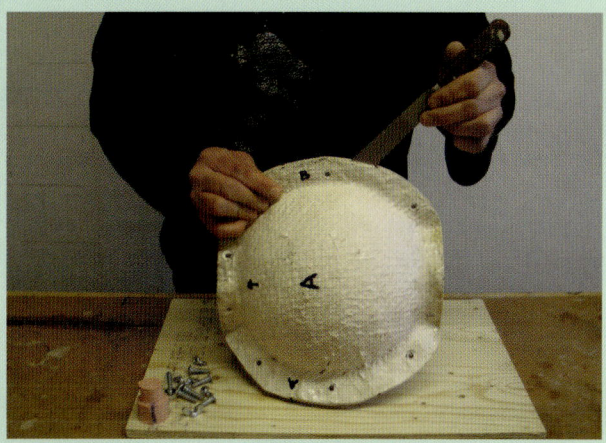

A knife is used to help the mould pieces apart once the Bioresin has set.

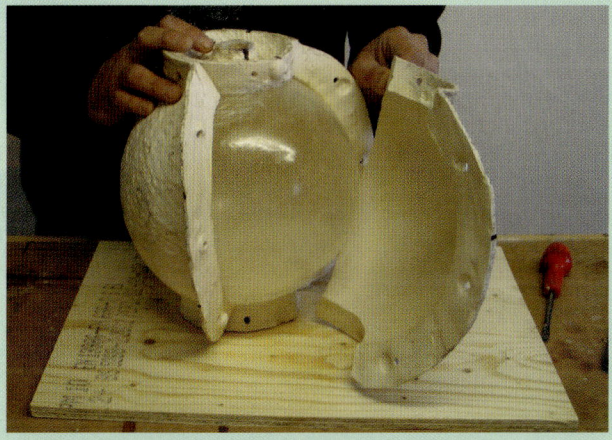

The mould pieces are removed carefully from the cast.

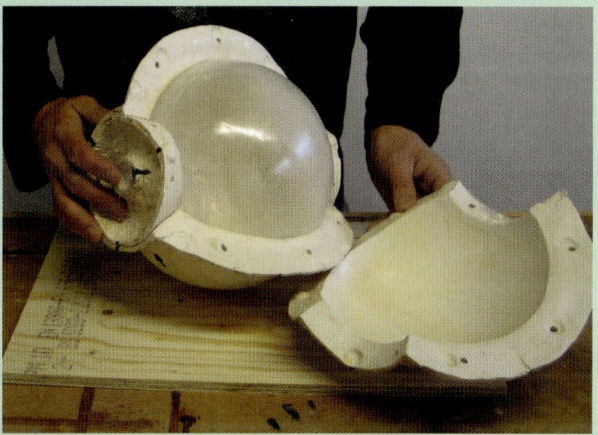

The mould pieces are removed carefully from the cast.

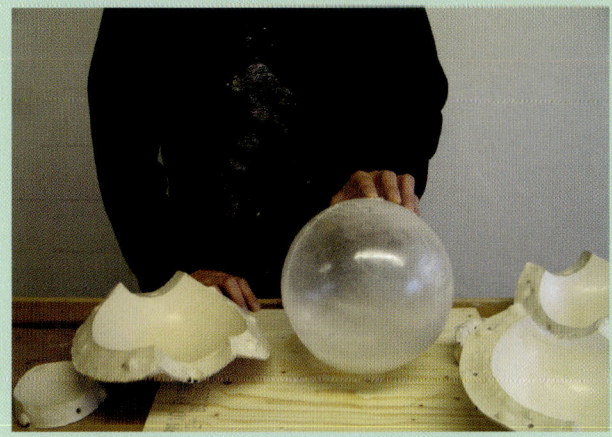

The mould pieces are removed carefully from the cast.

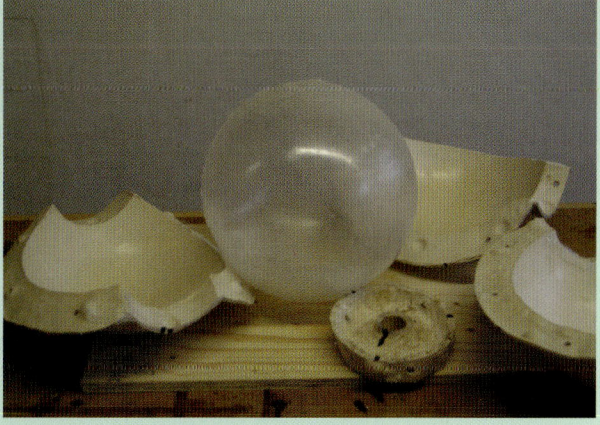

The mould pieces are removed carefully from the cast.

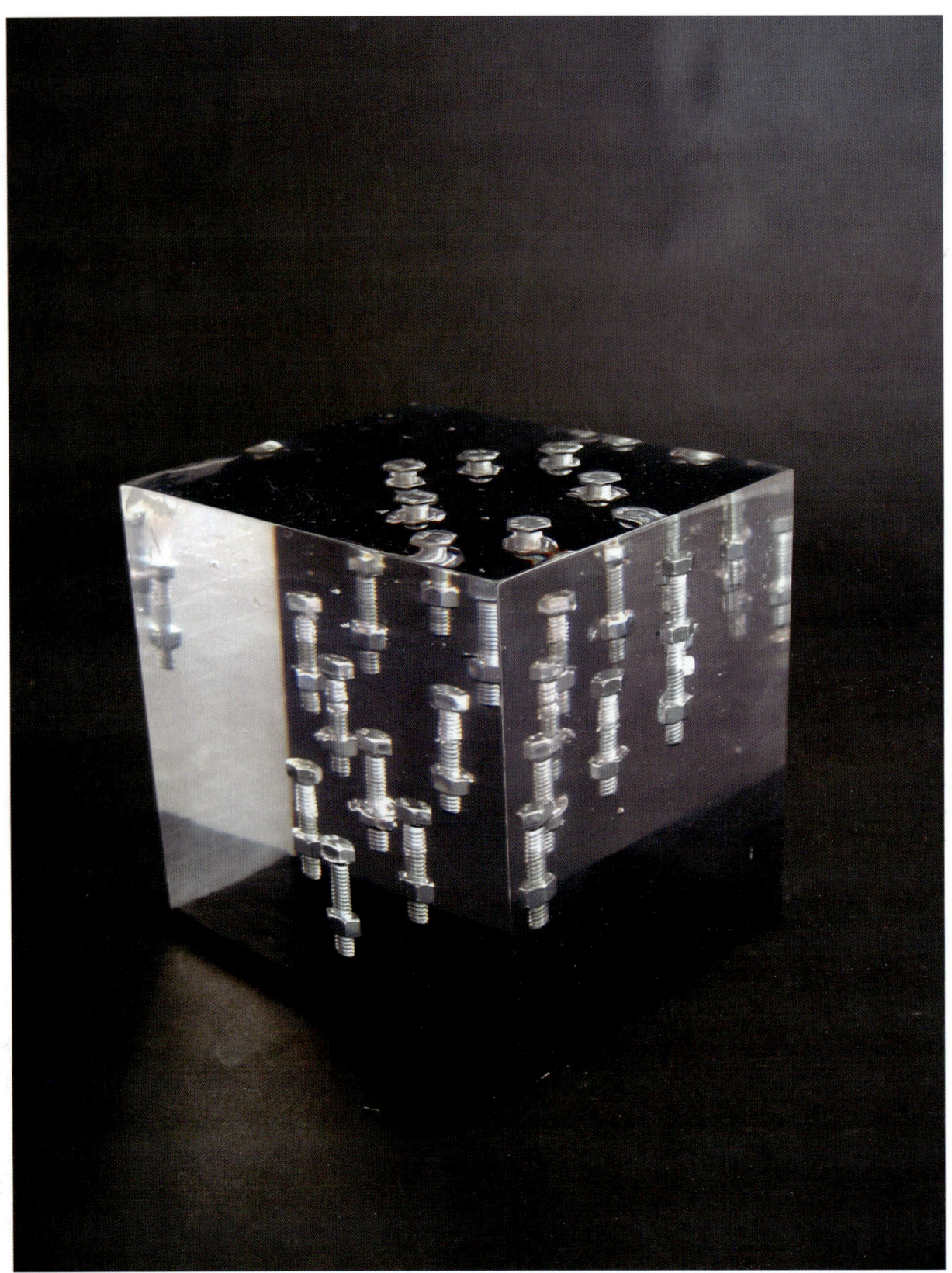

Embedded polyester resin cube (H: 115mm; W: 120mm; D: 95mm).

CHAPTER TEN

EMBEDDING IN CLEAR RESIN

There are number of resin systems that are capable of embedding objects within them in a liquid state and allowing them to set to a solid. The process is a relatively simple one but there are a number of potential difficulties that can produce unsatisfactory castings.

Virtually any mould type is suitable for the process, the only criteria being adequate access into the mould to embed the object and the use of appropriate release agent systems for the type of mould being used.

Another and very important consideration is the finishing time of the casting. Casting clear resins rarely produces a high-quality finish directly from the mould and usually requires substantial labour-intensive finishing processes to achieve good results.

Materials

Polyester

This traditional clear casting and embedding resin system has been around for years (see Chapter 11 in *Mouldmaking and Casting* for specification details).

- **Advantages**   Readily available and cheap.
- **Disadvantages**   Toxicity, size restriction, brittleness, high exotherm, long finishing times, shrinkage and slow setting times.

Polyurethane

Polyurethane is a slightly more versatile clear casting and embedding system. Some polyurethane systems provide a 'pre-coat resin' that is applied to the mould surface prior to the main casting and provides a practically finish-free cast surface. (See Chapter 8 for full specifications.)

- **Advantages**   A wide versatility of casting possibilities, high-impact resistance, the ability of some systems to produce a higher degree of finish straight from the mould, less toxicity and shrinkage than polyester systems, fast setting times, hollow slush casting possibilities.
- **Disadvantages**   More expensive.

Bioresin

Bioresin is a relatively new addition to the clear casting and embedding resin range. (See Chapter 9 for specifications.)

- **Advantages**   Very minimal toxicological concerns, low viscosity, high impact resistance, UV stability.
- **Disadvantages**   Availability, high cost, some restrictions on post-moulded surface finishing.

Pigments

Pigments can be added to all resins to produce varying degrees of translucent colour to castings.

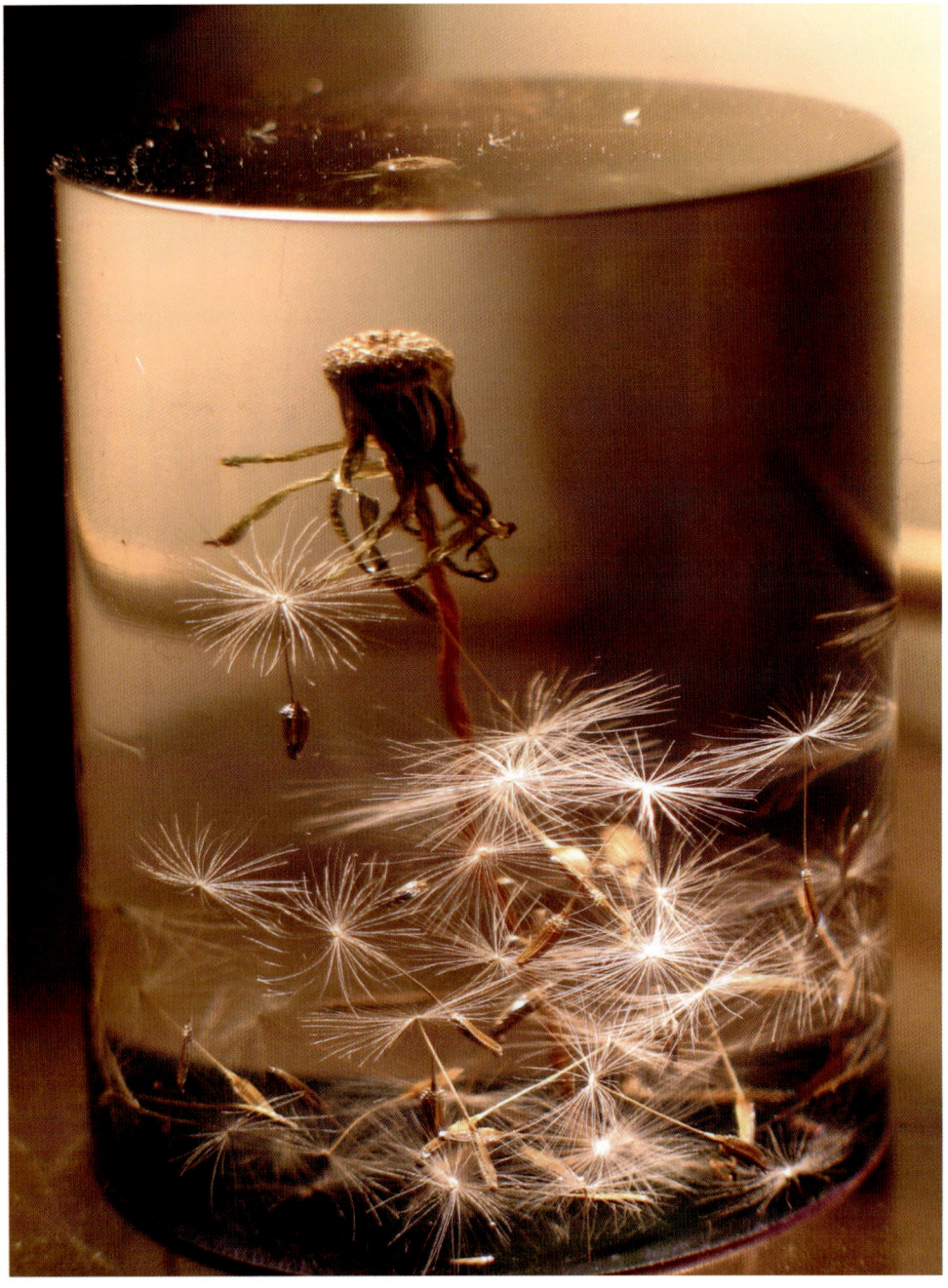

Embedded polyester resin.

Principal Techniques and Problems

The different systems described in the previous section are all capable of embedding objects in their liquid state to produce set clear blocks of resin encapsulating an object.

Some principal techniques are common to all three.

Setting or Packing Objects in Single Poured Castings

It is possible to set single objects or multiple objects in blocks of resin in one pouring operation.

114

- Will the object float or sink? An object that will float in the liquid resin will not fully embed, with some of the object potentially protruding from the surface of the casting. An object that will sink also may not embed properly, potentially protruding from the base of the casting. Pouring a thin layer of resin into the mould prior to the main pour can solve these problems.
- For objects that may float this initial thin layer should be allowed to set to a point where it is still tacky. The object can then be introduced onto the surface of the thin layer. The thin layer is then allowed to set fully, sticking the object to it. The main pour is then performed.
- Objects that may sink should be set upon a thin pre-poured layer that has been allowed to set, which will suspend it from the bottom of the casting when the main casting is poured.
- These two principles should be applied when setting multiple objects in layers throughout a block casting.
- Multiple objects can be embedded in high volumes, as far as the amount of resin required to hold the objects together will tolerate. This is a finite amount that will depend on the objects being embedded; in order to embed multiple objects there will need to be enough space between them for the resin to surround them and form a bond.

Suspending Objects

It is possible to suspend an object within a block of resin so that it appears to float in the set casting, or to suspend multiple objects set at different levels within a block.

- Will the object float or sink? This consideration is similar to that described in the previous section but on a larger scale.
- A layer of resin will need to be poured to the level at which the object is required to be set and either allowed to set sufficiently to stick down an object that will float or to suspend an object that will sink.
- The next layer is then poured over the first set layer, embedding the object at the level of the first layer.
- Multiple objects can continue to be set at different levels throughout a casting in the same way.
- Note: In order to achieve the illusion of suspension it is important to maintain equal quantities, catalytic

additions and setting temperatures for each layer of resin. If these amounts are not kept consistent and equal with each pour a line may be visible between layers. In practice this can be very difficult to achieve and, at certain angles of vision, lines between layers will inevitably be visible.
- It is important to cover the mould while layers are setting to stop dust settling on the surface. This should be done with a sheet of paper to allow heat generated from the exothermic reaction of the setting resin to escape.

Exotherm and Shrinkage

Different resins will have different levels of exotherm (heat generation) and shrinkage when setting. Exotherm and shrinkage have inherent fundamental effects on the success of castings. If exotherm is excessive, cracks and warping can occur. Equally, shrinkage between layers of resin can produce compromised surfaces to castings.

- Exotherm occurs when the catalytic reaction of the setting resin starts. The specifications of catalyst addition for the specific resin being used should be adhered to strictly. A general rule is that higher volumes of resin require less catalyst because they produce more exotherm, which in itself speeds up the setting of the resin.
- A block or thick layer of resin will require less catalyst because of the large amount of exotherm generated. Likewise a very small block or thin layer of resin may require more catalyst because of the lack of exotherm it generates. Only specified maximum and minimum amounts of catalyst addition should be used, however. Too little and castings may not set or will remain sticky when remoulded; too much and warping or cracking may occur.
- Moulds containing high-volume castings that are likely to generate large amounts of exotherm can be cooled while the reaction takes place. This can involve suspending the mould in water or air-cooling (with a domestic fan) until the exotherm subsides. If air-cooling be careful not to blow dust into the mould.
- Shrinkage of some resins, particularly between layers, can be a problem. Once a layer has been poured it will start to shrink during the setting time, sometimes

up to 5 per cent in total. If a layer is allowed to shrink away from the sides of a mould, it will produce a gap between the surface of the resin and the mould surface. The next layer poured will partially fill this gap, producing a fine layer of resin that seeps onto the surface of the first layer. When demoulded the excess seepage will need to be cut back to achieve a uniform surface on the casting.

■ Shrinkage cannot be avoided, but by pouring a second layer before the first has begun to shrink it can prevent or a least reduce seepage between layers.

■ Shrinkage should obviously be taken into consideration when considering the final dimensions of any clear resin casting.

Air and Moisture Entrapment

Air or moisture entrapment in a casting can occur in two ways. First, by the physical action of mixing and pouring the liquid resin into the mould and, second, by air or moisture being trapped in the object to be embedded and its subsequent release when the resin is poured over.

BUBBLES

Air entrapment from pouring will produce tiny bubbles in the body of the casting. These will naturally gravitate towards the surface of the casting and pop. This usually happens before it sets, thus not creating a problem. If small bubbles cannot escape, however, they will be trapped in the set resin. There are several methods for preventing this.

■ One way to reduce air entrapment is with a degasser. A degasser is a chamber that when pressurized creates a vacuum, forcing the air out. Filled moulds are placed in the chamber, pressurized and then depressurized to release the air from the mould. In the same way mixed batches of resin can be degassed before pouring into a mould.

■ The traditional methods of tapping the mould to bring up trapped air can be employed to some success.

■ Bubbles can also sometimes be teased up physically, by pushing them out with a pointed cane while the resin is still in a very liquid form. Do not do this when the resin starts to gel.

■ Low-viscosity resins can reduce air entrapment to a great extent.

SILVERING

When porous and therefore air-filled objects are embedded it can cause 'silvering'. This is the appearance that the object has turned silver and is caused by an air bubbles tightly covering the form of the object and reflecting light back through the casting. Moisture can also cause silvering. This can be quite attractive, but in practice is difficult to control.

■ Moisture entrapment can cause setting failure or result in surface tackiness of the castings. Objects to be embedded should therefore be thoroughly dry. A mixture of silica gel and table salt can be used to dehydrate organic objects prior to embedding.

■ Porous objects can be pre-dipped in resin before embedding to reduce silvering.

■ Pre-dipping and allowing the resin covering an object to set before embedding can also reduce silvering.

■ Non-porous objects will sometimes trap air as they are embedded and cause silvering. The pre-dipping methods described can help to reduce the likelihood of this.

■ Degassing can be employed to reduce silvering.

■ Low-viscosity resins can reduce silvering.

Size and Volume

The size and volume of castings are important factors to consider when casting and embedding with clear resins.

■ There will be size restrictions on maximum volumes of specific resins that can be cast successfully in one pour. The amount of exotherm a particular resin produces during setting will have a direct result on the maximum size of casting that can be created. The larger the volume of resin poured, the larger the amount of exotherm created when the resin sets. When allowed to exceed appropriate limits, exotherm can potentially warp and crack a casting.

■ Adhere to maximum size and volume specifications according to the manufacturer's instructions.

- Adhere to catalytic addition specifications. There will be a range, given as a percentage, of catalyst addition which should be used with the resin. Generally speaking low percentages are for larger volumes and vice versa.
- To create large castings over the specified maximum volumes of resin pour batches of resin as separate layers.
- Hollow castings of very large size can be produced with fast-setting resins using slush casting methods (*see* Chapters 9 and 12).

Moulds

Virtually any mould type is suitable for use with clear resins, the only criteria being adequate access into the mould to embed the object and use of the appropriate release agent systems for the type of mould being used. However, the surface finish of castings can vary greatly depending on mould type.

- Non-porous highly polished moulds such as glass, plastic or metal will produce castings that need very little surface treatment after demoulding, as will commercially available plastic moulds with very highly polished surfaces.
- Porous moulds such as plaster or Jesmonite and pre-fabricated wooden moulds can produce castings with a frosted appearance that will need to be cut and polished back to clarity. These types of moulds will need a series of applications of release agents appropriate to the resin being used (usually the 'combination' system described in Chapter 3 of *Mouldmaking and Casting*).
- Non-porous pre-fabricated moulds of metal, glass and plastic will help to minimize demould surface work to castings.

Trimming and Cutting Back

Once the cast has been demoulded any excess cast and seam lines (flashing) can be trimmed back.

1. Initially the extremities of any excess can be broken off carefully by hand or with a pair of pliers, but be careful not to break off too much. Then a

number of tools can be employed depending on the size of the cast and how much resin is to be removed (chisels, hacksaw blades, surforms, rasps and so on).
2. The initial trim should not be taken right back to the surface of the cast and should only be used to remove bulk excess.
3. Smaller and smaller tools should be used as you work closer to the cast surface.
4. Final cutting back to the surface of the cast should be achieved with increasingly finer grades of abrasive paper. Fine files including needle files can be useful for getting into difficult-to-access area of the cast (a fine brass or wire brush is also useful to clear clogged files).
5. Once excess flashing has been taken back to the surface final cutting back and/or polishing of the entire cast surface can be tackled.

Surface Finishing and Polishing

Clear casting resins will usually come out of moulds with a matt surface finish. To obtain the full effect of glass clear surfaces, castings will need to be cut back with abrasive papers and then polished.

CUTTING BACK WITH ABRASIVES

Wet-and-dry abrasive papers should be used to cut back cast surfaces and these should be used wet to avoid dust (which can be carcinogenic) and prevent paper from clogging. The papers are graded by the number of particles of grit per square inch of paper and a variety of grades should be used in sequence from coarse to fine. Depending on the job 100–800/1200 grit paper (100 being coarsest and 1200 finest) should be used in succession.

1. Standard sheets of paper should be cut up into pieces that are suitable for the size of the job and laid out in sequence.
2. Initially use the coarsest grade just to take off the worst of any seam lines and to give the whole surface 'bite'. Where there are smooth areas or areas that have little detail coarse papers should be used sparingly and it may be possible to start with a finer paper.

3. As the paper becomes clogged either rinse it under a running tap or in large bowl of water.

4. Once the whole surface has been cut back with one grit size wash the cast, change your rinsing water and move on to the next grit size. In this way the whole surface of the cast is cut back progressively using finer and finer paper, with scratches created by the coarser grades being removed by the finer grades.

5. Clear resins will remain cloudy even after the finest grade and will not become clear until polished unless pre-coated.

6. It is difficult to gauge whether casts have been thoroughly abraded enough until after polishing, but thorough and methodical abrading will produce better polished results. If polished results are not good it will usually mean returning to abrasives before polishing again.

POLISHING

Polishing can be done either mechanically or by hand using specifically designed polishing compounds. Polishing compounds come as either a hard waxy block or as a cream and are applied to the cast surface with a lint-free cloth or a mechanically spun polishing mop.

Cloth polishing mops for block compounds and sponge mops for cream compounds can be mounted, using the correct arbour, to a standard electric drill with variable speed control, or can be mounted in a dedicated polishing machine. Polishing machines are bench-mounted so this will restrict the size of the cast that can be polished mechanically. Electric drills can be used freehand or bench-mounted securely using a clamping system specific to the machine you are using. Care should be taken when using electric drills for polishing as they have no guards; goggles should always be worn whichever system of polishing is being used.

Polishing compounds are a very fine level of abrasive and come in grades of coarseness like the abrasive papers. They should be used in sequence from coarse to fine methodically over the entire surface of the cast. Compounds usually come in two or three grades and castings should be washed between grades of polish.

If after polishing through the grades of compound the levels of gloss, brightness or clarity required have not been achieved it may be necessary to return to the abrasive papers to cut back more and then to repolish.

TIPS

■ When cutting back any casting with abrasives the object is to remove the surface layer of scratches or frosting to allow for polishing back to clarity. On castings with very fine detail this process may remove some detail; there is no way round this so the balance of how far to cut back without losing too much should be considered carefully.

■ Castings with areas of high and low detail will produce areas that are clearer on the high points.

■ Different levels of clarity can be achieved by controlling the amounts of cutting back and polishing.

■ Toothpaste is an ultra fine abrasive polish and can be a good final polishing compound.

■ Note that some clear casting resins are not suitable for cutting back and polishing, so always check the specification of the resin used.

PROJECT

Specification

A polyester clear resin cube with eleven M6 × 30mm hex nuts and bolts set at ten 10mm layers throughout the casting. From a pre-fabricated glass mould. Size 115mm (H) × 120mm (W) × 95mm (D).

Time Required

Allowing for setting times this project can be carried out over approximately 5 hours.

Materials

MOULD

■ Pieces of 10mm plate glass × 5;
■ methylated spirit;
■ silicone sealant (building-grade mastic sealer);
■ 25mm masking tape;
■ acrylic sheet 115 × 120 × 4mm; and
■ a small amount of clay.

CAST

■ Polyester clear casting resin (supplied by Alec Tiranti Ltd)
■ polyester resin catalyst;
■ polyester resin pigment (to colour base of casting);
■ wax spray release agent; and
■ M6 × 30mm hex nuts and bolts × 11

Tools

■ A permanent marker;
■ mixing beakers;
■ wooden spatulas/sticks;
■ a spirit level;
■ digital scales;
■ a craft knife;
■ a thin-bladed filling knife or palette knife;
■ tweezers;
■ disposable rubber gloves; and
■ a sheet of A4 paper.

Method

SET-UP AND PREPARATION

As with any project, careful preparation before the start of the job is crucial. Knowing the material quantities and tools needed, undertaking repairs to the original and setting-up the working area will all help to complete the job accurately and efficiently. (Tip: make sure you have enough materials to complete the job before you start. Running out of material halfway through the job is at least a waste of time and, at worst, a loss of previously executed work.)

1. Ensure all work surfaces are clean, clear and well lit. This may sound obvious, but preparation of this sort prior to casting will help greatly in production. This is particularly important when casting with clear resin as airborne dust can contaminate castings.

PRE-FABRICATED MOULD

The pre-fabricated material of the mould in this case is five pre-cut pieces of 10mm thick glass. Ideally have the edges of each piece of glass ground to ensure a square edge.

If using glass or plastic to prefabricate a mould to cast resin the pieces need to be thick enough to maintain their shape while the exothermic heat is generated by the setting resin. If it is too thin it will shatter or warp with the heat generated by the chemical reaction of the setting resin.

1. Clean all pieces with methylated spirit to ensure a good bond with the silicone sealer.
2. Dispense a small bead of silicone sealer along one edge of one of the side pieces of glass.
3. Butt this up against the next side piece at right angles and secure temporarily with masking tape.
4. Continue with the next two sides to create the four sides of the mould.
5. Apply a bead of sealer along the top edge of the glass box.
6. Adhere the fifth piece of glass to create the base of the mould.
7. Secure the base to the walls with masking tape and turn the whole mould over onto a modelling board.
8. Apply a bead of silicone sealer to the outside joins of the mould to ensure it is watertight.
9. Allow the sealer to set fully.

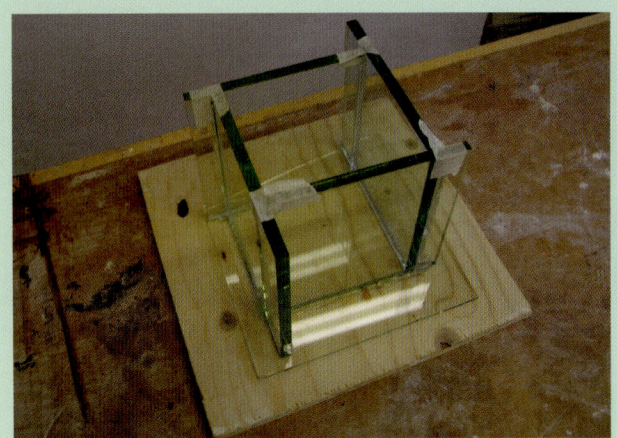

A prefabricated mould is created using plate glass.

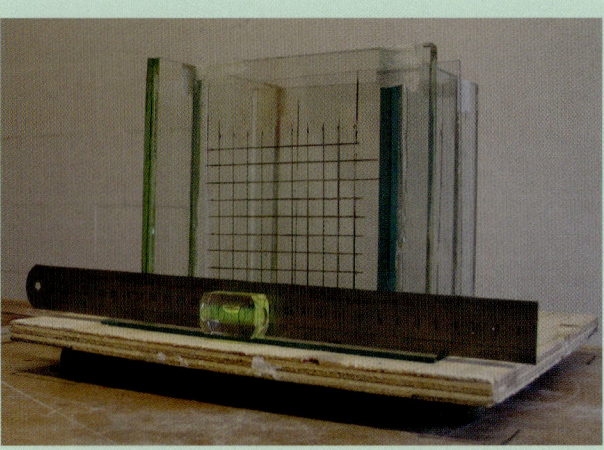

The mould is levelled and a grid drawn up on a separate piece of acrylic sheet, which is placed on the outside of the mould.

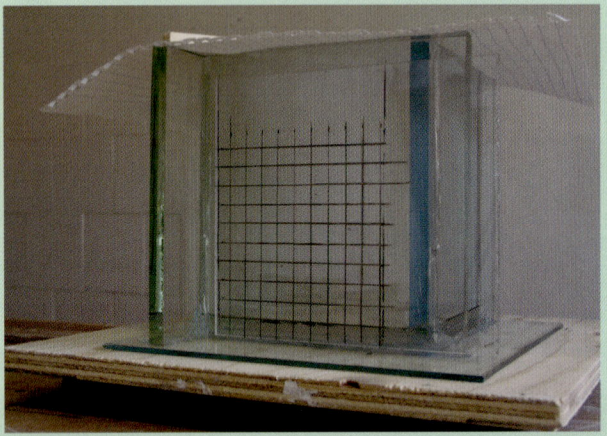

The first layer of resin is poured to a level on the grid and allowed to set.

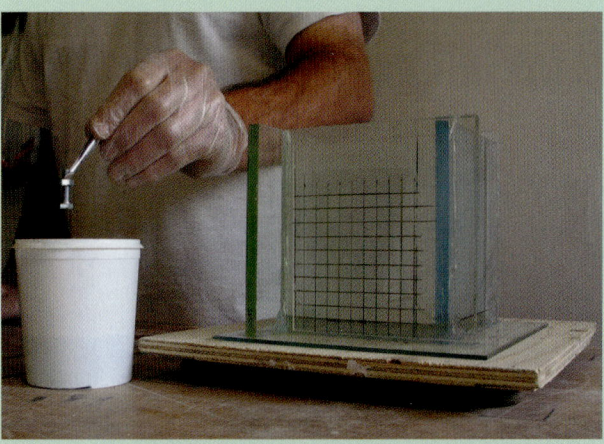

The first object is dipped in resin.

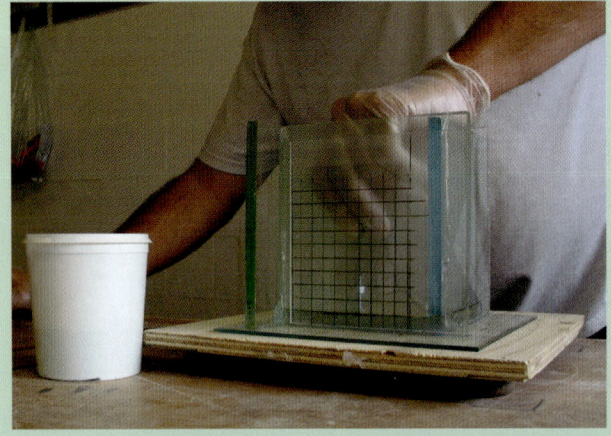

The first object is placed in position on the set first layer.

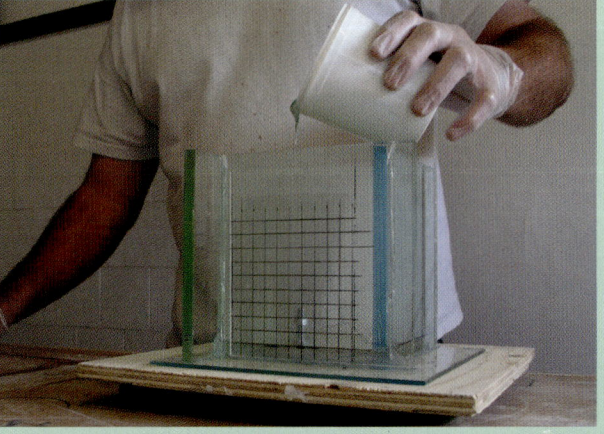

The second layer of resin is poured.

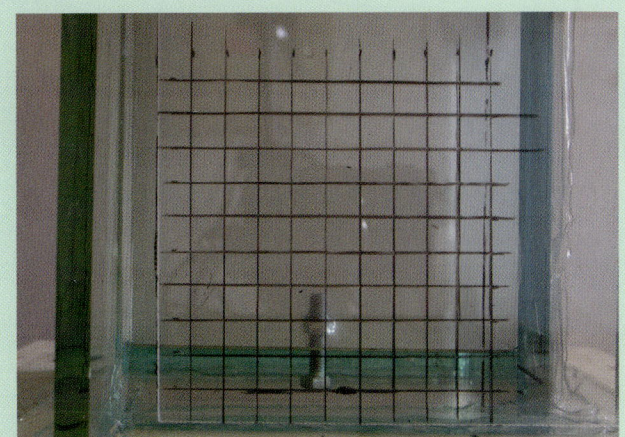

The object embedded in the second layer of resin.

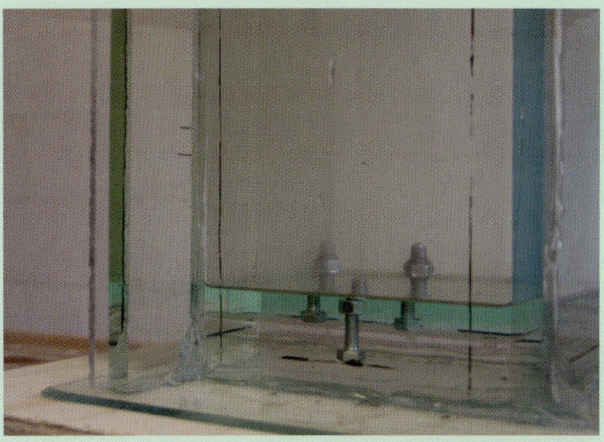

The second-layer objects are placed and a third resin layer is poured.

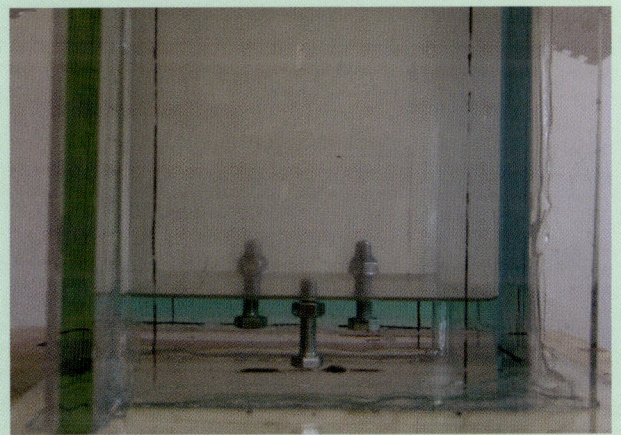

The second-layer objects are placed and a third resin layer is poured.

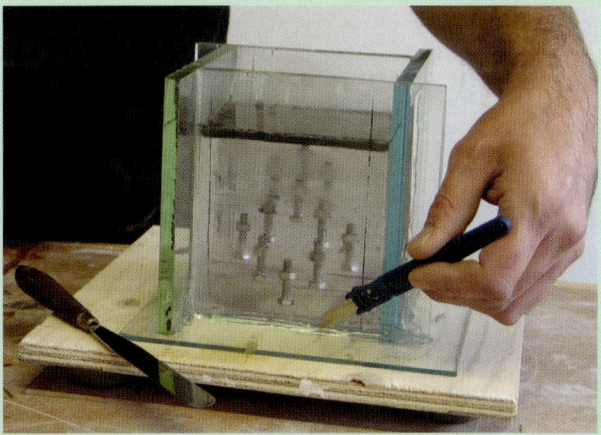

Silicone sealer is cut on the prefabricated mould seams.

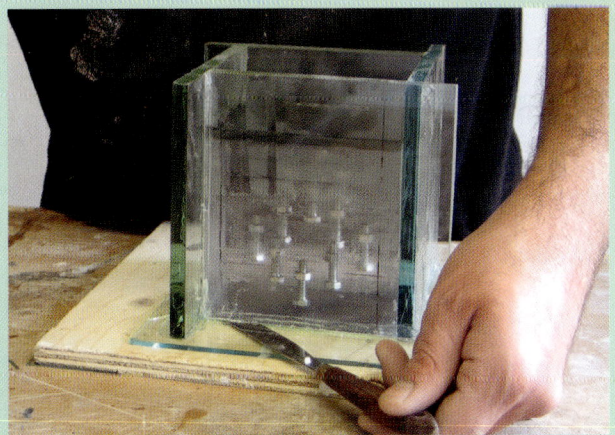

Silicone sealer is cut between the mould and the base.

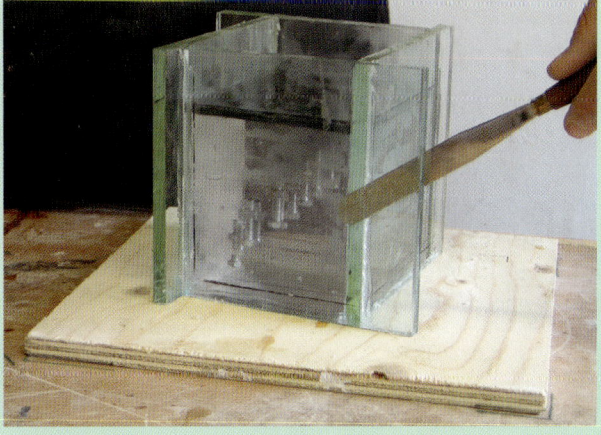

A palette knife is introduced between the cast and the mould wall.

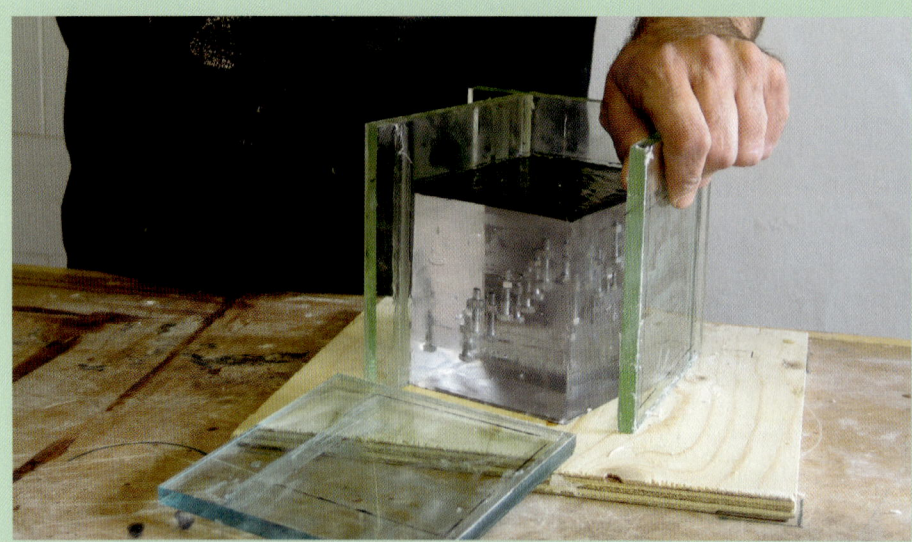

The mould walls are pulled way.

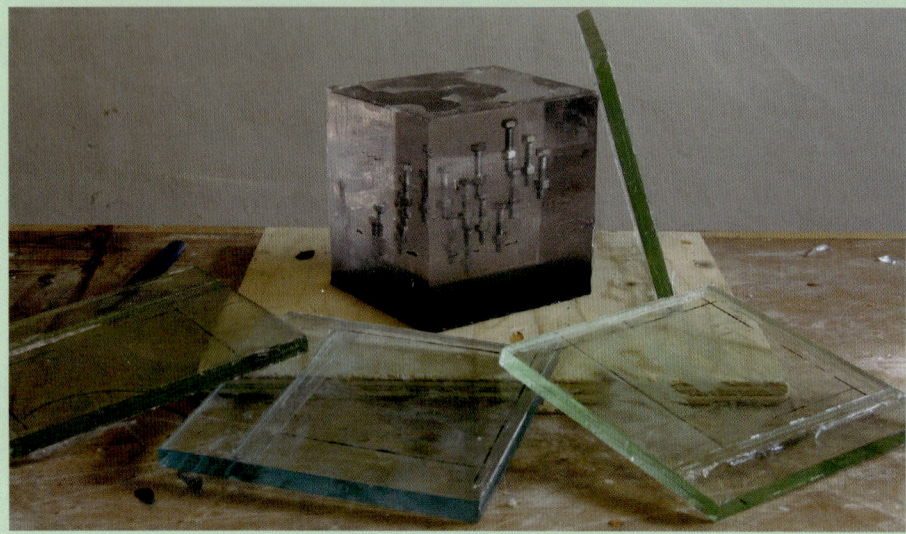

The cast demoulded.

10. With the acrylic sheet draw up a 10mm grid reference with the permanent marker. This will be placed on the outside of the mould as a guide when setting objects to be embedded.

11. When the silicone sealer has set fully use a craft knife to trim any excess silicone from the inside corners of the mould that may have been squeezed out when joining the mould pieces.

CASTING

1. To determine the amount of resin to dispense for each layer of the casting, make a mark on the outside of the mould to the thickness of the layer and fill to that level with water. Pour the water into a clear mixing beaker and mark the level of the water. Dry the cup thoroughly and dispense resin to the level marked on the beaker. Weigh this amount of resin to determine how much resin to dispense for each layer of the casting. Thoroughly dry the mould.

2. Set the modelling board with the mould on it on top of four small balls of clay.

3. Use a spirit level to create an even level by pushing the modeling board down into the clay balls. Do this in two directions to ensure the whole mould is level. It may seem obvious but the resin is a liquid

that will only settle to one level when poured into a mould.

4. Apply spray wax release agent.

5. Because the nuts and bolts to be embedded within the casting have a wide stable head the cast is created upside down within the mould. The first layer is clear and the first nut and bolt is set in the second layer.

6. Dispense and catalyze the predetermined amount of resin for the first layer and pour from one point into the mould in an even and steady flow. Pouring from one point will reduce air entrapment.

7. Cover the mould with a sheet of paper to stop dust settling on the cast surface. Dust between layers of the casting will show up as lines.

8. Allow this layer to set to a point where it is firm enough to support the first nut and bolt. Do not allow it to set so much that it starts to shrink away from the sides of the mould, however. Check and if necessary test the setting times and shrinkage of the resin being used.

9. Set the acrylic sheet with the grid against the outside surface of the front of the mould. The grid is to guide the setting of the bolts evenly throughout the casting.

10. Dispense and catalyze the resin for the second layer. Before pouring, use the tweezers to dip the first nut and bolt into the resin and set at a pre-determined point on the first layer of resin. Use the grid to set it in the desired position.

11. Pour the second layer of resin. The grid can be used to ensure the layer is equal to the first.

12. Repeat this process for the whole casting, ensuring the amounts of resin, levels, catalyst additions and setting times of each layer are equal.

13. Note: To cast a block of resin this big with one object embedded in the middle, the midway point of the casting may still need to be built up in layers to reduce exotherm and the chance of warping and cracking. Once the midway point is reached, the object can then be set and the second half of the casting built up in layers in the same way as the first.

14. Once all the layers have been poured and the objects embedded a last thin layer of pigmented resin can be poured to create a contrasting col-oured base to the casting. Ensure that the pig-mented layer is poured before the last clear layer starts to shrink back.

15. Allow to set fully, cool and cure before demoulding.

DEMOULDING

1. With a craft knife cut through the silicone seal between the mould walls. Be careful not to cut through to the cast.

2. Carefully lever the walls away from the casting, if necessary using a thin-bladed filling knife or palette knife between the cast and the mould wall. Be careful not to scratch the surface of the cast; if you do, scratches can be rubbed back with abrasives and repolished to clarity.

3. Once demoulded the casting can be washed and dried to remove any wax residue from the release agent before cutting back and polishing.

FINISHING

1. Follow the steps described earlier in this chapter for trimming and cutting back and surface finishing and polishing as necessary.

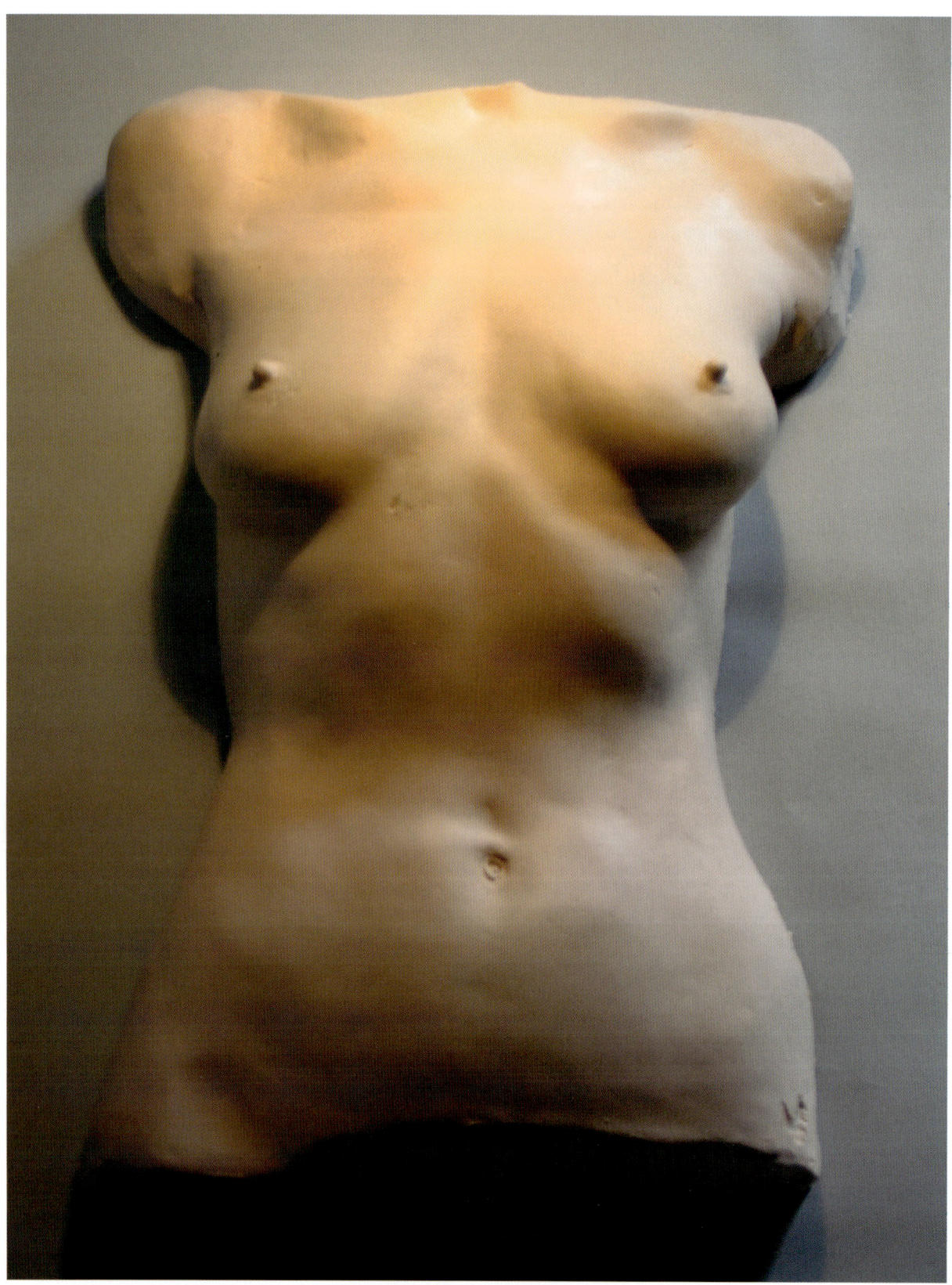

Silicone rubber life cast.

CHAPTER ELEVEN

SILICONE RUBBER

Although primarily used as a mouldmaking material, silicone rubber can be an attractive and versatile casting material in its own right. Silicone rubber can be pigmented to many colour specifications and is available in a multitude of different hardnesses, ranging from a very firm or hard rubber to an extremely soft jelly consistency.

Materials

Silicone rubber has a unique tactile quality and can have all sorts of casting applications, from creating skin-like prosthetics, for example, to producing a glass silicone that will shatter just like glass. The properties of silicone rubber include:

- extreme flexibility;
- excellent stretch capabilities;
- being available with a clear or semi-translucent appearance;
- ability to take surface colouring and/or integral pigmentation;
- being food safe; and
- suitability for solid or hollow casting.

To achieve interesting and attractive castings using silicone rubbers it is important to understand the capabilities and specifications of the wide range of silicone rubbers available.

Shore Hardness

'Shore hardness' is a scale used to determine the hardness of a material. Shore hardness is measured with a gauge that

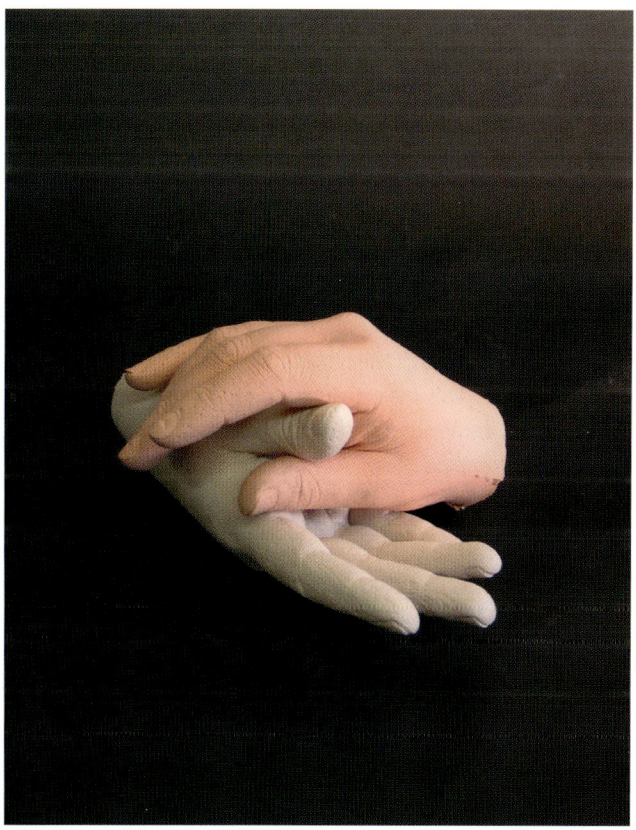

A silicone rubber life cast.

incorporates a sprung pin which is placed on a material and indented until it stops, producing a Shore hardness reading on a scale.

The hardness of a casting material will clearly have a tactile bearing on the physical properties of a casting. The Shore hardness of a rubber can have a significant correlation to its flexibility, stretch capability and tear strength.

SHORE HARDNESS SCALES

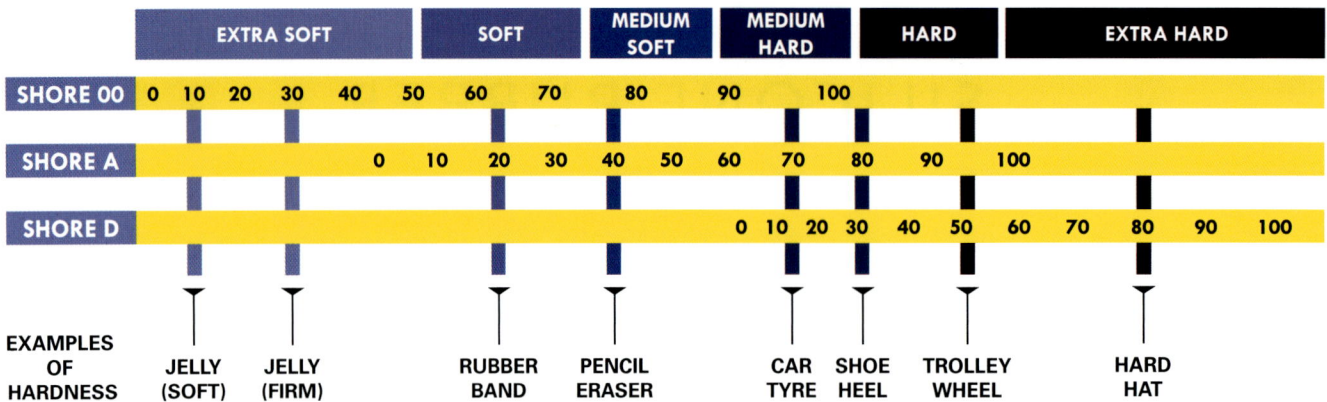

The Shore scale can be measured from 0–100 on three different sub-scales that overlap at certain points. These are:

- **Shore 00**   A scale of rubbers and gels that are extra soft.
- **Shore A**   A scale of rubbers that range from very soft and flexible to medium and moderately flexible to hard with very little flexibility.
- **Shore D**   This measures the hardness of hard rubbers, semi-rigid plastics and hard plastics.

Silicone Rubber Categories

Silicone rubbers fall into two basic categories: tin or condensation cure and platinum or addition cure.

- **Tin cure**   These are two-part component silicones that cure at room temperature and set to a flexible rubber. They have variable degrees of flexibility and tear strength and lie within the Shore A hardness range.
- **Platinum cure**   These are two-part component silicone rubbers that are characterized by their very high tear strength and flexibility. These silicones are available at hardnesses in the very soft Shore 00 scale.

Additions

- **Catalysts and accelerators/boosters**   All silicone rubbers require a catalyst to enable them to set from a liquid to a solid. Some silicone systems have a range of different catalysts and accelerators/boosters than can be used to adjust working, setting and demoulding times. Beware of working within pot life times when using extra-fast catalysts. Additions are added to the silicone as a ratio or percentage by weight and accurate digital scales should be used to dispense the correct amounts. Some silicone rubbers use a two-part system, which should be used according to specification.
- **Thixotropic additive**   This is added to silicones at variable percentages to create variable degrees of viscosity when applying them.
- **Silicone oil**   This is used to thin silicone to make it more fluid on application or pouring. It can also be used to lower the Shore hardness of some silicones, being added at amounts of up to 20 per cent by weight. Beware that excessive amounts may leach from set silicone.
- **Primers**   These promote the adhesion of silicone rubbers to other materials.
- **Deadeners/tactile mutators**   These materials are used in the production of prosthetics. They are added by volume of silicone and can vary the feel of the casting to make them more skin-like. They can be used to produce softer silicones with variable degrees

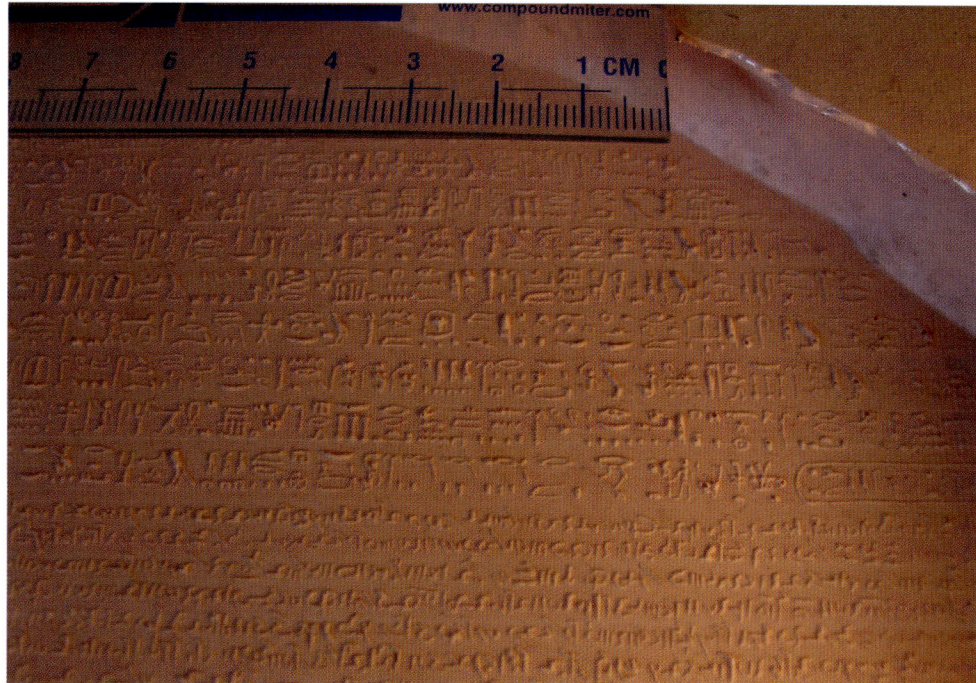

Detail of a silicone rubber 'Rosetta stone' mould.

of flex-and-return properties. Surface tackiness can also be adjusted to produce self-sticking silicone castings (useful for sticking prosthetic skin sections to the body). Gels can be produced that have an almost liquid quality to them, and can be layered with other grades of silicone to produce very effective prosthetic body parts.

Pigmentation and Colouring

There are specific pigments available for use with all silicone rubbers. Added to the rubber in its liquid state they will provide integral or surface colour to castings.

- Translucent or clear silicones, usually found in the platinum cure range, will take pigmentation more readily.
- Pre-mixed skin tone pigments are available in fair, mid and dark tones to produce background skin colour.
- Post-cure surface colours can be painted onto set silicone to produce infinitely variable colour combinations to castings. The range is suitable for platinum cure silicones.
- It is possible to colour some silicones with oil-based artists' paints. Testing should be conducted.

- Luminescent additive can be added to silicone castings and will give off a glow when exposed to UV light source.

Moulds and Release Agents

Silicone can be cast in most mould types, although various specifications and compatibility issues should be considered.

- Silicone moulds need to be primed with non-silicone-based wax release agents. The spray systems are convenient and effective.
- Some platinum cure silicones are only compatible with platinum cure moulds and vice versa.
- Porous moulds should be sealed and primed with non-silicone-based wax release agent before use.
- Multiple-piece moulds can sometimes be made with less undercutting consideration if casting in silicone. A silicone cast often has enough flexibility to bend past a certain amount of undercutting in a mould.
- Consideration should be given to adequate tear strength of castings taken from deeply undercut moulds.

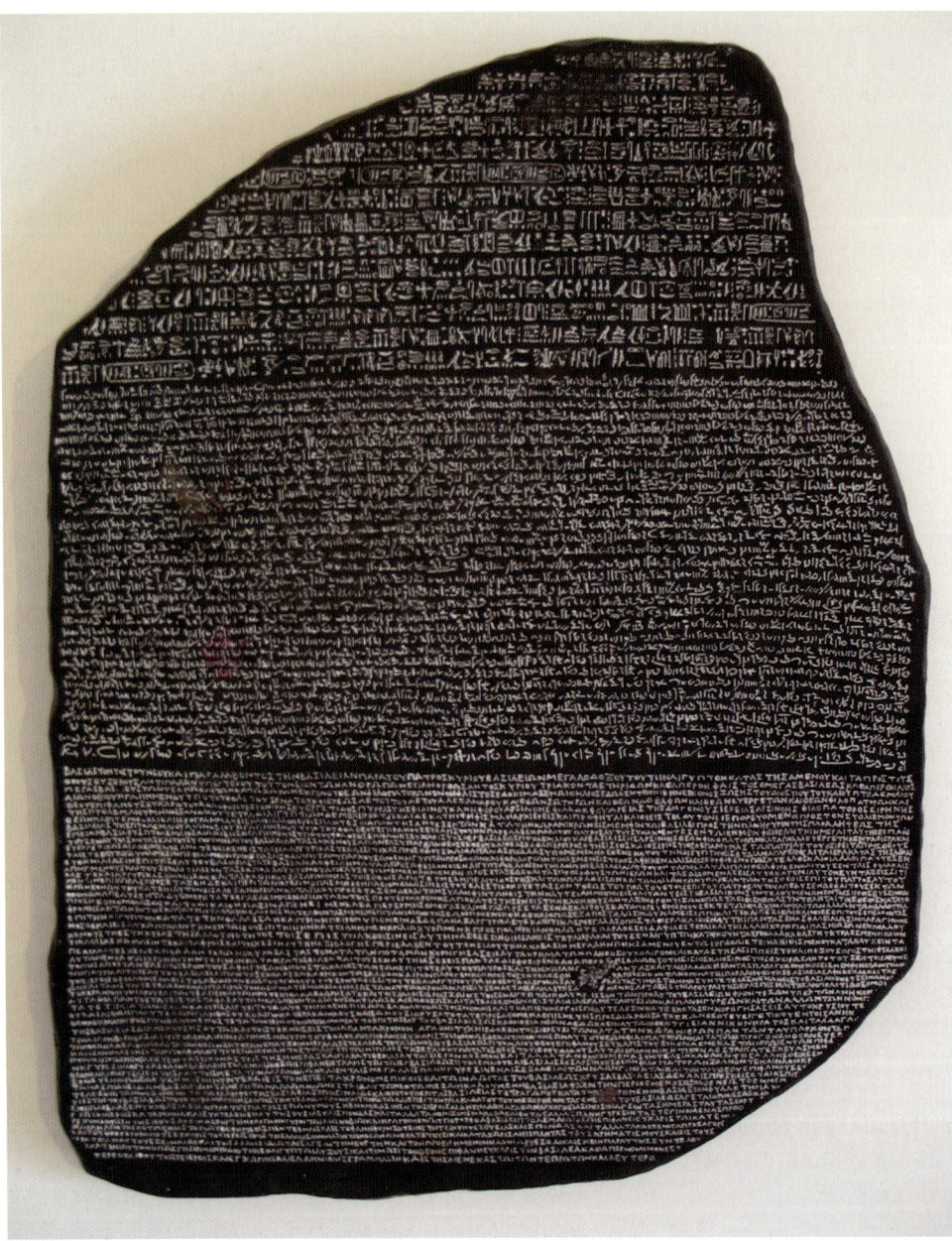

Rosetta stone copy, in pigmented polyester resin (H: 330mm).

Principal Techniques

Surface Coating

A decorative surface coat of silicone can be applied to a mould surface prior to filling or laminating with either neat silicone or other material. There are several reasons for using this method:

- To ensure maximum pick-up of detail from the mould surface lamination can be employed by applying a surface coat of silicone to the mould surface before backing up with thixotropic addition silicone.
- Decorative pigments can be applied via a surface coat and then backed up with neat silicone or other casting material as a method of being economical with the decorative pigment.

■ Platinum cure very soft Shore 00 silicones are relatively expensive. If very low shore hardness is just required on the surface of the cast an adequate layer of Shore 00 silicone can be built up initially and then it can be backed up with an economy silicone.

■ Prosthetic castings can benefit from having a neat surface layer of unpigmented translucent silicone applied before a pigmented layer.

■ Multiple-coloured layers can be built up to create depths of colour and different colours can be blended together on the surface of a mould. This can be particularly useful when trying to achieve realistic skin tones.

Solid and Backfilled Casting

Silicone rubber can simply be poured into a mould, with the appropriate release agents applied, to produce a solid casting. Alternatively surface-layered decorative silicones can be back-filled with other materials for economy.

■ When pouring silicone into a mould, pour from one spot and allow it to rise and fill the mould, pushing out any air entrapment as it does.

■ When pouring solid castings it may be necessary to degas some silicone rubbers to reduce air entrapment within the cast (*see* Chapter 9 for degassing information).

■ In theory any material could be used to backfill a previously applied decorative surface silicone. However, most materials will not adhere to silicone rubbers except other silicone rubbers. Where this is a problem a way of fixing the backfill material mechanically to the surface should be considered. The use of registration buttons or blocks is one way of anchoring a backfilling material to the surface silicone (*see* Project section).

■ If a hard backfilling material like plaster is to be used, consideration should be given to the flexibility and surface tactility of the finished casting. It may be necessary to lay up enough surface silicone to maintain surface tactility.

■ Expanding polyurethane foam rubbers can make an excellent lightweight backfilling material. Backfilling with expanding flexible foams can maintain cast flexibility. (*See* Project section and Chapter 8 for specifications.)

Laminated and Hollow Casting

Silicone rubbers can be cast hollow as well as poured solid. This is achieved by laminating or 'laying up' silicone in layers to an adequate thickness. This method can be useful for economy of casting material, when the desired surface can be achieved with minimal casting material and then backed up with a more economical reinforcing material.

■ After an application of decorative surface silicone, castings can be backed up with an economy thixotropic addition silicone for durability. If tactility is important it will be necessary to apply enough surface silicone to achieve the desired surface look and feel before backing up. Ensure the backfill silicone is compatible with the surface silicone used.

■ The thickness of the casting will depend on the specifications of the silicone being used and the specifications of the casting required.

■ Hessian jute or cotton scrim can be used to reinforce surface layer silicone. Ensure a good layer of silicone is applied underneath as well as on top of reinforcing scrims. Push out any air between layers to avoid air pockets within the casting.

■ It is possible to slush cast silicone. Silicones will need to be thinned to make them fluid and have fast setting times and a high tear strength. They may also need to be applied in several layers (*see* Chapter 12).

PROJECT

Specification

A laminated life-size torso, backfilled with flexible polyurethane foam. From a one-piece silicone rubber and Jesmonite case mould (*see* Chapter 5).

Time Required

The project was carried out over three and a half hours, not including setting times.

Materials

- T20 tin cured silicone rubber (supplied by Alec Tiranti Ltd);
- Mid-tone silicone flesh pigment (supplied by Notcutt Ltd);
- Silastic 3498 tin-cured silicone rubber (supplied by Notcutt Ltd);
- silicone oil;
- hessian jute scrim;
- self-skinning flexible polyurethane foam (supplied by Alec Tiranti Ltd);
- non-silicone spray wax release agent; and
- pre-made silicone registration buttons or blocks.

Tools

- Dispensing and mixing containers;
- wooden spatulas;
- laminating brushes;
- scissors;
- clamps; and
- disposable gloves.

Method

SET-UP AND PREPARATION

As with any project, careful preparation before the start of the job is crucial. Knowing the material quantities and tools needed, undertaking repairs to the original and setting-up the working area will all help to complete the job accurately and efficiently. (Tip: make sure you have enough materials to complete the job before you start. Running out of material halfway through the job is at least a waste of time and, at worst, a loss of previously executed work.)

1. Ensure all work surfaces are clean, clear and well lit. This may sound obvious, but preparation of this sort prior to casting will help greatly in production. It easy to miss parts of the mould surface when in a badly lit work space!
2. Clean and dry the mould surfaces.
3. Support the mould on a work surface. Make sure the mould is secure and will not move about during casting. Ensure there is adequate access all around the mould, particularly that you can reach all areas of the mould surface.
4. Apply spray wax release agent in three layers, allowing it to dry between layers.

APPLICATION OF THE SURFACE COAT

1. Dispense a batch of silicone large enough to cover the whole mould surface.
2. Add silicone mid-tone skin pigment to the batch. Pigments are usually very concentrated, so add just a little at a time until the desired colour has been achieved. Mix very thoroughly, scraping the sides and the bottom of the container to ensure thorough pigment dispersion. To properly ensure thorough mixing decant the mix into a new container and mix again.
3. Add the required amount of catalyst and mix thoroughly.
4. With a soft brush paint the mixture onto the mould surface to a depth of 1–2mm. Without the addition of thixotropic additive this is about the maximum thickness of coverage that can be achieved.
5. Allow surface coat to set fully.
6. Moulds with fine surface detail can benefit from having several applications of surface coat in this way to ensure good detail pick-up. Allow the silicone to set between layers.

LAMINATED LAYERS

The surface layer on its own will not be adequate and this needs to be built up to an appropriate thickness with a further layer of silicone. In this case this layer does not necessarily have to be pigmented.

1. Mix batches of thixotropic addition silicone and build up the layer in the mould to an appropriate thickness. In this case the thickness only needs to be approximately 10mm as the cast is going to be backfilled with flexible foam.

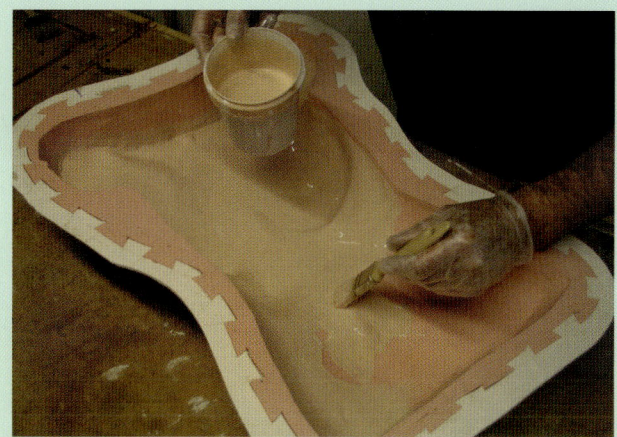

A thin coat of pigmented silicone is applied to pick up the mould detail.

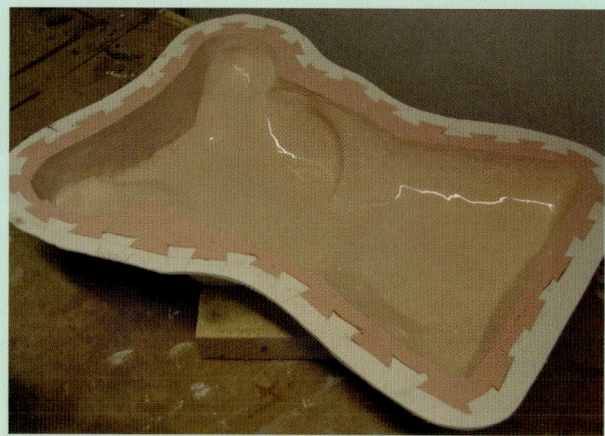

The detail coat is allowed to set fully.

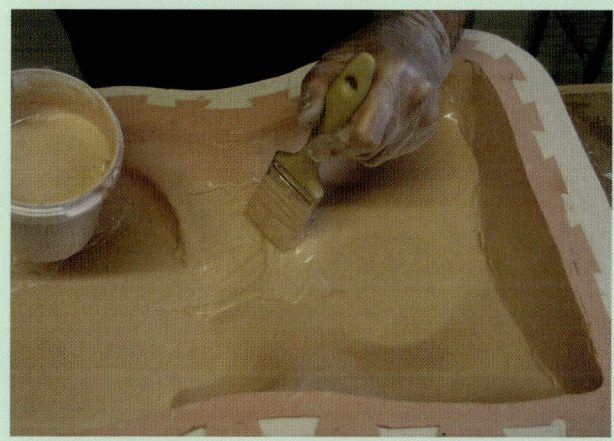

A second thin coat of silicone is applied to reinforce the detail cost.

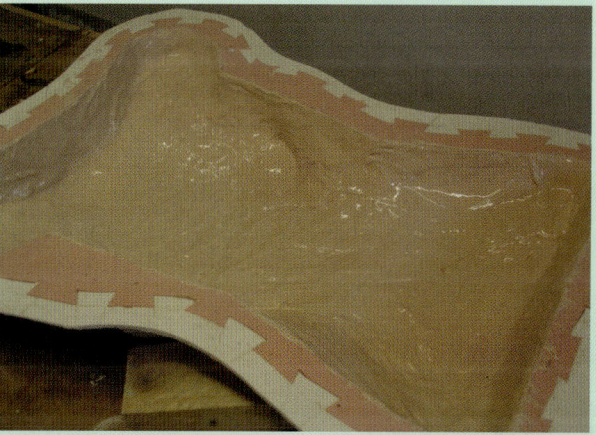

An additional pigmented thixotropic coat of silicone is applied to build up the thickness.

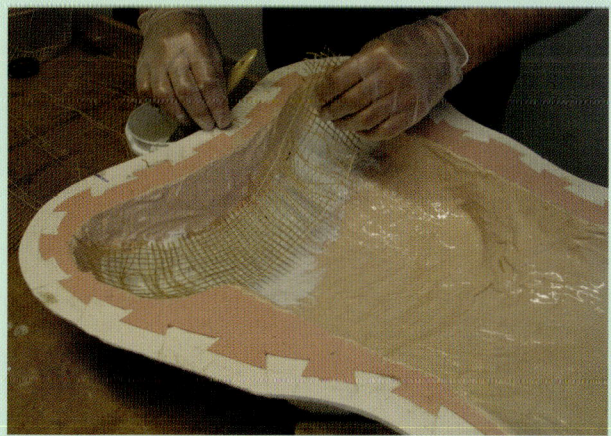

Hessian scrim and unpigmented silicone is applied to build the thickness further.

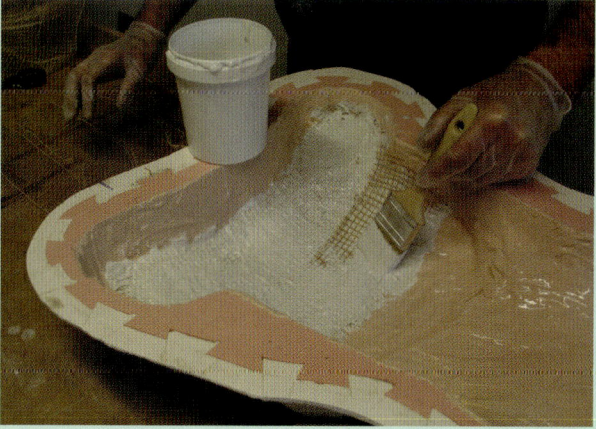

The hessian is saturated with silicone.

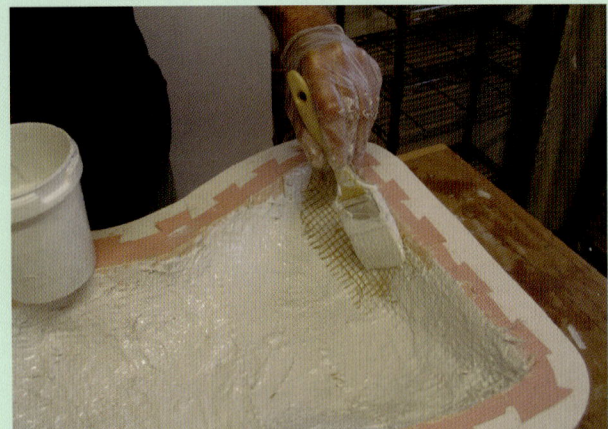

Extra hessian can be used on areas that need more reinforcement.

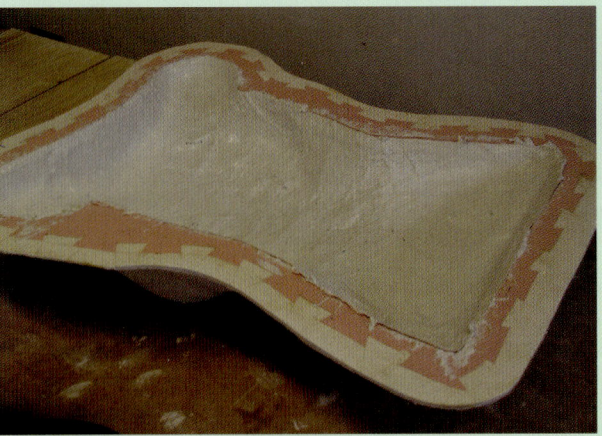

Once the desired thickness has been achieved the cast is allowed to set fully.

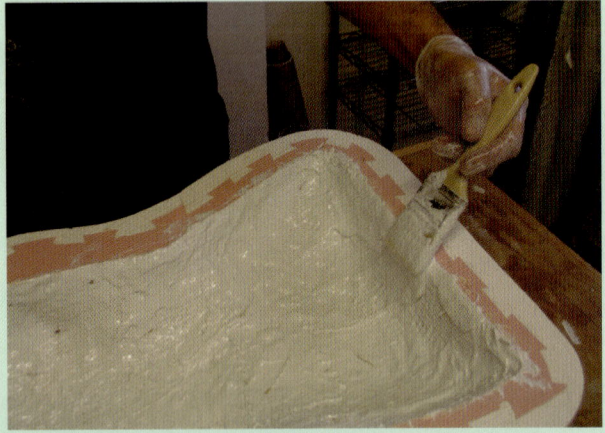

Additional thickness can be built up on cast edges for strength.

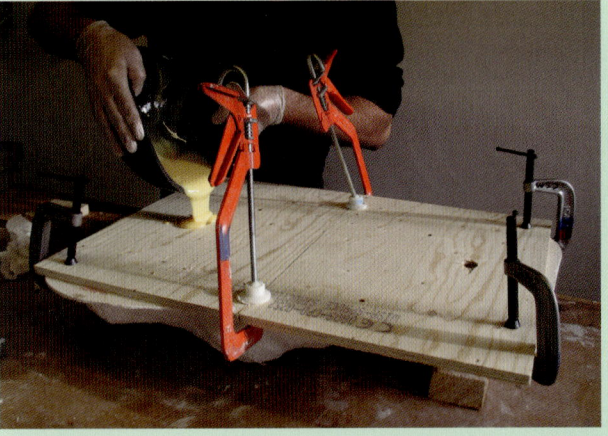

A top board with vent holes is clamped over the mould opening and polyurethane foam is poured into the mould.

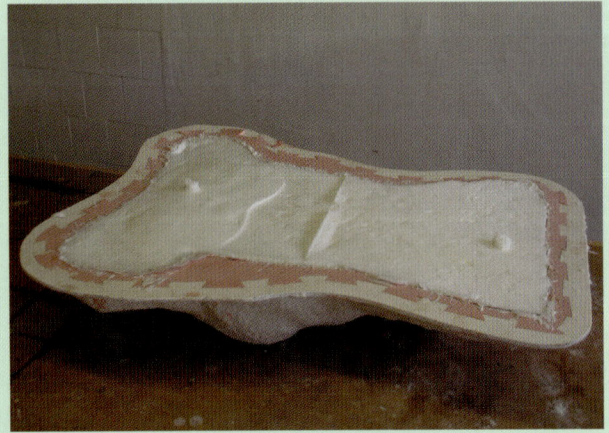

The top board is removed to reveal the foam backfilled cast.

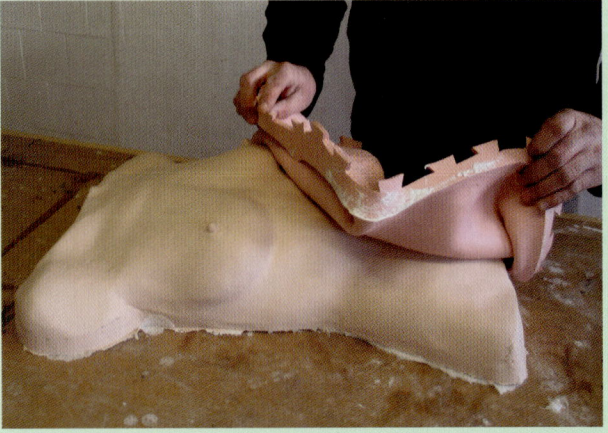

The cast is demoulded from the silicone mould.

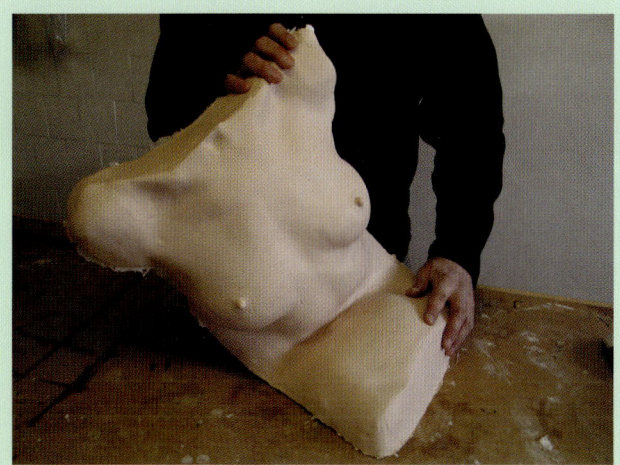

Showing the flexibility of the cast.

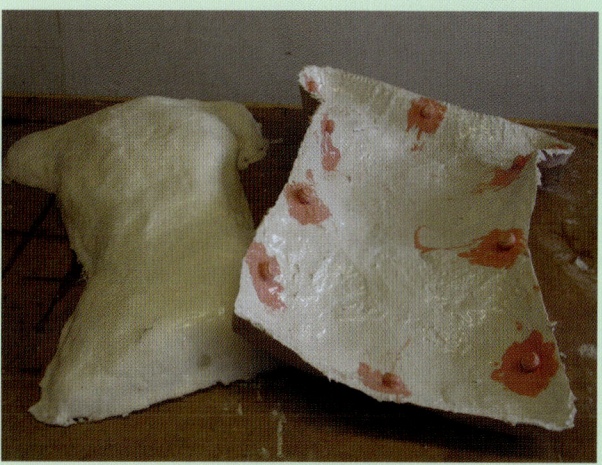

The silicone buttons inside the cast locate into holes in the foam backfiller.

2. Paint the thixotropic mix onto the surface of the pre-applied surface coat.
3. Hessian scrim can be used to increase durability and/or economize on the amount of silicone required to achieve cast thickness. Use non-thixotropic silicone when using the scrim to allow it to saturate into the fibres.
4. Once the full thickness of the cast has been achieved, before it sets, apply registration buttons or blocks to the unset surface. These will locate and secure the silicone cast into the foam backfill.
5. Allow all layers to set fully.

BACKFILLING

For this project a flexible polyurethane foam is used to maintain the flexibility of the finished casting.

1. Trim any excess cast silicone protruding from the mould opening.
2. Secure a board, with two 20mm holes drilled at either end, to cover the mould opening. One hole will be the pouring hole for the foam rubber, the other will allow the air to escape as it expands.
3. Pour the required amount of foam to expand and fill the casting and allow to set fully (*see* Chapter 8 for specifications).

DEMOULDING

1. The same demoulding procedures should be employed as for other casting materials from different moulds.

2. Sometimes castings may need quite a bit of effort to peel them away from the mould surface; however, silicone rubber castings can have the advantage of flexibility to aid demoulding.
3. Ensure that full material specifications for silicones have been achieved before demoulding. Thin castings may tear if not allowed to fully cure, for example.

TRIMMING AND FINISHING

1. Once demoulded, silicone castings should be trimmed. The initial trimming can be done with a Stanley knife, craft knife or nail scissors, and secondary or fine trimming can be done with a scalpel or razor blade.
2. For the final trim flexible silicone castings can be stretched a little, with tweezers if necessary, cut, and then allowed to spring back to achieve a close-to-the-surface cut.
3. Once trimming has taken place, the cast can be surface painted using post-cure silicone colour systems. These can be airbrushed as well.
4. Talcum powder can be applied to sticky cast surfaces to remove tackiness.
5. Silicone polish can be used to achieve shiny cast surfaces. This is available from sex/fetish shops!
6. Silicone castings can be cleaned with mild washing-up detergent.

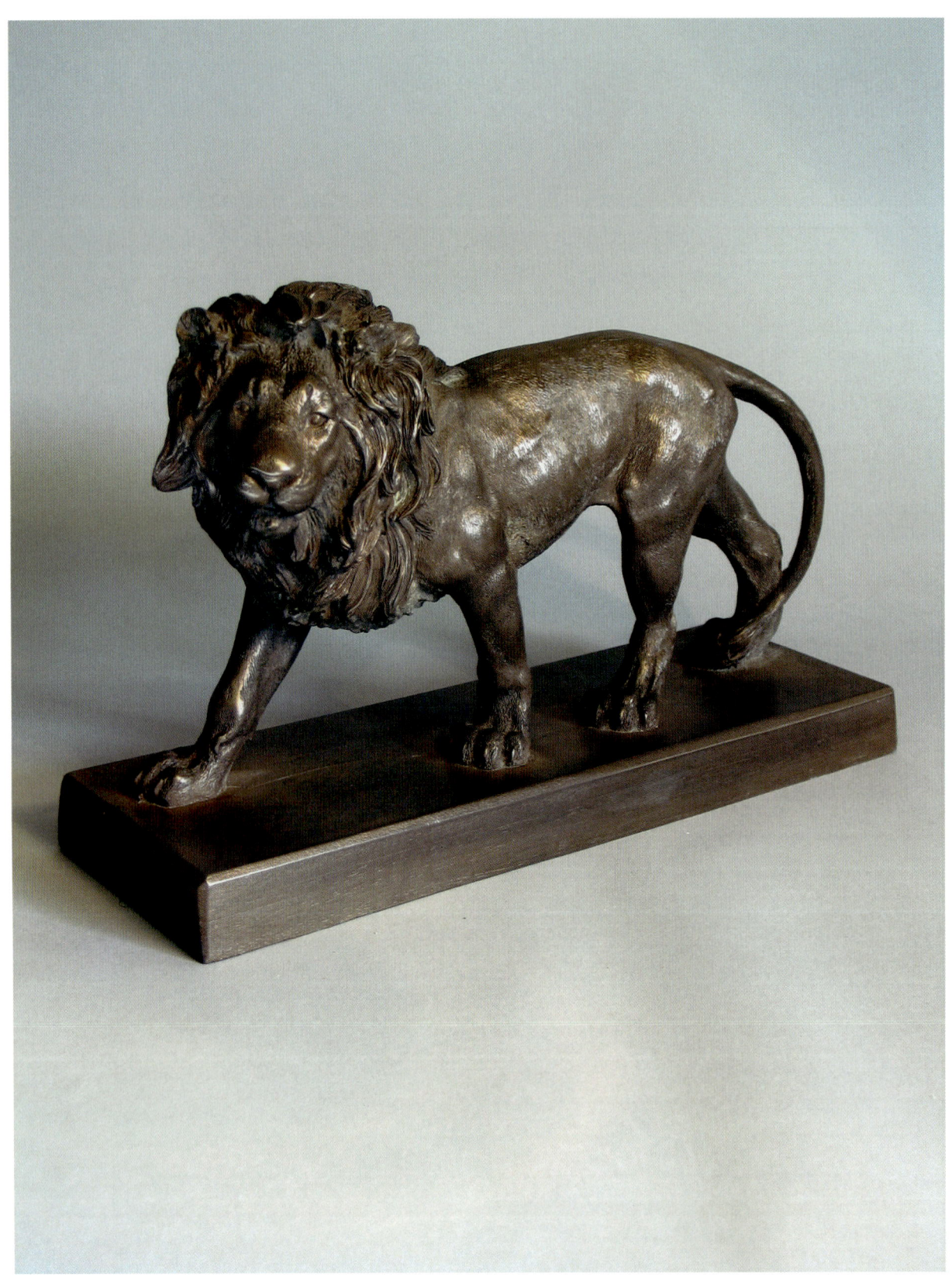

'Slush cast' bronze-filled polyester resin cast (L: 320mm; W: 110mm; H: 200mm).

CHAPTER TWELVE

SLUSH CASTING

Slush casting can be a useful method of producing a hollow cast from a mould. The process involves introducing an amount of the chosen casting material into the mould and 'slushing' it around and over the mould surface to pick up the detail. This method can be used with any mould but is particularly useful on multiple-piece moulds that would otherwise require an application of casting material separately on each piece and would then have to be joined. It can also be used on completely sealed moulds with just a pouring hole for access.

Slush casting can be employed to produce either hollow casts or decorative gel-coated casts that are then backfilled to produce a solid casting. Slush casting methods can provide time-saving benefits as the application of gel coats can be achieved very quickly, rather than having to apply them slowly by brush.

Materials

Slush casting methods can use many different casting materials that are fluid enough to move around the inside of a mould to coat it.

- **Plaster**   Casting plasters of any sort can be used. Alpha plasters of high strength are preferable due to their strength even in thin sections, but any casting plaster built up to an appropriate thickness could be used.
- **Resins**   Many different types of resin systems are suitable for slush casting. Resin systems with fast setting times and low viscosities are preferable.
- **Gel coat resins**   Metal/stone-filled gel coat resins can be employed as long as they are fluid enough to move around the mould surface. In order to make metal-filled gel coats fluid enough it may be necessary to reduce the amount of filler addition. This can compromise the surface quality of castings, however, so batch testing prior to slush casting is essential.
- **Clear resins**   Bioresin and fast-cast polyurethane resins are suitable.
- **Wax**   Most types of casting wax are suitable.
- **Silicone rubber**   This can be used for slush casting but the consistency should be very liquid and it should be employed with fast catalysts.

Principal Casting Techniques

The principal technique could not be simpler: a fluid casting material is poured into the mould and the mould is rotated until the material coats the surface of the mould and sets. It is important to cover the mould surface as evenly as possible and several factors should to be taken into consideration to ensure good results.

Mould type

OPEN MOULDS
Open moulds – those with a wide opening that constitutes the base of the casting – are probably the easiest moulds to use, as it is possible to look into the mould as it is slushed to ensure an even coat has been applied.

1.   Fill the mould to approximately a third full with casting material.

2. Rotate and tilt the mould to move material over the surface.

3. Ensure that the casting material covers right up to the lip of the mould. A brush can be used to get the casting material accurately up to the lip of the mould.

4. Maintain the rotating and tilting action until the casting material has set and stopped flowing.

SEALED MOULDS

Sealed moulds have only a pouring hole or very narrow point of access into the mould. This type of mould can be more difficult to slush as there is no visual confirmation that the casting material has completely covered the mould surface.

■ Consider your intended rotation pattern. When filling sealed moulds it is important to cover the mould surface evenly. A pre-planned rotational action that ensures casting material covers the inside of the mould, repeated consistently until the casting material has set, will assist this process.

■ A pouring hole plug for the mould should be constructed to plug the pouring hole and contain the casting material as it is setting. This can be constructed in the mouldmaking process or as a separate addition afterwards.

■ Fill the mould to approximately a third full with casting material.

■ Employ the rotation pattern repeatedly until the casting material has set and stopped flowing.

■ You will need to remove the mould plug and tip out the casting material a little to gauge whether it has set or not.

Mould Size

Size is a factor of obvious importance as the mould needs to be moved and rotated constantly until the casting material has set. Practical restrictions on the size of mould for employing slush casting methods is really dependent on the physical capabilities of the mouldmaker and the setting time of the casting material used. Remember that the mould will need to be kept moving until the casting material has set.

Machine 'roto-dye' systems can be employed to perform the rotational action of slush casting mechanically. It is possible to construct your own roto-dye machine, although time will need to be spent in research and testing.

Casting Material Consistency

This is important on a number of levels and will vary according to the casting material being used. Material consistency needs to have free-flowing capabilities, be thin enough to pick up mould detail and have maximum strength when set. These three factors may not be compatible, however. For instance, reducing the viscosity of some plasters to maintain free-flow may affect the physical properties of the set casting, and creating free-flowing metal/stone-filled resin gel coats may compromise the decorative surface finish. Clearly, some compromises may be necessary.

To maintain strength but accomplish a good pick up of detail a coat as thick as possible but thin enough to flow freely should be applied and then backed up with subsequently thicker coats. For metal/stone-filled gel coat resins as much filler as possible should be employed in the first coat while retaining a free-flowing consistency. This may require testing it in small amounts on the mould surface before casting to ensure an adequate surface finish. The dilemma is that a material that is too thick will not pick up detail and may contain air bubbles when set, and an appropriate consistency can only really be determined by testing.

Hollow Castings

It is possible to produce hollow castings using slush casting methods. These will need to be built up over several layers or coats of casting material to attain maximum strength.

How many coats to apply will wholly depend on the casting material being used. Adherence to casting material tolerances and specifications are important; testing on a small scale can determine these specifications with most accuracy.

Allow coats to set fully before applying the next coat. This is particularly important for the first coat because it will pick up mould detail and should not be disturbed until set. Subsequent coats should also be allowed to set before another coat is applied otherwise they will not cover properly.

When using pigmented, metal-filled or stone-filled gel coats the initial decorative coat can be backed up with subsequent coats of neat casting material. Back-up coats can be filled with inert fillers to reduce the casting costs. Filled back-up coats of casting material should be free flowing to ensure an even covering. To ensure good lamination do not allow the plaster to dry out between layers. (*See* Chapter 9 for an illustrated example of hollow slush casting.)

Solid Castings

Where solid castings are required a surface coat or decorative gel coat layer can be slush cast and allowed to set fully. Neat or filler addition casting material is then poured into the mould to fill it and back up the surface layer. This method has clear advantages in terms of time and cost savings.

PROJECT

Specification

A cold-cast bronze polyester resin gel coat and backfilled solid casting of a model lion on a base. From a silicone rubber 'core' mould (*see* Chapter 1). Size: 320mm (L), 110mm (W) and 200mm (H).

Time Required

This project takes about one hour, not including setting times.

Materials

- General-purpose polyester resin (supplied by Alec Tiranti Ltd);
- a medium-reactivity catalyst for polyester resin;
- bronze powder filler;
- Fillite® filler
- petroleum jelly; and
- clay.

Tools

- Beakers for dispensing, mixing and pouring;
- digital scales for weighing cast materials;
- wooden spatulas for mixing;
- a plaster mixing bowl;
- a spirit level;
- a container for pouring out excess casting material;
- a brush; and
- disposable rubber gloves.

Method

SET-UP AND PREPARATION

As with any project, careful preparation before the start of the job is crucial. Knowing the material quantities and tools needed, undertaking repairs to the original and setting-up the working area will all help to complete the job accurately and efficiently. (Tip: make sure you have enough materials to complete the job before you start. Running out of material halfway through the job is at least a waste of time and, at worst, a loss of previously executed work.)

RELEASE AGENT

It is a good idea to apply a release agent around all seams and flanges on multiple-piece moulds, to ensure the mould is thoroughly sealed.

1. Apply release agent thoroughly to any area of the mould opening where excess casting material may be poured out to ensure coverage.

APPLICATION OF THE GEL COAT

The gel coat layer of the casting is the most important layer because this picks up the detail of the mould and contains the surface treatment of the casting.

1. Make up enough gel coat mix to fill the mould a third full. The consistency should be pourable.
2. Fill the mould to a third full.
3. Rotate and tilt the mould in a pre-determined rotation pattern.
4. Ensure the casting material covers the whole interior surface of the mould as you do this.
5. It may be necessary to completely invert the mould, allowing a little casting material to be poured out around the mould opening to ensure coverage. Have a container available to pour out excess casting material.

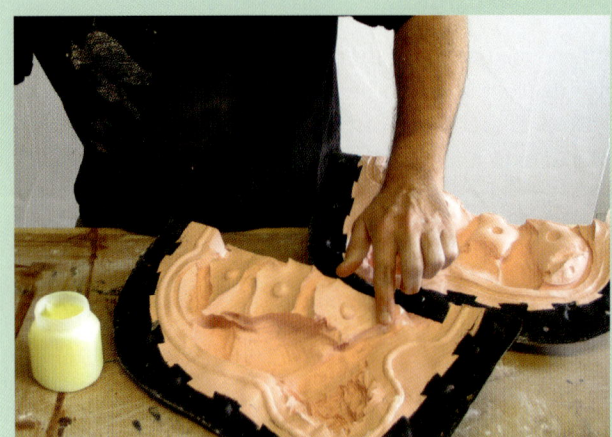

The silicone mould seam flanges are prepared with petroleum jelly.

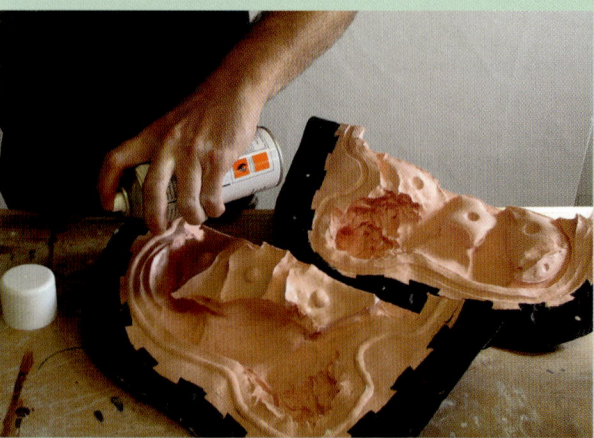

The case flanges are prepared with wax spray release agent.

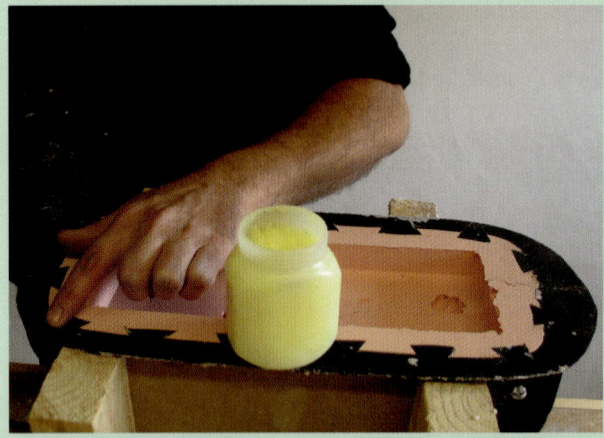

The mould case opening flange is prepared with release agent to prevent the casting material from sticking when poured over.

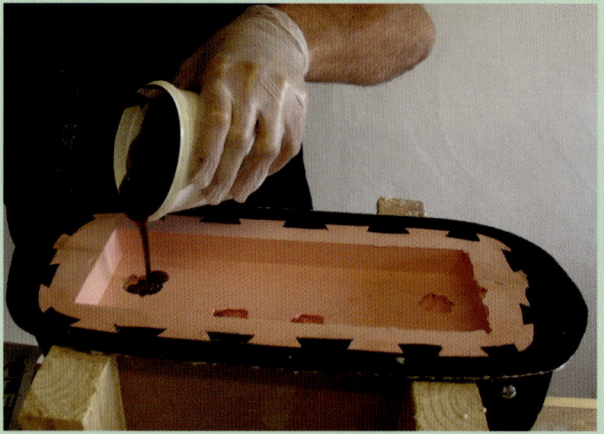

The mould is filled to one third with a bronze-filled polyester resin gel coat.

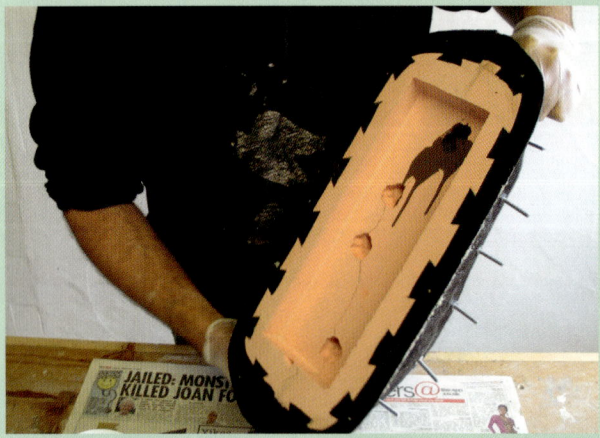

The mould is repeatedly tilted in a pattern to cover the inside of the mould surface with casting material.

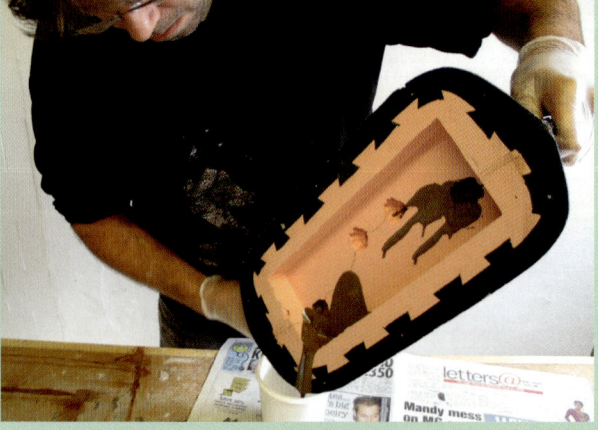

The mould is repeatedly tilted in a pattern to cover the inside of the mould surface with casting material.

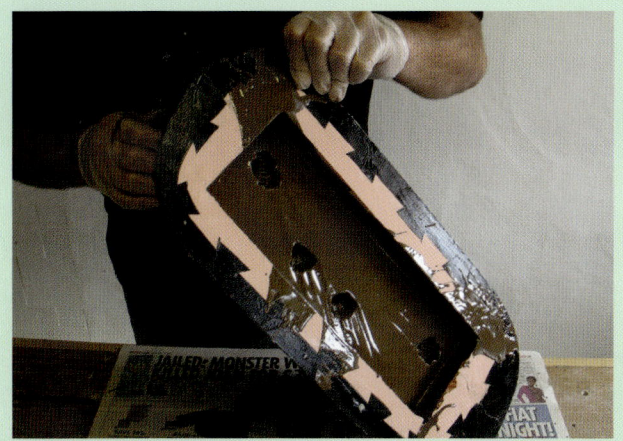

The mould is repeatedly tilted in a pattern to cover the inside of the mould surface with casting material.

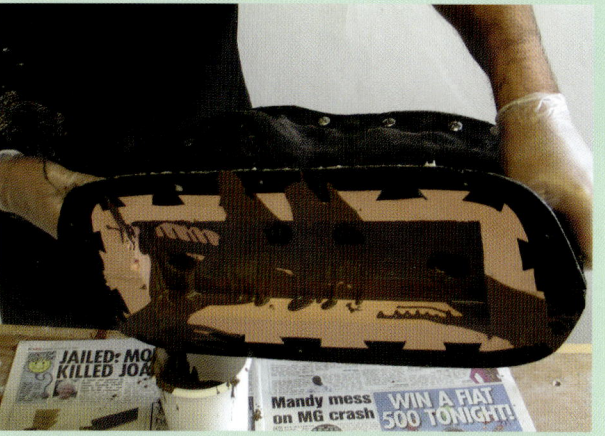

The mould may need to be inverted and some casting material poured out to ensure complete coverage inside.

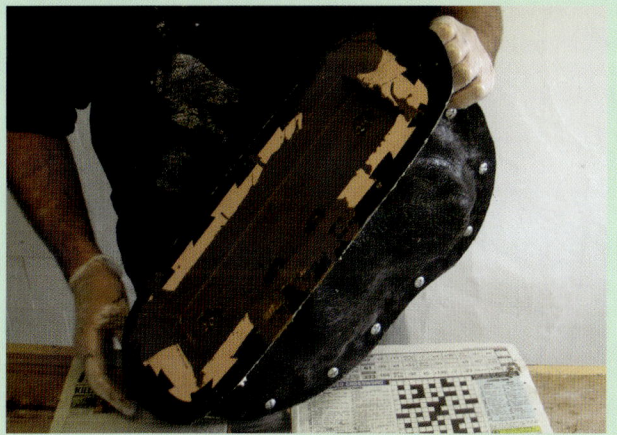

The mould may need to be inverted and some casting material poured out to ensure complete coverage inside.

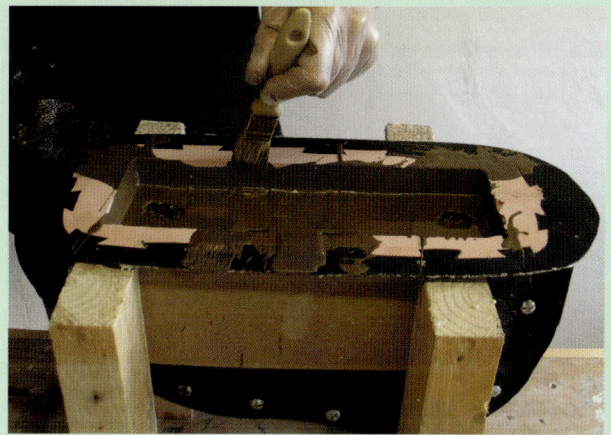

A brush can be used to ensure coverage up to the mould opening.

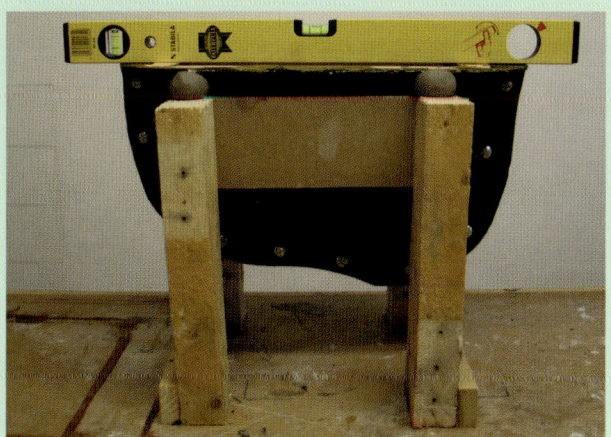

The gel coat is allowed to set fully, with the mould resting level on the support.

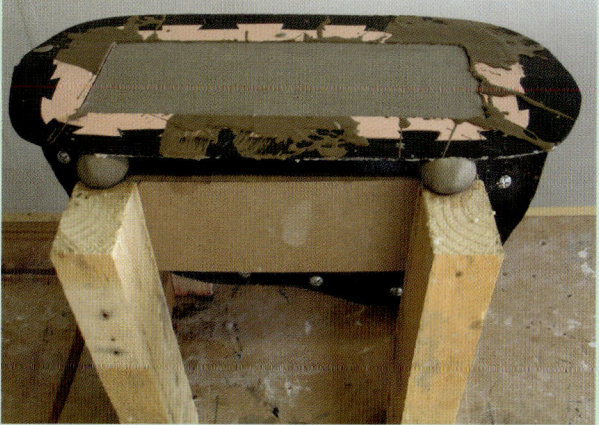

A filler addition resin is used to backfill the slushed gel coat.

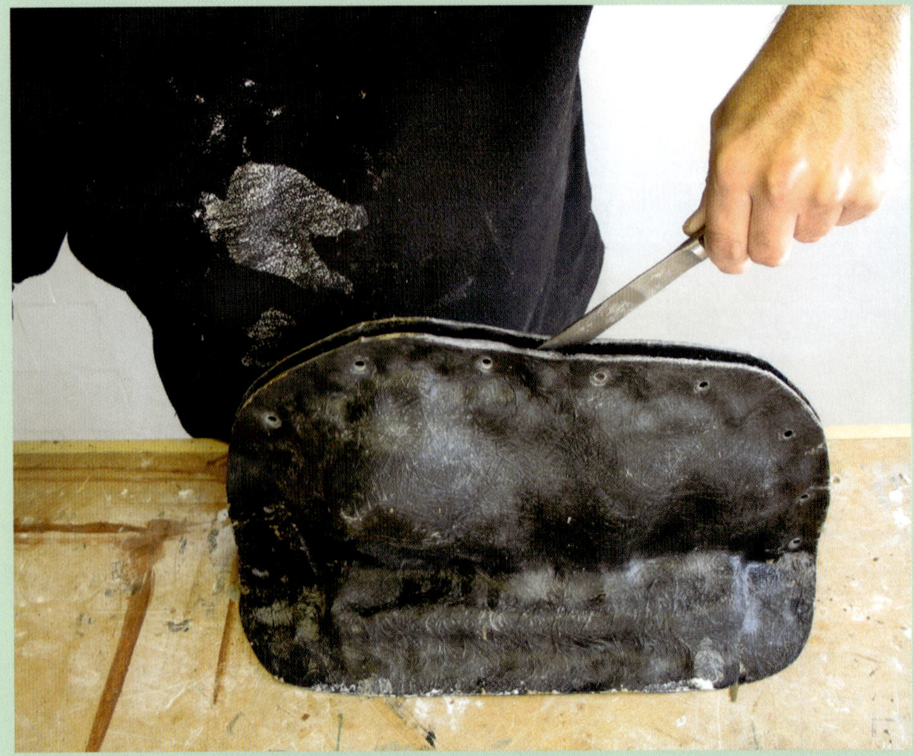

The mould case is separated and removed.

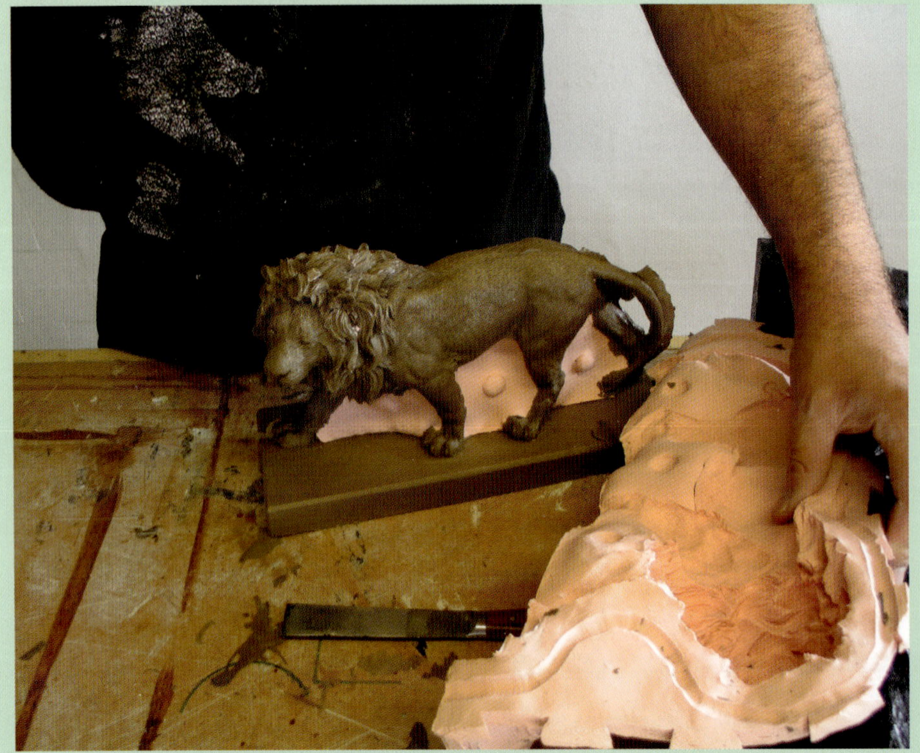

The casting is demoulded from the silicone mould.

6. If access allows, a brush may be used to bring casting material up to the mould opening.
7. Continue with the rotation pattern until the casting material has set.
8. It is usually a good idea to apply two gel coat layers to ensure good coverage of mould surface.
9. Allow the gel coats to set thoroughly.

BACKFILLING

The gel coat layer will not have enough strength on its own and will need to be backfilled. Backfilling with filler addition in the casting material can cut down on cost.

Backfilling casting material will need to be of a consistency that can be poured.

Solid Castings

1. Backfilling material will be a pourable liquid and will therefore fill to a level, so the mould should be levelled. A good way to set a mould level is by placing four small balls of clay under the mould at each corner. With a spirit level set across the top of the mould, it can be pushed down into the clay balls to set a level. Remember to set the levels in two different directions.
2. Fill the mould with backfilling casting material from one point, allowing the level to rise and release air entrapment as it does.
3. Allow the backfilling material to set fully before demoulding.

Hollow Castings

1. Hollow backfilled castings can be achieved by pouring backfilling material into the gel coated mould to a third full.
2. Apply a pre-determined rotation pattern until the material has set.
3. Repeat until an acceptable thickness of material has built up.

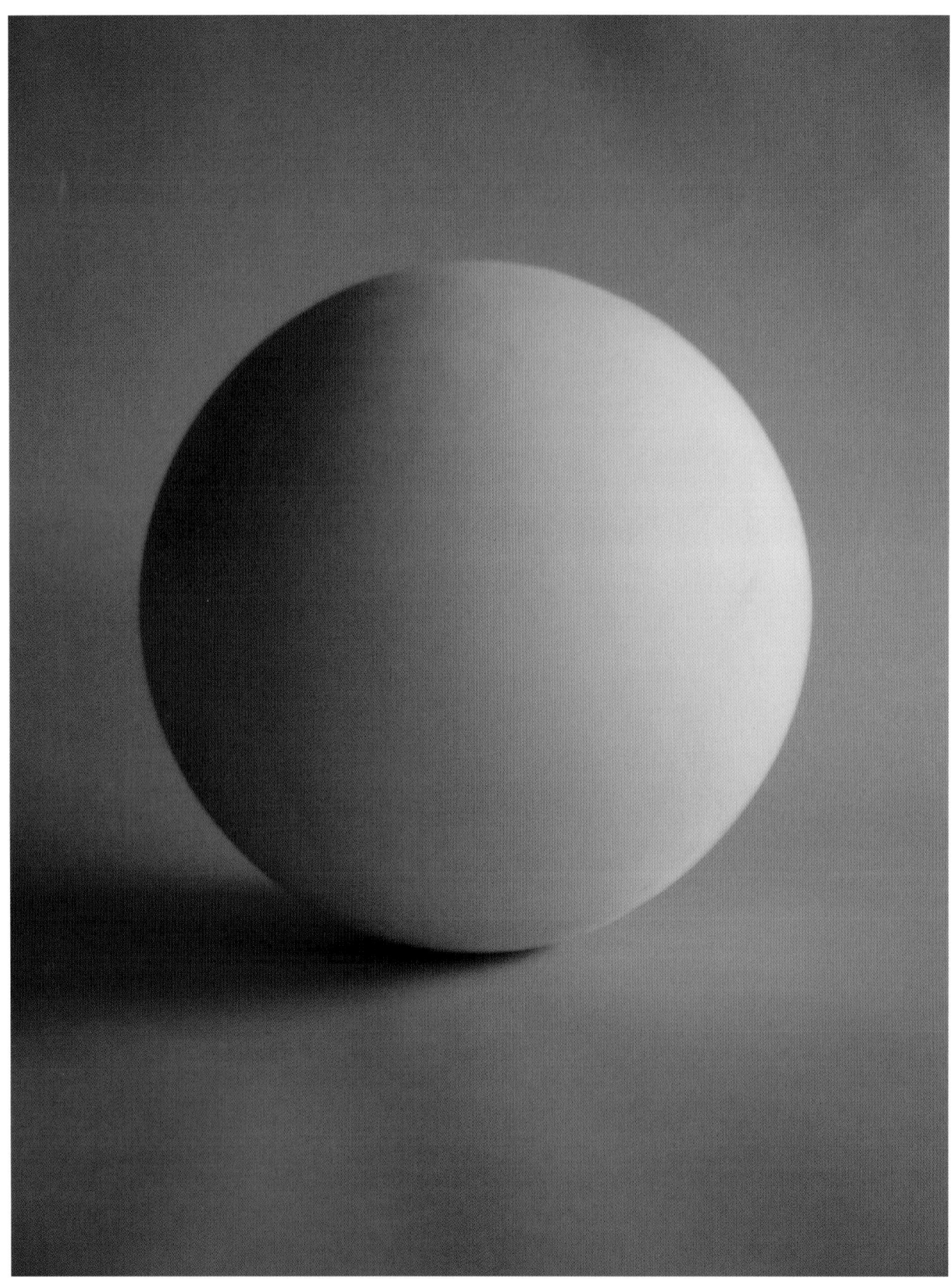

Multiple piece pigmented Alpha plaster sphere cast (700mm circumference).

CHAPTER THIRTEEN

MULTIPLE-PIECE CASTING

Multiple-piece casting involves creating a cast from a multiple-piece mould. This is explained in principle in my first book, *Mouldmaking and Casting*, but it seems useful to explain and illustrate multiple-piece casting in a little more detail here. Although the principles of the process are not complex it can be tricky to execute with accuracy. Once understood in principle, the process is generic to most multiple-piece casting tasks.

Generally speaking a mould created in multiple pieces can be cast in three ways:

1. **Solid**   Casting material is poured into a joined multiple-piece mould to create a solid casting.
2. **Hollow slush cast (one-piece)**   Casting material is poured into a joined multiple-piece mould and slushed around the inside until set (*see* Chapter 12).
3. **Hollow laminated (multiple-piece)**   Casting material is applied in layers to individual pieces of a multiple-piece mould and then joined together.

There may be a number of reasons why creating a multiple-piece cast by building up mould pieces individually would be preferable:

1. **Economy of materials**   Casting solid will obviously use more casting material than hollow castings.
2. **Scale**   For castings of a large size it may not physically be practical to cast solid or slush cast hollow.
3. **Weight**   For castings of a large scale it may not physically be practical or desirable aesthetically to cast solid.
4. **Mould access**   It may not be possible to cast a joined multiple-piece mould if there is inadequate access for applying the casting material. This would be the case, for instance, with a mould with a 'footprint' smaller than the body of the mould or where there is only a pouring hole as access. The mouldmaker needs to be able to access the inside of a mould physically in order to apply the casting material.

The project illustrated uses plaster but these principles could be applied to most casting materials and more complex multiple-piece castings.

PROJECT

Specification

An Alpha casting plaster and fibreglass laminated cast, slightly tinted with yellow earth pigment for demonstration, from a five-piece Jesmonite mould. Size: 300mm circumference.

Time Required

Approximately one and a half hours.

Materials

- Spray wax release agent;
- basic Alpha casting plaster (supplied by Alec Tiranti Ltd);
- heavy fibreglass mat;
- Yellow Ochre earth pigment; and
- a small amount of grey clay.

Tools

- A plaster mixing bowl;
- a plastic jug;
- a clay knife; and
- a small sponge.

Method

The basic principles of multiple-piece casting involve the application of the casting material to an open multiple-piece mould. In terms of the seams, it is always easier to apply casting material to as few mould pieces as possible and subsequently to join the cast pieces together from inside the mould.

If the mould is in two pieces, casting material is applied to each piece separately. The mould pieces are then joined and the separately applied cast pieces are joined from inside the mould. Moulds that are in more than two pieces could be cast separately and joined in the same way – although it is obviously an advantage if you can join a cast in as few pieces as possible. For this reason you should join as many mould pieces as possible but still allow access to apply the casting material and then cast and join any remaining piece or pieces of the mould.

In the example illustrated a five-piece Jesmonite mould is used. It would be possible to apply casting material to each mould piece separately and then join all five pieces to be sealed together from inside. In this case, however, it is preferable to join four pieces of the mould and apply casting material to all four at the same time. The last mould piece is cast separately and then joined to the other four pieces in one operation. This effectively means that only two cast pieces need to be joined internally in the mould.

SET-UP AND PREPARATION

As with any project, careful preparation before the start of the job is crucial. Knowing the material quantities and tools needed, undertaking repairs to the original and setting-up the working area will all help to complete the job accurately and efficiently. (Tip: make sure you have enough materials to complete the job before you start. Running out of material halfway through the job is at least a waste of time and, at worst, a loss of previously executed work.)

1. Ensure all work surfaces are clean, clear and well lit. This may sound obvious, but preparation of this sort prior to casting will greatly help in production. It easy to miss parts of the mould surface in a badly lit work space.
2. Ensure all mould pieces are clean and dry.
3. Ensure all mould fastenings are present.

MOULD PREPARATION

1. Join and secure four pieces of the mould, allowing access from the missing single piece.
2. Apply release agent to the surfaces of the four joined mould pieces and the one separate mould piece.
3. Apply release agent to all exposed mould flanges. With any multiple-piece mould you should ensure that any casting material leakage from the seam to be joined internally does not stick the mould flanges together. Obviously the more accurately the mould is made the less seam leakage there will be, but it is better to err on the side of caution.

APPLICATION OF CASTING MATERIAL

For this project a cast is produced using Alpha casting plaster.

1. Apply a layer of plaster to the surfaces of the joined four mould pieces and the single separate piece.

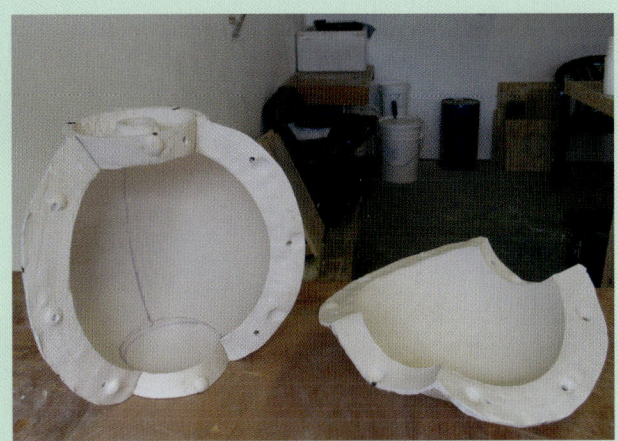

Four pieces of the mould are securely joined, leaving one piece open.

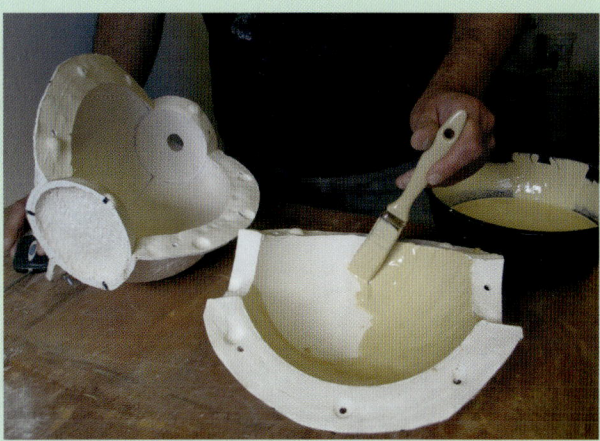

A first coat of plaster is applied to the single mould surface.

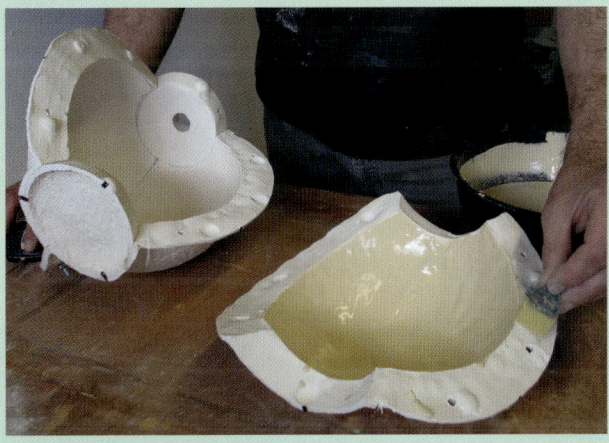

Mould flanges are cleaned of excess plaster.

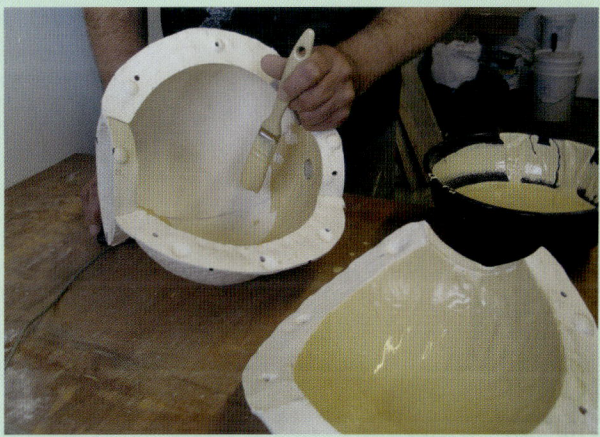

A first coat of plaster is applied to the joined remaining mould pieces and allowed to set.

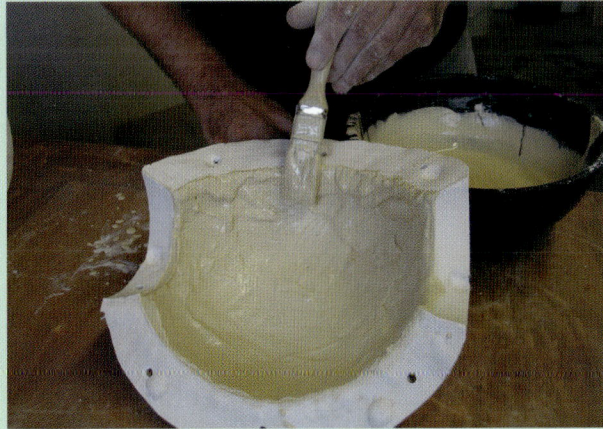

As the plaster is built up in lamination the edges of the cast are thickened.

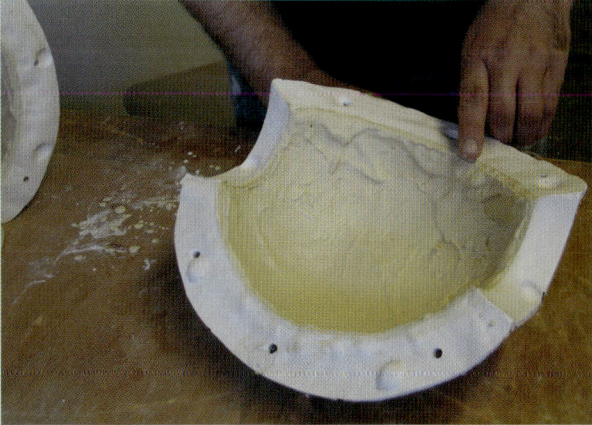

The cast piece edges are chamfered downward using a finger.

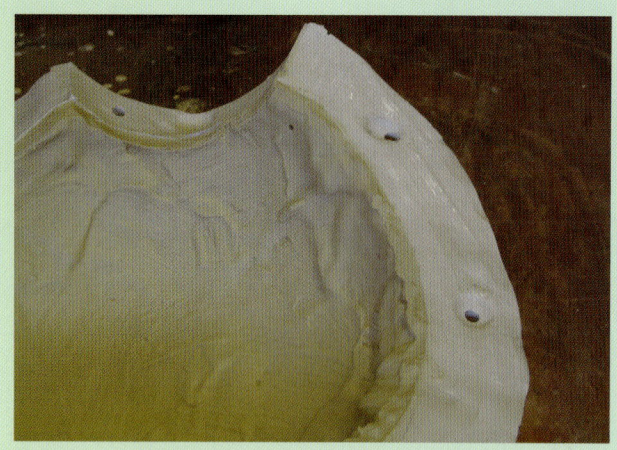

The chamfered edges of the cast pieces.

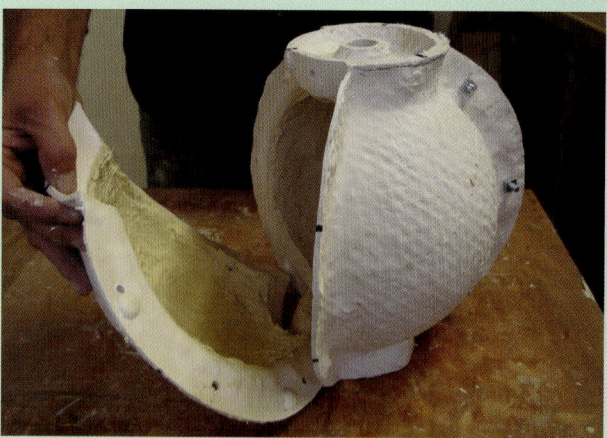

The mould is joined and secured.

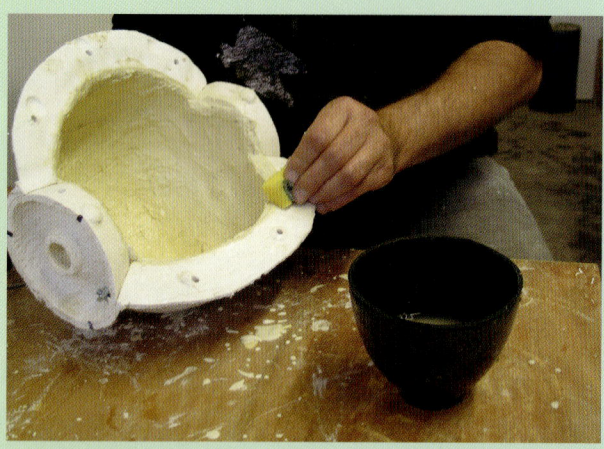

Keep the mould flanges clean of any excess material.

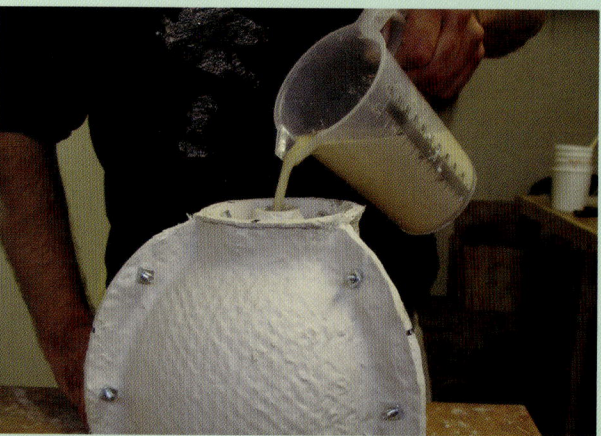

Plaster is poured into the mould via the pouring hole.

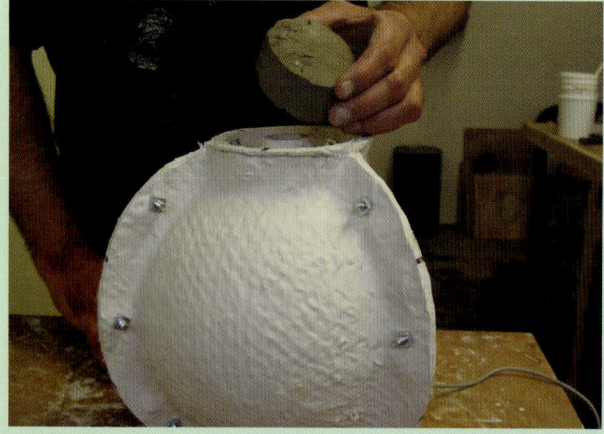

A pre-made bung is inserted to seal the pouring hole.

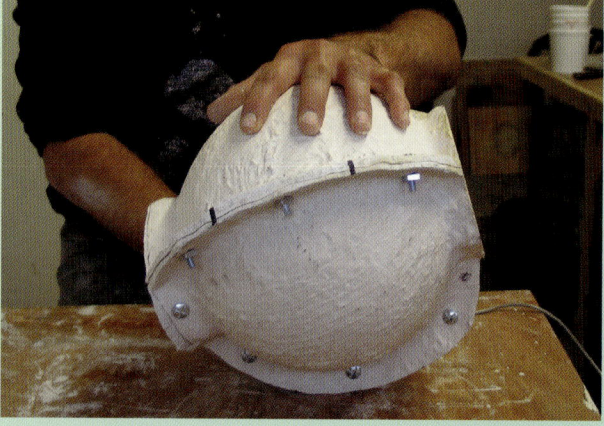

The mould is tilted at the seams to allow the plaster to cover them internally.

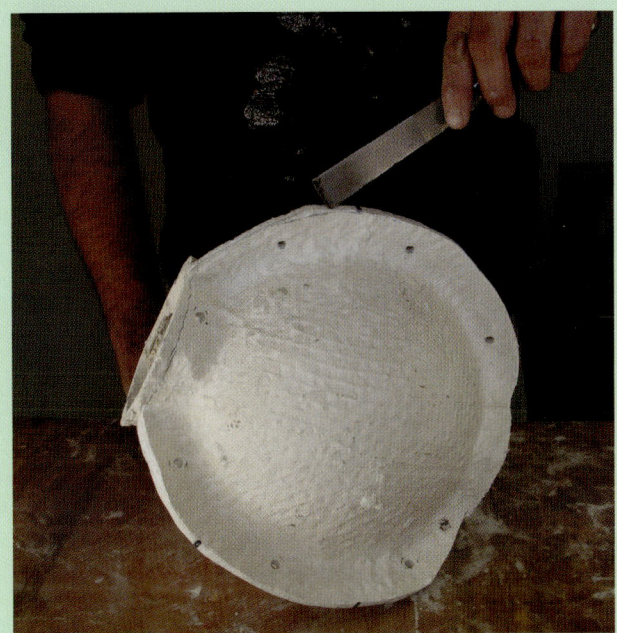

Once the cast has set the mould pieces are helped open with a knife.

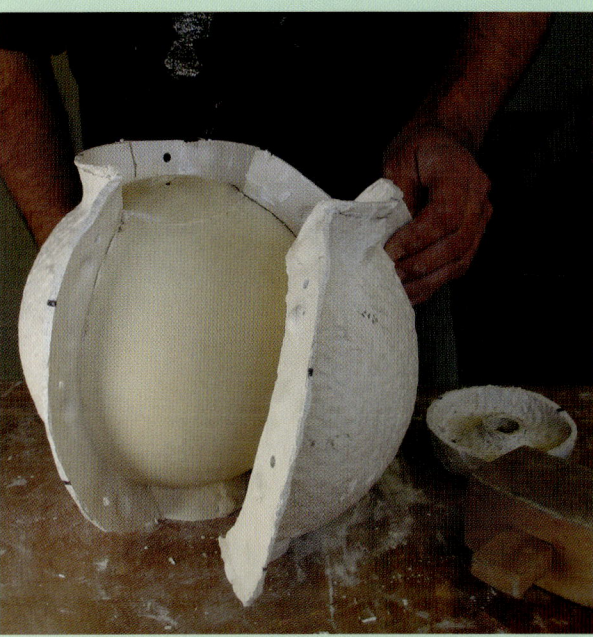

The five mould pieces are carefully removed to demould the cast.

2. Work right up to the edges of the mould pieces. Avoid getting any casting material on the exposed mould flanges. If necessary, clean off any casting material from the mould flanges.
3. Allow this layer to set before applying further layers.
4. Apply further layers to the required thickness as above.
5. As the layers build up create a chamfered edge angled down from the mould edge. This can be done by running a finger or sponge around the mould edges. The casting material needs to be applied right up to the edges of the mould surfaces but then chamfered down to avoid excess casting material preventing accurate registration when joining the final mould piece.
6. Apply laminating material as necessary to achieve full cast thickness and strength.
7. Ensure that the pouring hole is kept clear as the layers are built up.
8. When the required thickness has been achieved allow the cast pieces to set but not dry out. The cast pieces need to be firm enough to move without breaking but wet enough to allow good adhesion when joining with more casting material.

JOINING THE CAST PIECES

1. Ensure there is no excess cast material on the mould flanges and around the pouring hole.
2. Ensure the cast edges are chamfered down from the mould flanges.
3. Carefully join and secure the mould pieces containing the cast pieces.
4. Make a small batch of casting material and pour this into the joined mould via the pouring hole.
5. Seal the pouring hole with clay or a pre-made bung.
6. Rotate and tilt the mould to allow the casting material to cover the seam lines inside the mould. The chamfered edges of the casting will allow the casting material to cover and join the cast seams efficiently.
7. Rotate and tilt the mould until the casting material has set.
8. Repeat this process several times to ensure a good deposit of casting material over the seam lines.
9. Allow the casting material to set fully before demoulding.

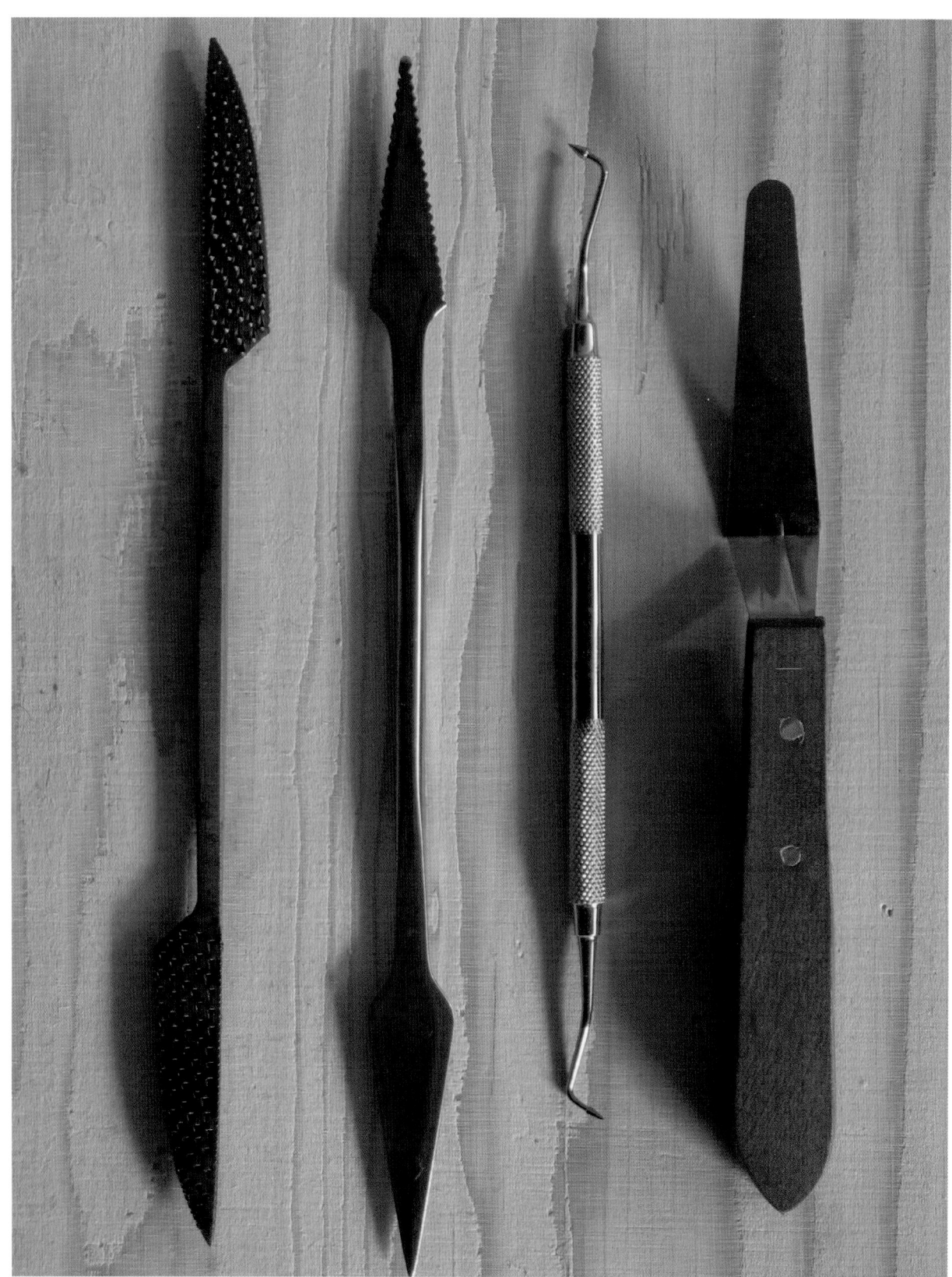

A selection of finishing tools.

CHAPTER FOURTEEN

FINISHING

The end result in any mouldmaking and casting project is only ever fully achieved in the finishing process. The quality of the final finished casting can vary greatly depending on the amount and quality of the finishing process and it should therefore be considered as taking at least a third of the whole length of the job, sometimes even half.

Mouldmaking and the production of the subsequent casting are not finite processes and there will always be a certain amount of finishing to do on any project. The degree and amount of finishing required will obviously depend on a number of factors. Accuracy in preparation and mouldmaking is of primary importance and this can reduce the amount of finishing a casting will require. Similarly, good preparation and accuracy in the casting process will help to reduce your labour at the finishing stage. Some mouldmaking techniques

inherently require more work at the finishing stage because of the nature of the process, as with life moulding for example. Also, some casting materials can be difficult to finish because of the nature of the material. Clear resin castings, for example, with seam lines can be particularly tricky due to the transparency of the casting showing up any imperfections. The quality of your castings will no doubt be improved and refined with experience, but never expect to have no finishing to do!

Before undertaking any finishing processes it is advisable to first assess the casting and then select the appropriate finishing system or systems. In your assessment determine how much finishing is actually required; it would be a mistake to wade into a programme of finishing processes that is too comprehensive for the job in hand. If one or two systems will achieve the required finished result do not go through ten systems.

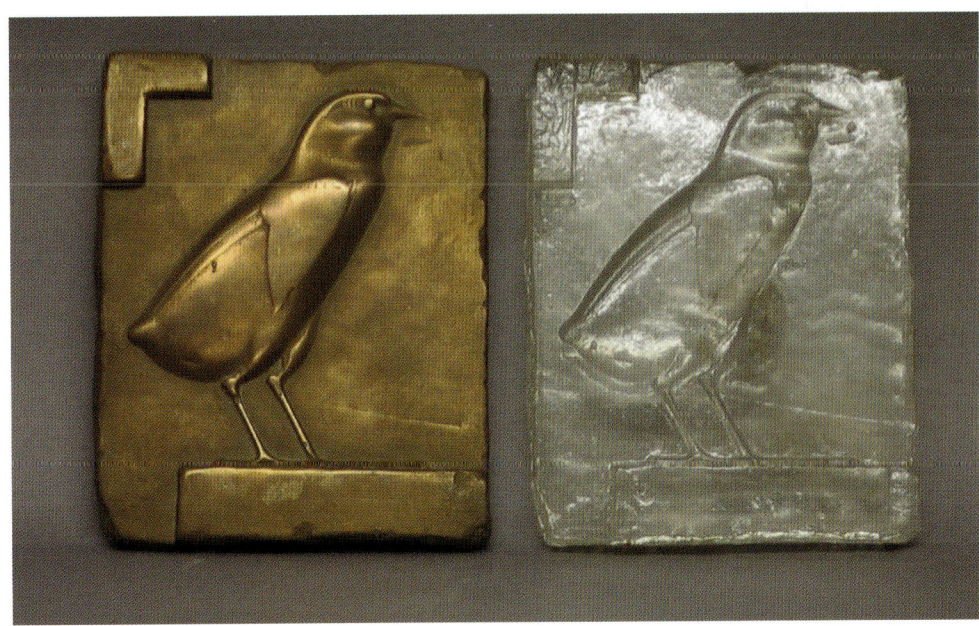

Cold-cast bronze and clear resin tablets (H: 120mm).

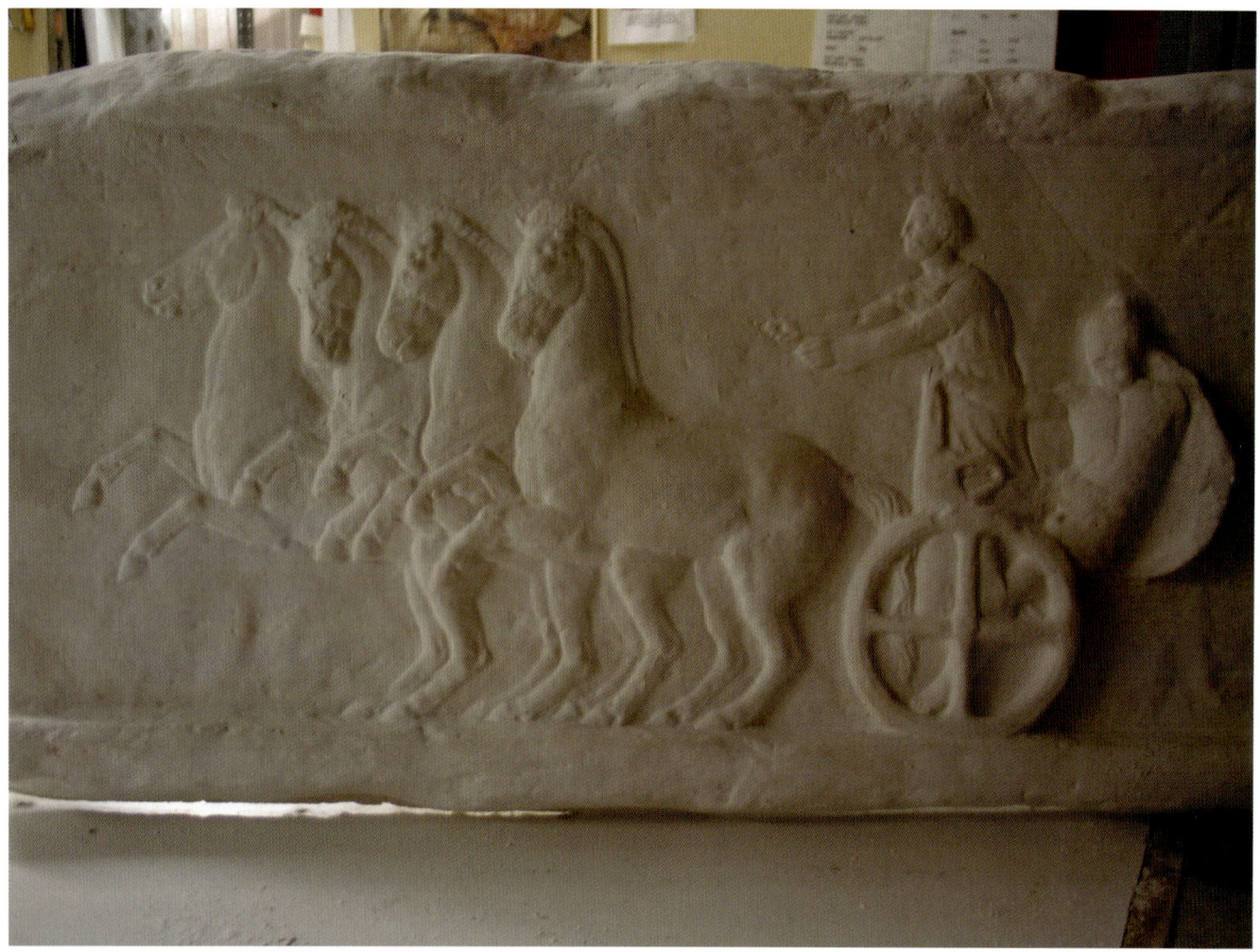

An Alpha plaster cast (W: 850mm).

Knowing where to start is obviously the crucial factor here, and defining what degree of finishing is required should be easy to judge from visual inspection. Finishing can be broken down into two categories: seam line and surface, or just surface. The finishing needed will be determined by the type of mould employed. A multiple-piece mould will produce seams on a casting and a one-piece mould will not, but both will require surface finishing of some sort.

Finishing systems incorporate a process of abrading from course to fine, with degrees of this within each system. The categories I have laid out therefore start with large chisels and end with polishing and buffing systems, with many decreasing levels in between. Within the scale of ten it will be necessary to assess the stage at which to start. Castings with very rough seam lines may need to be taken through all ten, but castings with smaller seam lines may only require work beginning at the finer levels. Similarly, choices of required finish will determine which finishing systems are employed. Some castings may look better polished and others not, for instance, and this may be an aesthetic choice for the mould-maker.

The tools used within each system described here can of course be expanded upon depending on the nature of the project. There are no rules, only possibilities and choices.

Whatever the requirements and choices, for the best results take finishing processes slowly and methodically and stand back frequently to look at the results progressively until satisfied.

1. Large chisels Old wood or stone-carving chisels of 5–25mm are ideal. They should be used only for the removal of large amounts of seam flashing or imperfections. Stop using these tools when you are within 2 or 3mm of the surface of castings. They can be used on most materials but will blunt more readily on stone composite or concrete-based castings.

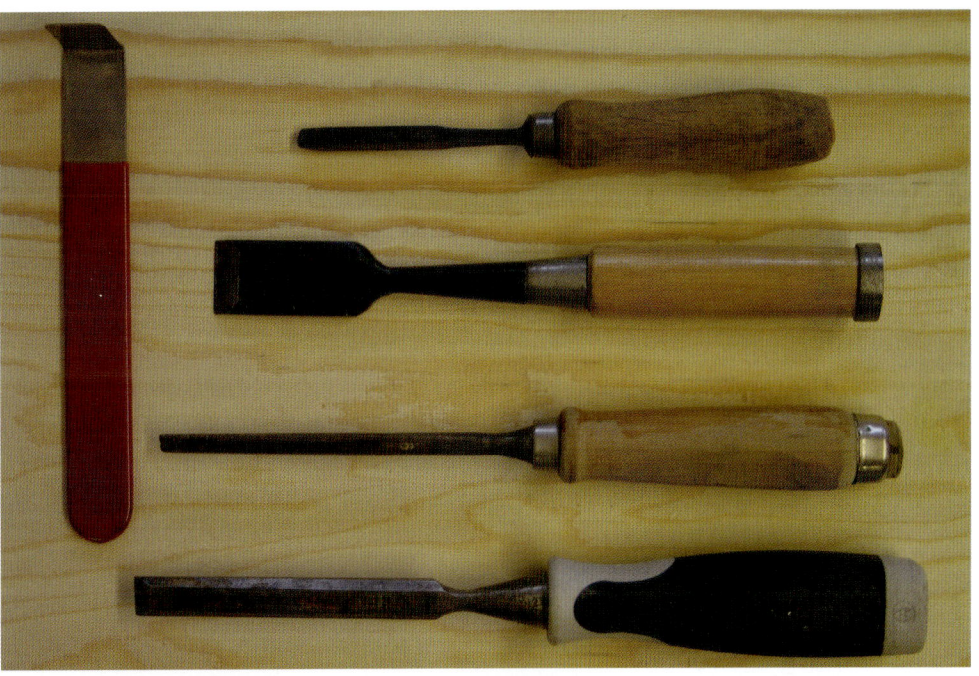

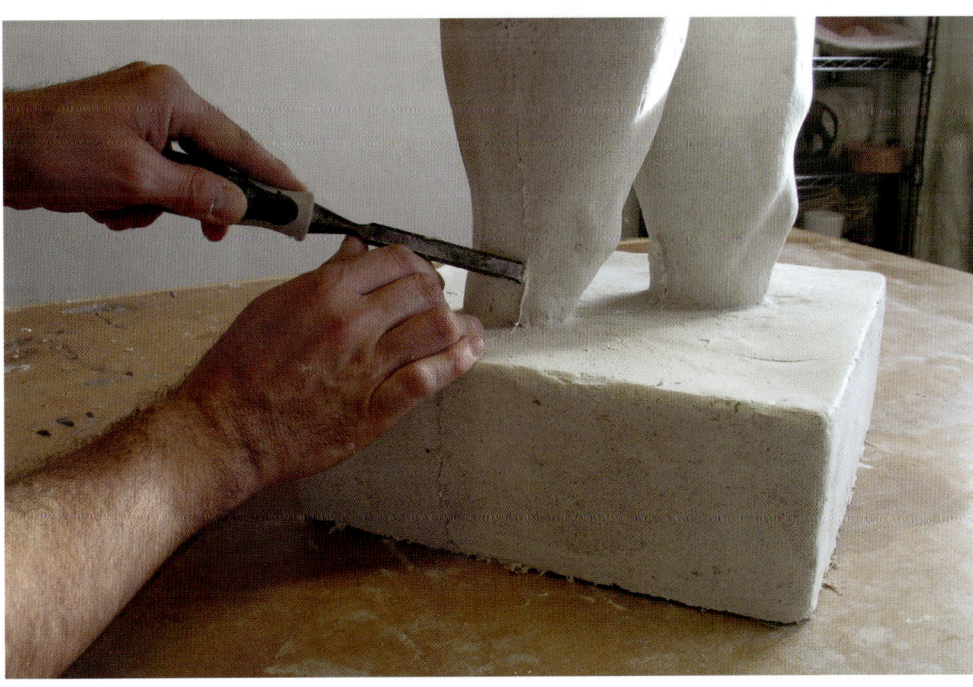

2. Surforms Surforms of various sizes and shapes can be used to remove seam flashing up to 2 or 3mm close to the casting surface. Standard surform plane bodies can be fitted with differently shaped blades to accommodate undulating casting surfaces and contours. They should be kept clean and unclogged with a coarse wire brush.

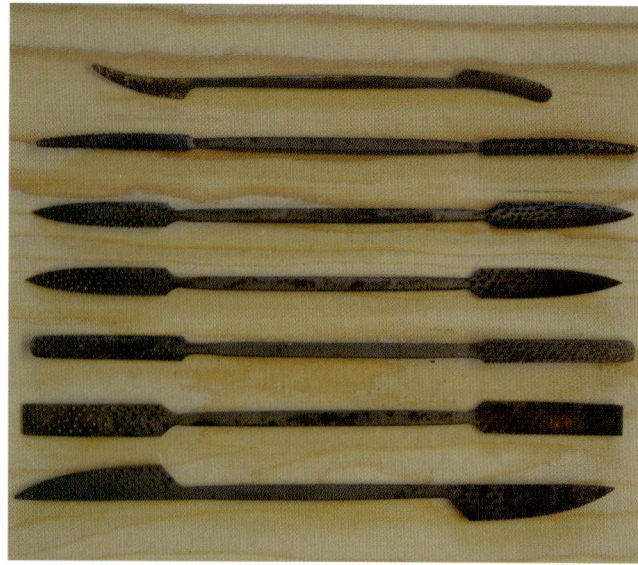

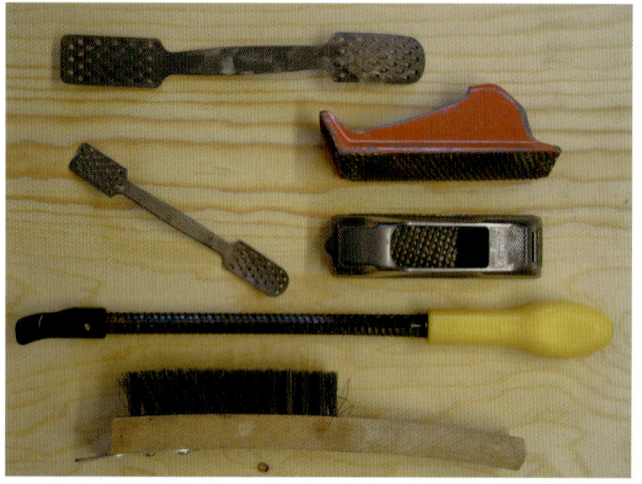

3. Rasps A further finer level of abrasive action following surforming can be achieved with rasps, working up to about 1mm to the casting surface. Multiple shapes and contours are available. These should be kept clean and unclogged with a fine wire brush.

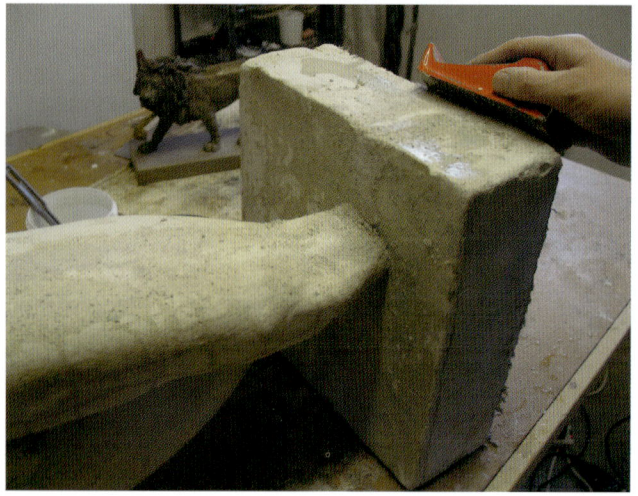

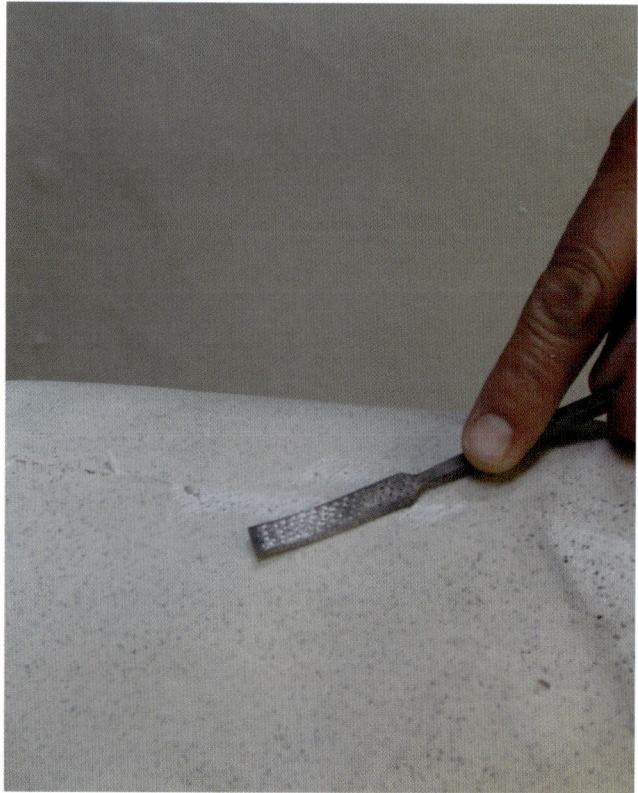

4. Leaf and spears (and other metal modelling tools) Leaf and spears are picking and scraping tools available in multiple sizes. Leafs can be used to scrape back fine seam lines to very near the cast surface and around the inside of concave surfaces. Spears can be used to pick imperfections out of difficult-to-access areas. These tools can be useful for opening up cracks or seams that need to be filled. Other metal modeling tools, usually sold for working with plaster, can be used as finishing tools and these come in a multitude of sizes and shapes. Use tools of an appropriate size and shape for the job in hand.

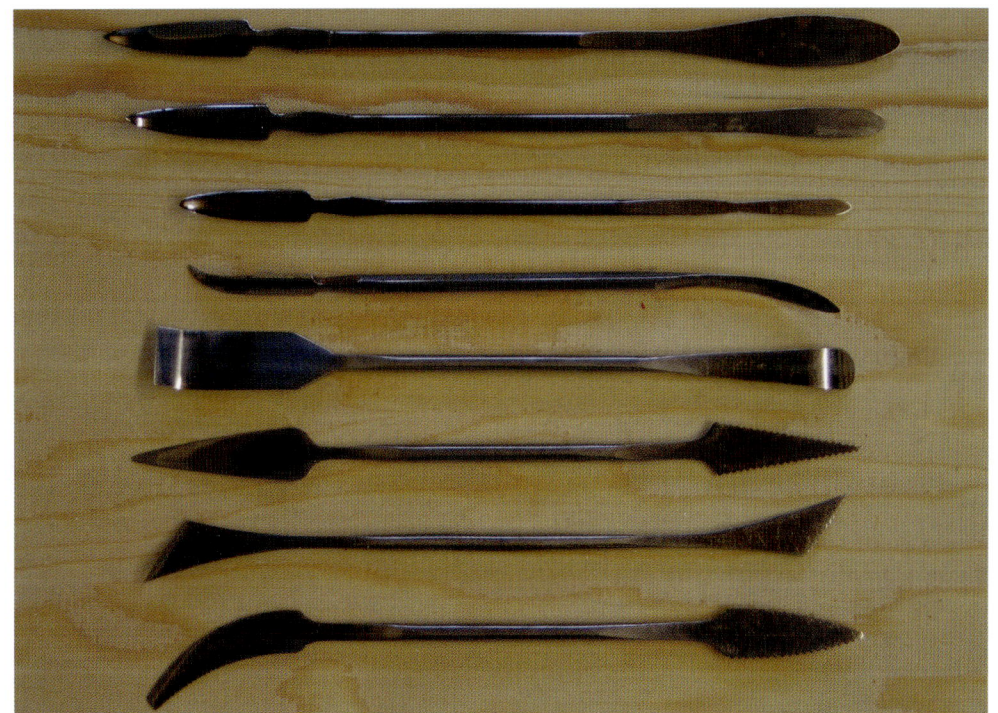

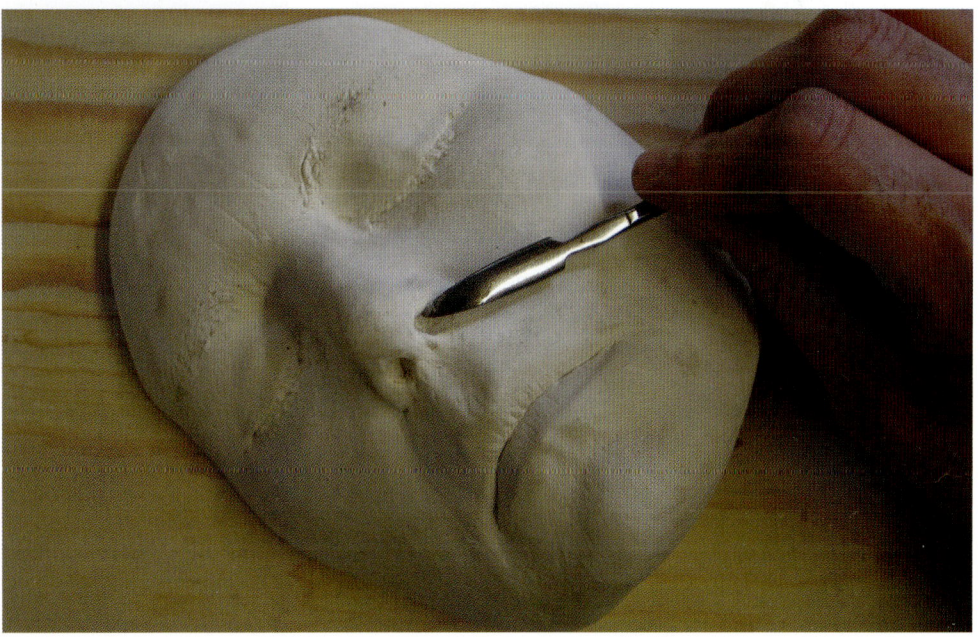

5. Small chisels and dental tools   Chisels of 5mm and smaller can be used to take back seam lines and very small imperfections very close to the cast surface. Small chisels can also be used to open up cracks and seams prior to filling. Sets of small wood-carving chisels come in multiple profile ranges. Dental tools in various shapes and sizes can be very useful to remove imperfections in very highly detailed areas that are difficult to access.

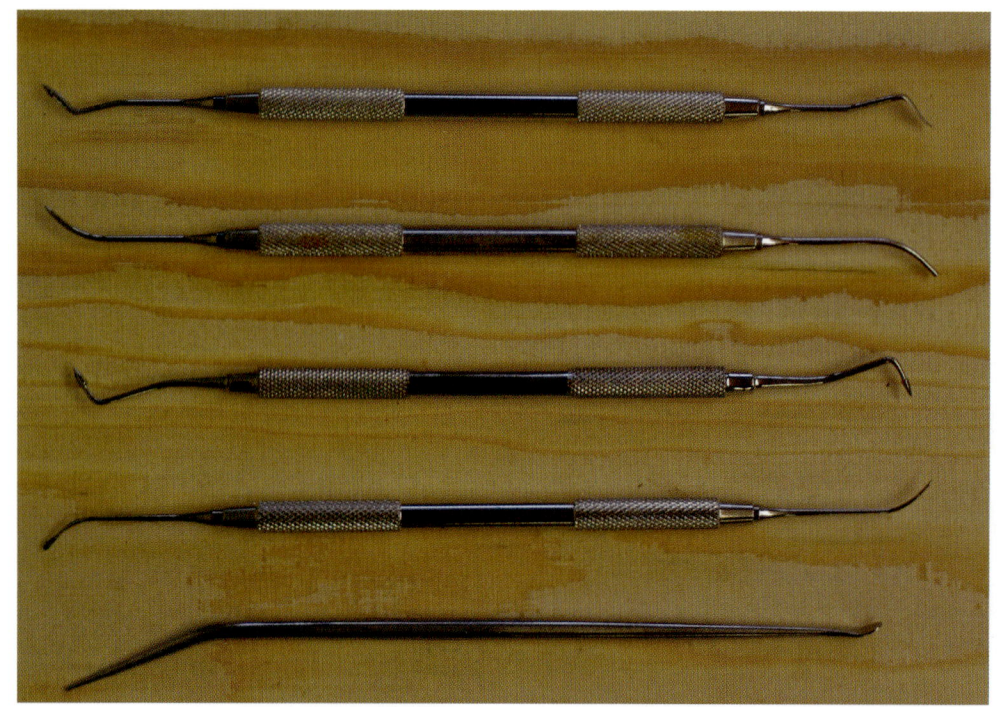

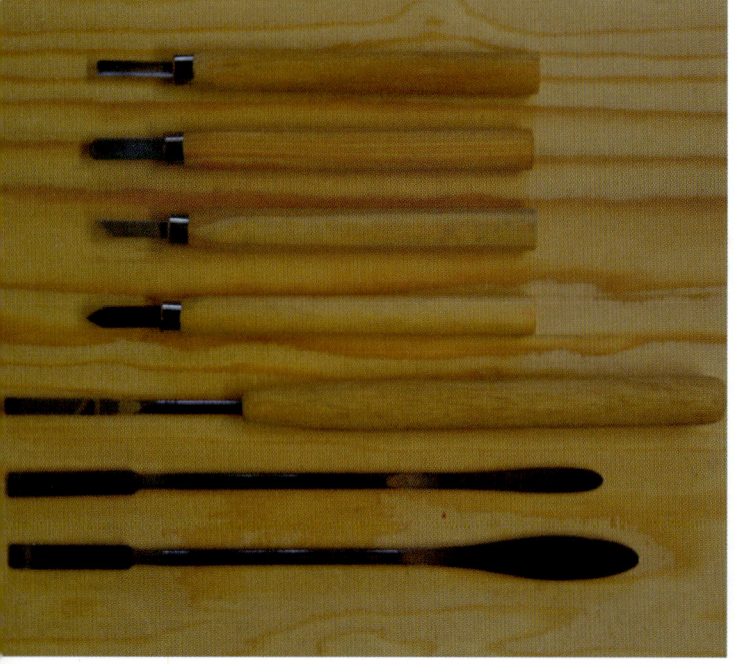

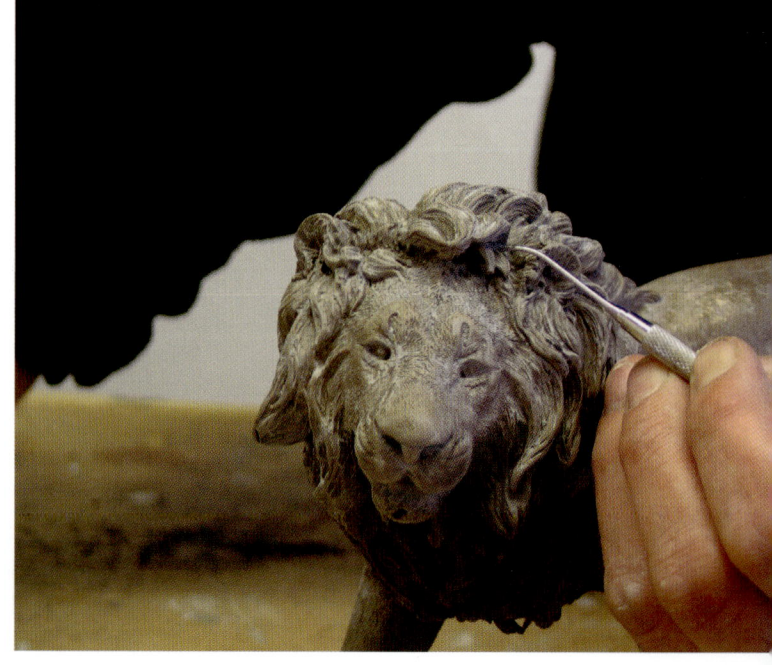

6. Filling Filling with the appropriate casting material may be necessary on areas with air bubbles, cracks or seam lines that have not joined properly. Various flexible tools can be used to apply the filling material (fingers are good as well!). Areas to be filled should be opened up a little to clear any loose material and to allow filler to get a good hold. When applying water-based filling materials the area should be primed beforehand with a water spray to allow good adhesion. For this reason areas to be filled should also be free of debris and clean. Always overfill a little to allow for potential shrinkage and accurate sanding back to the cast surface when set. It is advisable to colour-match and test any filling materials before application.

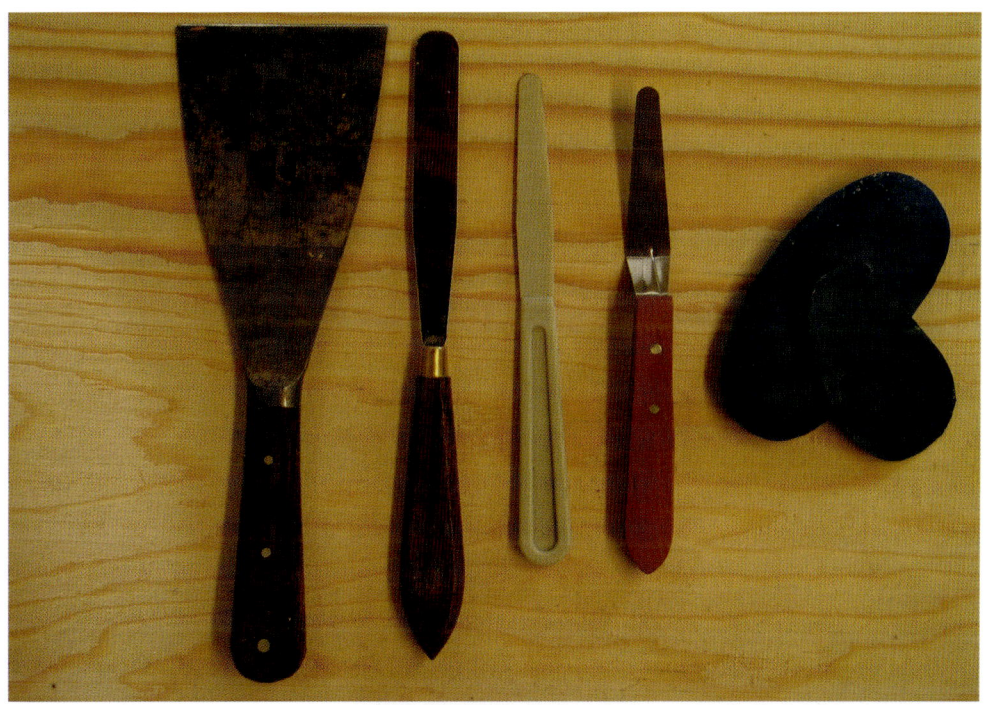

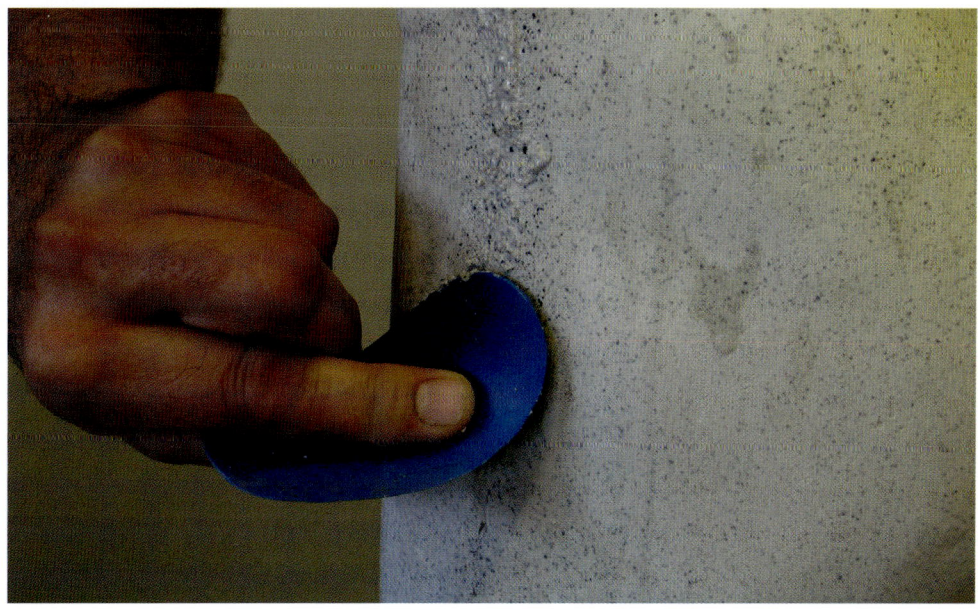

7. Mechanical sanding Small-scale mechanical sanding apparatus can be used on medium-level seam flashing and imperfections (of 2–3mm). Small sanding drums and attachments for cordless drills are useful, as are electric 'delta' sanders with interchangeable profiles and different paper grit sizes. Do not wet sand with mains electric tools. Be wary of sanding too far too quickly when sanding mechanically, particularly when exposing metal or stone composites. Work progressively through the coarse levels of abrasive to finer levels. Be aware of dust control measures.

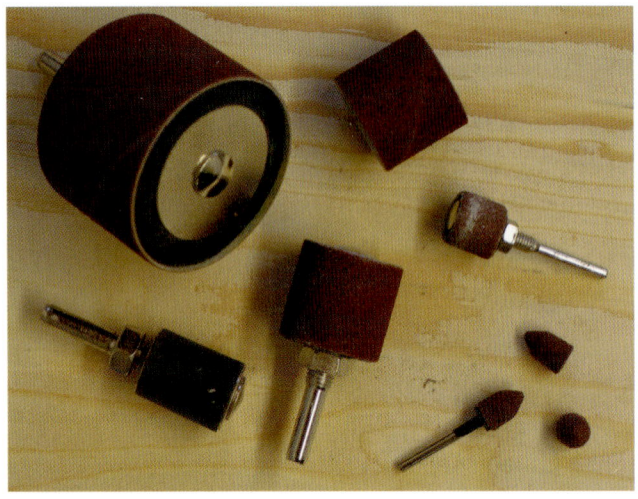
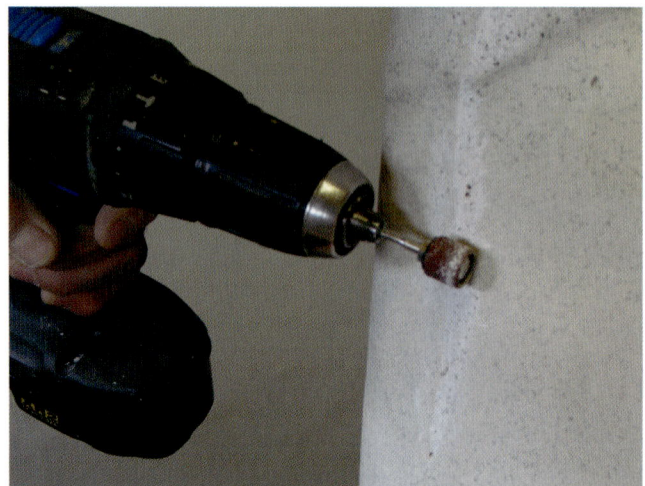

8. Hand sanding Hand sanding systems should be employed to take seam lines, raised imperfections or set filled areas of castings down to the cast surface. They are also used for exposing metal or stone composites. Wet sand with water-proof papers and sanding blocks, rinsing frequently during use and changing water between abrasive grades. A little washing-up liquid can assist wet sanding, particularly when cutting back clear resin castings. Wire wool can be used effectively to expose metal composites. Heavy duty nylon kitchen scourers are useful for exposing Jesmonite stone composites; dry and view the work frequently to determine levels of exposure. Work progressively through the coarse levels of abrasive to the finer levels. Be aware of dust control measures.

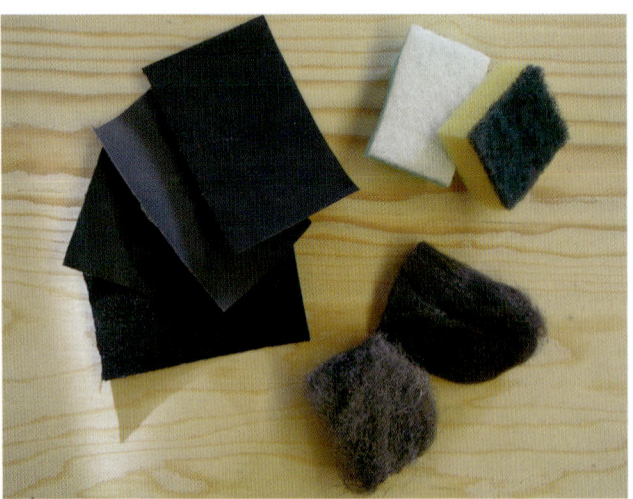
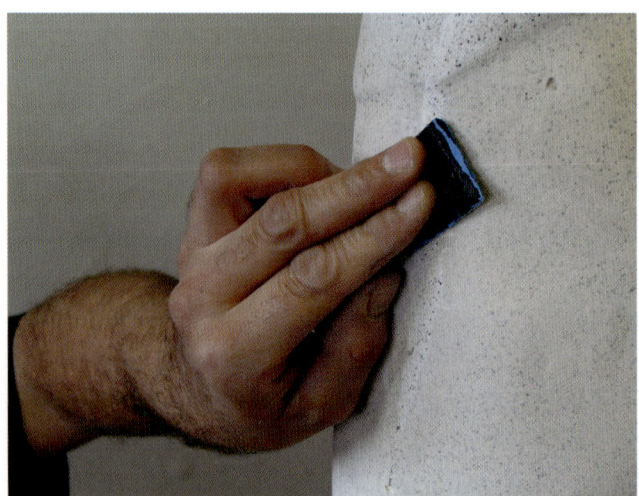

9. Polishing Some castings may benefit from or require polishing. Different polishing systems are available, including wax-based blocks or cream systems applied to mechanically driven mops and hand-applied wax or cream polishes. Polishing with cutting compounds should be considered as another level of abrasion; grades should be worked through progressively and then it should be finished off with polishing systems. Levels of polishing can only really be determined after buffing.

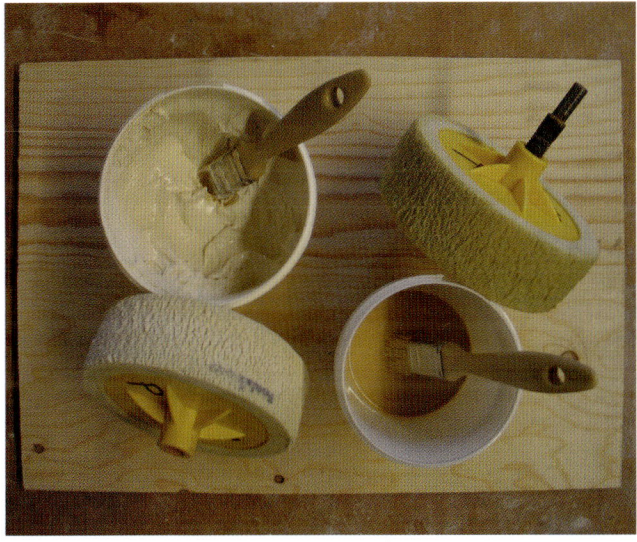

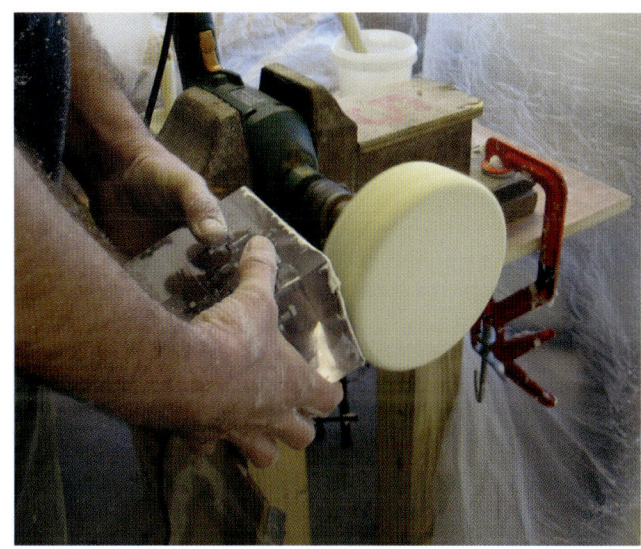

10. Buffing The final sheen or shine can be achieved by buffing pre-polished castings. Soft lint-free cloths or mechanical fleece buffing mops can be used. If the required levels are not achieved then revert to polishing, or if necessary to sanding levels and then polishing, and repeat.

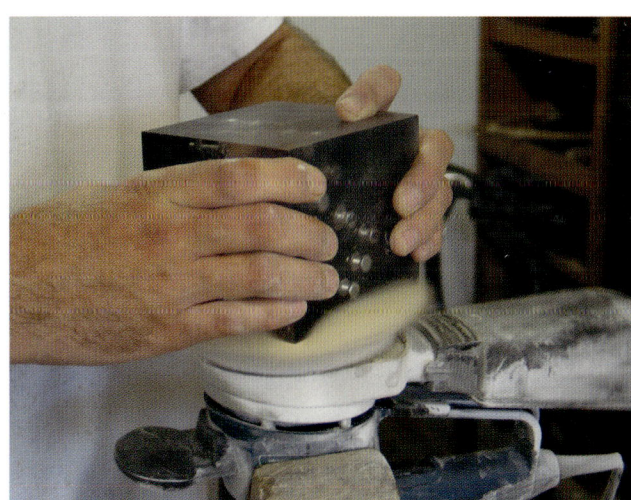

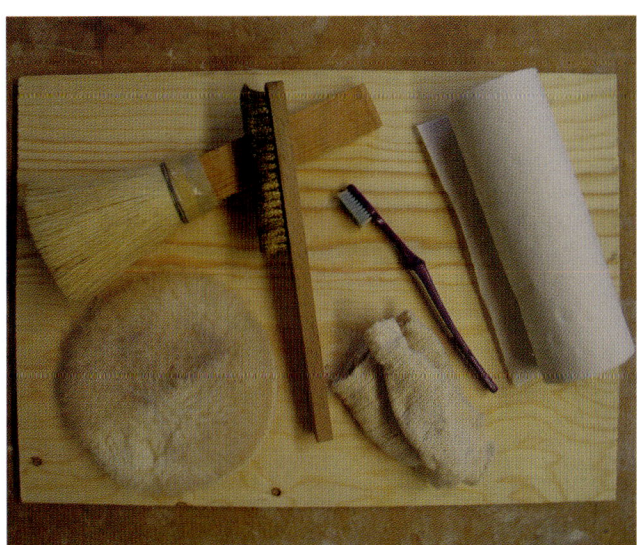

MANUFACTURERS AND SUPPLIERS

For courses and commissions, see the author's website www.mouldmakingandcasting.com

4D MODELSHOP LTD
The Arches
120 Leman St
London
E1 8EU
Tel: 0207 264 1288
Fax: 0207 264 1299
Email: info@modelshop.co.uk
Website: www.modelshop.co.uk
(Model-making supplies)

ALEC TIRANTI LTD
3 Pipers Court
Berkshire Drive
Thatcham
Berkshire
RG19 4ER
Tel: 0845 123 2100
Fax: 0845 123 2101
Email: enquiries@tiranti.co.uk
Website: www.tiranti.co.uk
(Mouldmaking, casting and sculpting supplies)

BENTLEY CHEMICALS LTD
Frederick Rd
Hoo Farm Industrial Estate
Kidderminster
Worcestershire
DY11 7RA
Tel: 01562 515121
Fax: 01562 515847

Email: info@bentleychemicals.co.uk
Website: www.bentleychemicals.co.uk
(Mouldmaking and casting supplies)

BIGHEAD BONDING FASTENERS LTD
Units 15/16 Elliot Rd
West Howe Industrial Estate
Bournemouth
BH11 8LZ
Tel: 01202 574 601
Fax: 01202 578 300
Email: info@bighead.co.uk
Website: www.bighead.co.uk
(Specialist fasteners)

CANONBURY ARTS LTD
65 Halliford St
London
N1 3HF
Tel: 0207 226 4652
Fax: 0207 704 1781
Email: sc@canonburyarts.co.uk
Website: www.canonburyarts.co.uk
(Bioresin and other sculpting and art supplies)

FLINT HIRE AND SUPPLY LTD
Queen's St
London
SE17 2PX
Tel: 0207 703 9786
Fax: 0207 708 4189
Email: sales@flints.co.uk
Website: www.flints.co.uk
(Theatrical chandlers)

NOTCUTT LTD
Homewood Farm
Newark Lane
Ripley
Surrey
GU23 6DJ
Tel: 01483 223311
Fax: 01483 479594
Email: sales@notcutt.co.uk
Website: www.notcutt.co.uk
(Mouldmaking and casting supplies)

SMOOTH-ON INC
2000 Saint John St
Easton
Pennsylvania 18042
USA
Tel: +1 610 252 5800
Fax: +1 610 252 6200
Website: www.smooth-on.com
(Specialist silicones and resins)

SOUTH WESTERN INDUSTRIAL PLASTERS
63 Netherstreet
Bromham
Chippenham
Wiltshire
SN15 2DP
Tel: 01380 850616
Fax: 01380 859638
Email: info@industrialplasters.com
Website: www.industrialplasters.com
(Tools and other mouldmaking and casting supplies)

ACKNOWLEDGEMENTS

All materials used in the production of this book were supplied by Notcutt Ltd, Alec Tiranti Ltd and Canonbury Arts Ltd.

Special thanks to Andrew Hill (Notcutt Ltd); Arthur Manzo (Notcutt Ltd); Richard Joplin (Alec Tiranti Ltd); Shaun Clifford (Canonbury Arts Ltd); Andrew Sinclair (Plas-ti-shim); also to Ken Adams for writing the Foreword; Jonathan Chapman (for invaluable assistance on the Chapter 4 project); Mitch, Rachel and Pallas (Chapter 3); Vivienne Fabb (Woodlands Farm); and to Linki for everything.

INDEX